LESLIE BAILY'S *BBC* SCRAPBOOKS

VOLUME ONE 1896–1914

by courtesy Lieut.-Colonel Sands

Hullo! Hullo! Who's your lady friend?
Who's the little girlie by your side?

The Brighton Pierrots, by the gay and zestful Walter Sickert, of all English painters in his day the nearest to the French impressionists in style, while his subjects were the nearest to 'ordinary' English life. This painting gives a vivid impression both of the scene and the mood of nights when the unpretentious concert party reigned supreme at the seaside. See note on p. 202.

Leslie Baily's BBC
SCRAPBOOKS

VOLUME ONE 1896-1914

*With a Calendar
of Significant Dates*

London

PUBLISHED BY ARRANGEMENT WITH THE
BRITISH BROADCASTING CORPORATION BY
GEORGE ALLEN AND UNWIN LTD

FIRST PUBLISHED IN 1966

PRINTED IN GREAT BRITAIN
BY JARROLD AND SONS LTD
NORWICH

ACKNOWLEDGEMENTS

The social history in this book is substantially reinforced by the first-hand memories of many people who have broadcast in the *Scrapbooks*; my thanks go to them for their permission to quote freely, and also to many colleagues at the BBC for their help, especially to Mr R. L. Collison (Librarian), Miss Joan Houlgate (Reference Librarian), Mr W. Sullivan (Popular Music Library), and Mr Bert Lally.

Valuable research assistance was given by the British Museum, Victoria and Albert Museum, the Science Museum, London Library, the National Film Archive, the Imperial War Museum, the public libraries of Bournemouth, Poole (Dorset), and Southampton; and by Sir William Hart (Clerk to Greater London Council), Mr A. Lindsay Clegg (Town Clerk, Bournemouth), Mr E. H. Turner (Town Clerk, Scarborough), Mr C. H. Gibbs-Smith, Mr Douglas Kennedy and the English Folk Dance and Song Society, the Boy Scouts Association, London Transport, the Automobile Association, the Electricity Council, the Gas Council, the Marconi Company, Marconi International Marine Ltd, Rolls-Royce Ltd, British Motor Federation, Dunlop Rubber Co., Bourneville Village Trust, Leslie Stuart Enterprises Ltd, the British Road Federation, the General Post Office, and the Ministries of Agriculture, Health, Labour, Transport, the Home Office, and the Central Office of Information.

Sir Edward Elgar's correspondence with Mr A. C. Benson is published by permission of Mrs Carice Elgar-Blake and the Elgar Trustees, and the Master and Fellows of Magdalene College, Cambridge.

My research into the subject of Hiring Fairs was assisted by the National Farmers' Union and their officers Mr Leslie Thomas and Mr Ernest E. Milner, the Museum of English Rural Life at the University of Reading, Dr E. R. C. Brinkworth of Banbury, *The Farmer's Weekly*, the BBC programme *On Your Farm*, and many farmers.

I acknowledge having plundered volumes of *Punch*, the *Illustrated London News*, *The Times*, the *Graphic*, the *Daily Mail*, the *Daily Express*, and *The Motor Cycle*.

Every effort has been made to trace copyright owners; if I have failed to obtain any permission I pray forgiveness.

For their helpful criticisms of the text I thank Miss Daphne Meier, B.A., Miss Gladys Burgess, B.A., and Mr Charles Brewer, M.C.

The *Scrapbook* staff as seen by the cartoonist of the
BBC staff magazine, *Ariel*, G. W. Smith

An old-established programme need not be (and should not be) old-fashioned – this is a guiding-line to us at the BBC in shaping the *Scrapbooks*, and I take this opportunity to give credit to the producers who have kept these programmes abreast of changing techniques during their long-life (more than thirty years); in turn Charles Brewer, Francis Worsley, Howard Agg, and Vernon Harris. Also working alongside me were Alan Paul with his advice on the music and his conducting of the orchestra, Freddy Grisewood as narrator, and too many backroom boys and girls to name – studio managers, tape editors, library assistants, engineers, secretaries: all those without whom no BBC programme would be borne on the air.

L.B.

CONTENTS

On 400 feet of aerial wire suspended from a kite, the first transatlantic wireless signal was received by Marconi at Signal Hill, Newfoundland, from Poldhu, Cornwall: 1901

On the Modern Way to Catch History on the Wing

I go to Broadcasting House in London, ascend to the largest library of recorded sounds in the world, and search in the file index for 'William – 1st; recorded at Hastings, 1066'. I get his disc from the racks, put it on a spinning turntable, and listen to the Conqueror after the battle, addressing crestfallen English knights in the tent that William of Normandy had pitched on the very spot where King Harold had fallen and where, so an ancient scrivener tells, William 'sate down to eat and drink among the dead'.

If this dream could be true, what revelation there might be of the mood of the feasting victor, and what facts, long lost to us, might be contained in an on-the-spot recording! – but through all the distant centuries we have to pick what clues we can from sometimes meagre writings, sometimes romanticized, not to say twisted for propaganda's dirty sake. The interpretation of much history would be shaken to its roots, I suspect, if we could hear its voices. Today we can take a disc from those racks at Broadcasting House and hear (for example) Montgomery speaking in 1945 to the crestfallen High Command surrendering before his caravan on Lüneburg Heath: 'The German Command to carry out at once and without argument or comment all further orders that will be issued by the Allied Powers on any subject.' Here is exact fact preserved for all time; here, too, in Monty's curt voice the mood is explicit.

The immense revolution in methods of history-preservation that has been made in the last thirty years is not generally appreciated because we are too familiar with it. Its significance is enormous. Students hundreds of years hence will hear and see Churchill as well as read about him. History will be more accurate, less legendary, more vivid, because the overtones of human personalities will be there. How I would like to hear a recording of that interview in the laboratory of the Royal Institution in 1831 when Michael Faraday was fiddling with bits of wire and a magnet, making an experiment in electro-dynamics, and was asked what was the use of such knowledge, and legend says he replied 'What is the use of a newborn child?'. A man who could make such a remark one would like to know more directly. Out of Faraday's embryo dynamo grew all modern electrical engineering. Just seventy years later Marconi sent the first radio signal across the Atlantic, and in this case the great innovator himself may

9

be heard describing it in a record he made exclusively for *Scrapbook for 1901*. The *Scrapbooks* have no monopoly in this modern history-collecting. Hundreds of other BBC men and programmes have brought together that priceless Archive Library at Broadcasting House; I mention this example to stress the fact that the *Scrapbooks* (which have now been a BBC feature for a third of a century) have made this one of their purposes, to catch history on the wing.

It was a novel idea when the first *Scrapbook* went on the air, *Scrapbook for 1913*, broadcast on December 11, 1933, compiled by myself, with Charles Brewer[1] as producer. Turning the pages now of that rather brash and sentimental old script, I can see how much the brickbats of critics were deserved; we had a lot to learn; but I can also see – and this is vital to all the *Scrapbooks* ever since, and is the essence of this book – that Brewer and I interpreted the word 'history' in its widest social terms. We took a look at life in Britain in the last full year of peace, 1913, when few people felt the breath of European war on the back of their necks but there was a ferment of affairs at home – the suffragettes, the brewing-up of Irish trouble, etc.; and we also brought to our microphone Robert Hale (father of Sonnie and Binnie) and Ida Crispi to sing Irving Berlin's explosive innovations of ragtime just as they had done in the revue *Everybody's Doing It* at the London Empire. Ragtime's youthfully impolite dismissal of the conventions we saw as part of that fermentation of 1913, just as social historians in future will examine the teenagers' pop-singer-idolatry as part of the gimmicky fabric of the Sixties.

We also used recorded voices ranging from Chaliapin to Marie Lloyd and Premier Asquith, surely the most varied cast of stars ever. Such a cross-section of life, now commonplace, was

[1] Charles Brewer, son of Sir Herbert Brewer, organist of Gloucester Cathedral; served First World War, infantry, later pilot in Royal Flying Corps, awarded Military Cross; joined BBC 1926 Cardiff, later specialized in light entertainment at Birmingham; producer in London from 1933, and later Assistant Director of Variety; applied his creative influence to *Scrapbook* until Second World War; served in RAF and Fleet Air Arm; 1944, led Allied Expeditionary Forces Programme's first unit to enter Paris after liberation; 1945, BBC North American Director, New York.

'Explosive innovations of ragtime' by Robert Hale and Ida Crispi (*left*), caricatured by H. M. Bateman in the Empire Theatre programme of *Everybody's Doing It*, 1913. (*Right*), Mr Hale again, in his burlesque of 'The Biograph Hounds'

Twenty years later: Ida Crispi and Robert Hale recall the ragtime days in the first BBC *Scrapbook* ever produced. This photograph was taken in a brand-new Broadcasting House, 1933 (Leslie Baily in centre)

unfamiliar in radio or anywhere else. Listeners were surprised, entranced, shocked (Asquith rubbing shoulders with Marie Lloyd! – tut-tut – whatever next!); but to find new things when they switched on was nothing unusual for listeners in the mid-Thirties, radio's exhilarating years of expansion and experiment under the towering leadership of Reith. Uninformed critics nowadays deride him as the puritan Director-General who fashioned Auntie BBC in his own image. Certainly, John Reith more than anyone created Auntie, but what a terrific kick she had in her! His vision of the influential part she must play in the nation's life was a positive inspiration to many of us during those (in many ways) negative years between the wars. Reith's idealism was not to be scoffed at then. And the immense creative energy within his BBC let no cobwebs grow at Broadcasting House, even if there were a few bats in the belfry.

I want to give these lines in affectionate memory of those days because I am grateful for them. I believe many others are, too, on both sides of the microphone – grateful for new horizons. After ten years of adolescence, radio had got right off the ground by 1932. Val Gielgud's radio-playwrights and producers had cut away from the conventions of the stage and were unfolding their dramas within everyone's imagination; philistines who pooh-poohed the radio-talk as though it was devoted to the habits of the common earthworm ignored what exciting new horizons of the intellect were opened when the voices of Bernard Shaw and H. G. Wells first spoke at millions of firesides; the new BBC Symphony Orchestra under Adrian Boult's direction was spearheading an unprecedented music-awareness among the people, such that the satirist could get a laugh at the new musical housewife:

> *Washing up to Shoobert,*
> *Cleaning boots to Brahms,*
> *Scrubbing sinks to Humperdinck's*
> *And Mozart's many charms . . .*[1]

Eric Maschwitz, too, directing BBC Variety in the early Thirties, was a catherine-wheel sparking off ideas in a cascade of gaiety, badly needed in time of mass-unemployment at home and Fascism's rise abroad, while comics like Gillie Potter and Stainless Stephen were juggling absurd figures in the imagination and blazing a crazy trail towards the later surrealism of *ITMA* (1939). And so on, and so on – these were great formative days in radio. This was the stimulating environment in which *Scrapbook* was tried out.

The audience grew rapidly. The millions listened. That was exciting, too – to feel the power of radio. I remember Margaret Bondfield, MP (Britain's first woman cabinet minister) telling me how one morning she happened to go into a London office employing hundreds of women – 'and the main topic of conversation was *Scrapbook for 1908* the night before, with its story of the suffragettes, the older women reviving memories and the younger ones thrilled by the speech that Mrs Pankhurst made from the dock at Bow Street: it presented a case they had not known. It was bringing history alive for them.' This touches one reason why the *Scrapbooks* found a public far greater than we had anticipated. Sir Philip Gibbs, a journalist very sensitive to the public mood, wrote:

'These are the dramatized albums of our own lives and memories – at least, if we are not very young; and in listening to these broadcast scenes we are aware of our own ghosts, and of "the years that the locusts have eaten", and of life as we knew it in the heyday of our own youth.

[1] Lyric in *The Gate Revue*, by Gerald Bryant, 1934.

We hear again old ballads sung by music-hall stars who were our favourites away back in our springtime. Good heavens! Is it possible that they are being sung again by the same voices? Yes. By some magic the BBC has found them. This microphone brings back the past into the present with such living reality that for a little while the illusion is very moving. . . . But young people also, as I know, have listened to the *Scrapbooks* with the same interest as their elders – though surely with something different in emotion. To them it is a revelation of history. So that's how it happened just before they were born! How very extraordinary! How very amusing! Their fathers and mothers spoke like that, thought like that, lived like that, behaved like that. How amazing! How touching! How absurd! – though that must be said in a whisper. Anyhow, here is history; and here are some of the very people who made that history. One gets into touch with their personalities. Some of them are the people who changed the world and made it all different – like Blériot, who crossed the Channel in an aeroplane. They spoke to us in these *Scrapbooks*, and no soul on earth could listen without a thrill.'

Scrapbook programmes have now looked at most of the years between 1896 and 1953. Some have been drastically revised and re-issued to meet the interests of new audiences that have grown up; and new techniques have broken fresh ground, especially with the tape-recorder. A couple of behind-the-scenes stories will show how the scope and style of sound-radio has changed. The first occurs in 1935, the other in 1962.

In 1935 when I had the idea of getting Marconi himself to describe that famous trans-atlantic wireless signal of his, my ambition was put in jeopardy by (of all things! – but so run the inner wheels) Mussolini's war in Abyssinia and the controversy over sanctions against Italy imposed by Britain and other countries, under the aegis of the League of Nations. Reith has since told how Marconi embarrassed him by writing to ask if he might broadcast over the BBC a talk on the Italian view of sanctions (Marconi, despite his many intimate connections with Britain, was an Italian citizen, and a marquis of the Italian nobility). Lord Reith says: 'I took him to lunch and we had a pleasant talk. He said he expected to be told that he could broadcast about anything under the sun except what he wanted to broadcast about. Quite right. I asked if Mussolini had put him up to this, and he did not deny it; a clever move.'[1] So when Reith had shut the door firmly at one level of the BBC it was hardly an auspicious time for a young script-writer to try to tempt Marconi to the microphone at another; but I wanted him very much. One afternoon I heard that Marconi had decided to leave England within twenty-four hours. I took a taxi to the Marconi offices on the Thames Embankment. A cautious secretary said the great man *might* be in for an hour or so next morning; after that he was away. I said I *must* have him for *Scrapbook*.

'How on earth?' asked the guardian.

'You have in your archives all the facts about this trans-atlantic affair. Have you anyone on your staff who was actually working on it with Marconi in 1901?'

'Yes, an engineer named Paget.'

'Good. Let me see him and the archives *now*. Overnight I'll write a script for Marconi. First thing tomorrow we'll have a microphone on his desk. When he comes in will you give him the script?'

'Good gracious!' exclaimed the secretary, not surprisingly. He mentioned the Mussolini business. My heart fell. 'On the other hand,' said Marconi's watchdog, 'he's the sort of man

[1] *Into the Wind*, by J. C. W. Reith (Hodder and Stoughton).

Marconi International Marine Ltd

Marconi in 1901, at St. John's, Newfoundland, with the apparatus he used to receive the
first transatlantic wireless signal

who might rise to a *fait accompli*.' My heart rose. 'Then again, if we fix things up without
consulting him he may go off the deep end.'

I urged my case like mad – the historic importance of getting this man to tell the story, etc.

'Very well. Let me have the script by half-past nine in the morning. I'll see what can be
done.'

I phoned Broadcasting House. Brewer arranged for one of the huge recording vans we used
in those days (complete with two engineers and driver) to park next morning on the Embankment, cables to be run into the building, and a microphone fixed in Marconi's office. I pumped
Paget's memory, swotted the archive material and sat up until the early hours writing the
script, trying to put the right words into Marconi's mouth. In those day we never dreamt of
working *without* a script. How strange it seems now.

Next morning everything was ready, the engineers standing by in their van, Brewer and I
in the ante-room to Marconi's office. An hour went by. Was he perhaps not coming in?
Another half-hour. Was he possibly going off the deep end? Then the door opened and the
guardian beckoned us in. Anxiously, we looked at a neat little man with one glass eye who
was sitting on the edge of the desk, the script in his hand. He smiled. Picking up the microphone, he said 'This won't take us long, gentlemen.' In the van outside history was recorded.
Then Marconi dashed off to catch the boat-train to Italy. He never returned.

Note the differences of method when in 1962 I was preparing a *Scrapbook for 1922* and wished to find an eye-witness of the ambush in which General Michael Collins, hero of the new Irish Free State, was killed by Sinn Fein gunmen in a desolate ravine called Beal na mBlath in County Cork. Eighteen IFS soldiers were in Collins's convoy on that day during the Irish civil war; forty years later I wanted to find one of them. What were the chances? With a tape-recorder slung over my shoulder I flew to Cork and started teasing out a few possible clues, eventually lurching in an ancient taxi through the pellucid green of an Irish countryside drenched in permanent rain, my destination a small town where I was told I should find an ex-bodyguard of 'Micky's'. My garrulous driver told me that this living link with 'the bad old days' was now a porter at a hospital. We went to his home address. The blinds were drawn. It was midday.

'Begob,' said the driver. 'You'll find him in the mortuary.'

Once before, in a London suburb, I had carried my tape-recorder up the front path of a house only to be met by someone coming out who told me that the person I wished to record had just expired. Had the man with the scythe once more beaten the man with the microphone? Had I come all the way from London for this? No. A genial fellow in his braces came to the door, sat me by a roaring fire, and there under the blazing sun of an unshaded electric lamp, behind the drawn blind, he told me the story of tragic Beal na mBlath. He had that gift for a phrase, that innate poetry, with which the Celts are blessed far more than the English. I swear that no script-writer on earth could have spun the words like the old soldier, and because he could talk *ad lib* at his own hearth instead of being dragged over to London to a frightening BBC studio he gave a remarkably idiomatic account of a piece of history.[1] (But I still don't know why the blinds were drawn.)

The tapes from such excursions are brought back to London where they are edited into the programme by Vernon Harris, who has been producer of *Scrapbook* for the past dozen years.[2]

The snag about all this is that the BBC transmits a programme perhaps two or three times and then it goes into the Archives, so these sources of history are not available for general ready-reference by the public (apart from a few that are on the commercial record market[3]). To make them available is the first purpose of this book. I shall quote many people who took part in the *Scrapbooks*. The speaker will be identified by this typeface – MR JOHN SMITH – to distinguish him from other sources of quoted material. Occasional passages have been published in my earlier books, but I trust that their reappearance is justified now that they can play their part in a wider panorama: as I have worked on more and more programmes much fresh material has been turned up. This brings me to the second aim of these two volumes.

Every time a *Scrapbook* is broadcast letters come from listeners with a hearty appetite for facts, from teachers, from students, from the enthusiastic planners of a local pageant celebrating some notable anniversary in the history of our town, our college, our Women's Institute, our this and that – all asking for copies of the *Scrapbook* scripts. This has been

---

[1] It will be printed in Volume 2, *Leslie Baily's BBC Scrapbooks*.

[2] Vernon Harris started his professional career in 1926 as an actor with Sir Frank Benson's Shakespearean Company; 1927 to 1935 in Plymouth, Manchester, and Birmingham Repertory Theatres, then West End, films, and radio. Joined BBC 1939 as producer. Since then has been responsible for hundreds of radio programmes. Also screen-writer, *Reach for the Sky*, *The Admirable Crichton*, etc.

[3] *Scrapbooks* so far issued under the Fontana label are those for *1914* (493 015 FDL), *1940* (493 014 FDL), and *1945* (493 016 FDL).

impossible but now I can offer them something more. As Professor Briggs has noted in his history of broadcasting, considerable research is invested in the *Scrapbooks*.[1]

Much information is gathered, but some never reaches the listener's ears, simply because everything can't be squeezed into an hour's programme. My research files are drawn upon extensively for the present book. I also add pictures to this, my new scrapbook; personally, I find the drawings by black-and-white artists in the old illustrated magazines especially delightful, evocative, and often more sensitive to the spirit of their day than photography; such cartoons are pure gems of social history, for they convey to us not only the shapes of motorcars, furniture, streets, clothing, houses, all the multifarious aspects of life as it changed, but also the attitudes of mind going with it. Look, for instance, at George Morrow's drawing (published 1910) called 'Progress', and you have a sequence of attitudes displayed in a flash, from the dejection of the 1900 motorist having to be helped home by stolid countryman and faithful horse, to the fun poked at the aeroplane ten years later; the horse looks on all these

[1] 'The *Scrapbook* programmes satisfied the Englishman's love of nostalgic reminiscence and at the same time drew on a powerful documentary element which earns them a certain place in the future interpretation of contemporary history.' – *The Golden Age of Wireless*, by Asa Briggs (Oxford University Press).

1900

1910

'Progress'   *Punch*

changes with as bland an expression on his face as animal ever had. I hope that my use of such pictures in this book will add to the reader's pleasure.

That last word brings me to my last, not least, purpose – your entertainment. When the *Scrapbook* series first got into its swing the *Manchester Guardian* analysed its formula as 'Not merely facts, but illustrations and impressions so selected and treated that they made a section of social history in the form of entertainment.' A good definition. But please be warned that for me 'entertainment' does not mean wallowing in Good Olde Tymes nostalgia – though some of the times *were* good.

So were some of the tunes. And some were awful. But it is magical how a crude common song, belted out in ages past by a slap-happy comedian, can transmute itself into gold when heard today, because it suddenly illuminates a page of history. Some songs have deep emotional associations not to be despised; 'Take Me Back To Dear Old Blighty' in one war, 'Lily Marlene' in another.

Kipling said of popular songs, 'They supply a gap in the national history, and people haven't yet realized how much they have to do with the national life.' That was years ago. People do realize it now. Since Noël Coward sent his Boer War troopship sailing away from Drury Lane to the strains of 'Soldiers of the Queen' in *Cavalcade* (1931), and since the first *Scrapbook* a couple of years later tried its experiment with ragtime, the evocative use of old songs has become common in radio, television, films, and theatre. 'How potent cheap music is,' says Coward.

There is another class of song even more valuable to historians than the emotion-stirrers: event-songs whose words provide us with contemporary running commentaries on things in the news. With a boisterous touch of prediction, for example, comedians on the late Victorian music-halls gave notice that 'the poor old horse will disappear':

> *Somehow it seems to me a diff'rence there will be*
> *Now we've got the motor-car;*
> *Poor cabby's looking blue, he'll have no work to do,*
> *Now we've got the motor-car.*
> *We'll have to send the fourwheel'd cabs to Margate on the sea,*
> *And as machines for bathers quite a luxury they'll be;*
> *The poor old horse will disappear, excepting one or two,*
> *That we'll show as a novelty to children at the zoo.*
>
> *All thro' the motor-car; the motor-car,*
> *We seem as if we dunno where we are;*
> *And it's all U.P. with the poor 'gee gee',*
> *Now we've got the motor-car!*[1]

The event-song belongs to a tradition as old as Man himself. In a BBC series called *There's A Song About It* I traced it from 'Bella the Barrage Balloon' (1941) back to 'The Song of Roland' (1066), and I could have gone further. In the *Scrapbooks* I have taken such songs from two distinct sources: first, the folk songs which in centuries past sprang from the heart of the people, a form of expression delightfully uncommercial and spontaneous, and second, the pop-songs

[1] 'All Through the Motor-car', words by A. J. Mills, music by Bennett Scott (reproduced by permission of Francis, Day and Hunter Ltd.).

16

of the music-hall. Both sources have virtually dried up in the present day, and modern society is the worse off for that. To be sure, there has been a revival of 'modern folk songs', often songs of protest (racialism, the bomb, etc.) sung by a limited number of folk. As for the commercialized pop-song of today, it makes a noise which is in great demand but its words rarely mean anything worth hearing now, let alone to the historian in the future. This is an anaemic change from the day when the music-hall song-writer turned out (alongside a lot of banalities) a good many ditties which swept the country with their light-spirited commentary on the latest topic.

New crazes, new fashions, and new inventions were favoured topics, and I shall quote some of their tell-tale lyrics in this book because (like the drawings of black-and-white artists) they are full of the atmosphere of their day. The general hilarious scepticism about the first motor-cars was expressed by a list of its awful consequences:

> *The pussy-cats have heard the news and now they're looking blue,*
> *They can't eat worn-out motor-cars, what will the poor things do?*

– roared the comedian over the footlights, climbing a mad pyramid of crazy prophecies such as (hold it, boys, this is a SCREAM!) motor-racing:

> *At Epsom racing course in pref'rence to a horse,*
> *Loates will mount a motor-car . . .*

to the pinnacle of all absurdities:

> *In future we shall see our mounted cavalry*
> *Charging on a motor-car!*

The date of that song is 1896. Which takes us back three score years and ten, to the beginning of our scrapbook.

From *Autocarbiography of Owen John* (Iliffe)

'Bus Driver (to Cabby, who is trying to lash his horse into something like a trot). "Wot's the matter with 'im, Willum? 'E don't seem 'isself this mornin'. I believe you've bin an' changed 'is Milk!"

Punch, 1899

Drawings that are in themselves social history: this one was by Phil May, one of the greatest of the black-and-white artists. The art was virile and full of atmosphere; the jokes were abysmal

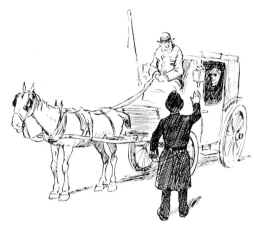

Sketch from the *Strand Magazine* by permission George Newnes Ltd
'It's all U.P. with the poor gee-gee', said the song of 1896, but the horse tradition died hard

In your home you could have a horse-substitute to stimulate the liver and brighten the mind: 1896 advertisement in the *Illustrated London News* (*below, left*)

In 1905 the Earl of Ranfurly had the idea of adapting the hansom-cab body to a Vauxhall motor chassis. It was not a success

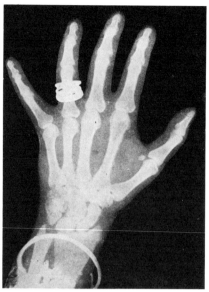

The X-ray picture that may cause 'a slight shock to loyal subjects': the hand of the Duchess of York, later Queen Mary, taken in 1896

The aerials at Poldhu, Cornwall, from which the first transatlantic wireless signal was sent in 1901, to Marconi listening in Newfoundland

A British administrator travels 10,000 miles through Africa and plays his phonograph to woo the admiration of a tribal chief in Barotseland, 1902

1 VICTORIAN

The Air is Full of Promises

'*We publish today two royal hands – one of the Duke and the other of the Duchess of York – taken by the Röntgen rays on the occasion of a recent visit of their Royal Highnesses to the Middlesex Hospital. They are excellent specimens of the new photography; the bones of hand and wrist have never come out with greater clearness.*'

In 1896 the *Illustrated London News* thus presented pictures taken by the X-rays discovered in the previous year by Wilhelm Konrad von Röntgen. The caption-writer hastened to soothe Victorian susceptibilities:

'*Possibly this representation of royal hands may cause a slight shock at first to loyal subjects; but the Röntgen ray is no respecter of persons and gives a touch of homeliness to the most illustrious anatomy.*'

It may amuse us now – this sense of shock when the penetrating eye of 'the new photography' showed prince and dustman to look very much the same under the skin, but it is worth noting that exactly forty years later, just after the abdication of King Edward VIII (son of the above Royal Highnesses), the *New Statesman* remarked that the British people had been shaken in 1936 because they 'had been taught that the monarchy was an impeccable, almost divine, institution, and the discovery that kings are human has been a shock'. In 1896 royalty, especially in the aged and rarely seen person of Queen Victoria, was as detached as Everest. There was no radio or television to bring the peak closer to ordinary man. From that faraway regal height, myth-shrouded, the Establishment's hierarchy descended steeply, like granite slopes moulded for eternity. The social classes were rigid castes; not a single Socialist sat at Westminster; not a woman was allowed to drop a vote into a ballot box. It was a social system puffed with privilege and riddled with deprivation: 42 per cent of men had no vote, 27 per cent of people had insufficient money and food to live in health and comfort. Yet towards the outer world almost every Britisher, high or low, felt himself to be top dog. As Cecil Rhodes had put it: 'I contend that we are the first race in the world, and that the more of the world we inhabit, the better it is for the human race. I contend that every acre added to our territory provides for the birth of more of the English race, who otherwise would not be brought into existence. Added to which, the absorption of the greater portion of the world under our rule simply means the end of all wars.'

It meant some blood-letting straight away. As one looks through newspapers and magazines of seventy years ago a striking difference compared with those of today is the rareness of reference to the rights of native races. In 1896 (when territory fifty times larger than Britain had been added to the Empire in ten years) the resentful natives of Rhodesia took their spears against the white settlers, a tenth of whom were killed before the Matabele 'rebellion' was broken. Far to the north, Kitchener was reconquering the Sudan. While the red-jacket carried the white man's burden into Darkest Africa and his martial feats were greeted at home with unabashed jingoism, the influence of Britain was also seen in a multitude of civilizing directions, from the emancipation of slaves to the coming of roads and railways – in 1897, for example, came the completion of 1,360 miles of railway from Cape Town to Bulawayo, and the same year saw the discovery of the malaria parasite by Ronald Ross of the Indian Medical Service, as great a boon as any brought to all people of the tropics. As the British made their mark, world-wide, so did the most humble little shop-assistant in England think himself a Somebody in the world, even if he was a serf *vis-à-vis* his own boss.

Conditions in Darkest England are described by one of its humble natives, MR PERCY ALLOTT: 'I worked at a big London drapery store. We lived in. This system meant that you slept and had your meals on the firm's premises. The food was poor and we were always hungry at the end of the day. We slept four in a room on hard beds. The conditions in crowded, dingy, and ill-ventilated dormitories were appalling. There was no heating and no covering on the bare boards. Occasional visitors were rats. There were only five bathrooms for several hundred employees. We washed each morning in cold water in zinc basins, in a room with a concrete floor. The shop assistant in those days was literally a wage slave, and fear of the sack prevented protest and virtually imprisoned him.' Hours of work in the drapery trade ranged from sixty-five to ninety a week.

The year 1896, though only a lifespan distant, seems in its scenes of almost Dickensian squalor and of Kiplingesque imperialism to belong to a remote age, yet it was also a time of immense richness and of promise for today, especially in science. Not only was the X-ray already entering medicine, and small studies were beginning into what we now call radio-activity, but significant advances were made in five other technologies which have since changed our lives: the motor-car, motion-pictures, wireless, flying, the telephone. Let us look at them one by one.

An advertisement by a Biggleswade firm of carriage builders notified the gentry that a landau cost 120 guineas, a victoria 70 guineas, a dog-cart 30 guineas, and an improved buggy 35 guineas. The horse was monarch of the roads. It was a sensational event if a motor-car disturbed the dust of centuries. The REV B. H. DAVIES ('Ixion' of *The Motor Cycle*) has told why almost every man's hand was against the motorist: 'There was not one square mile of tarred road in the whole country, and when the horseless-carriage passed down a deep Devon lane in summer it raised a cloud of dust 20 feet high and a mile long. Gritty particles penetrated everybody's eyes and nose and ears, and left them choking, besides ruining all dark clothing. Clergymen and magistrates adjured us to abandon our crazy hobby. They said we were mad. The little car shook like a jelly and rattled like a reaping machine. It was so unreliable that I carried a bicycle strapped to its tail. We had to push up all really steep hills. Sometimes we doubted our own sanity.'

In the whole country there were probably less than fifty cars. The early horseless-carriage had been severely hobbled by the law but November 14, 1896 was its Emancipation Day. A procession of thirty-three cars set out to Brighton from London (and thirteen finished) to celebrate the freeing of motor-vehicles from a speed limit of 4 miles per hour (increased to 12), and from the legal necessity to be preceded by a walking Jeremiah who usually carried a flag, red for danger. This landmark in the story of motoring is perpetuated by the annual London–Brighton run.

Prophetic opinion in *The Times* of 1896: 'It is highly probable that motor-cars will be brought largely into use before there has been time or opportunity to train an adequate number of drivers, and if so we must be prepared for a considerable catalogue of collisions and other accidents.'

The motor was also hated for aesthetic reasons. A horse pulling a carriage of any kind was a delight to the eye, whether a great farm-waggon in the country or a hansom-cab in towns where the clippety-clop of hooves made exuberant music, muted when straw was laid in a street where someone was seriously ill; but a car that was horseless lacked grace, it roared, stank, went berserk. When in 1896 an adventurous young aristocrat, the Hon. C. S. Rolls, drove his $3\frac{1}{2}$ horse-power Peugot from London to his home in Monmouth the journey took three days and in the coaching yard of the New Inn at Gloucester Rolls managed to be run over by his own monster. He had not yet met Royce. Almost all motor-cars were imported from the Continent, but in the previous year F. W. Lanchester, mathematician and engineer, of Birmingham, had built a single-cylinder machine, probably the first four-wheeled petrol vehicle made in this country. At a Crystal Palace exhibition in 1896 a tiller-steered three-wheeler appeared, designed by Herbert Austin, also of Birmingham. These two were Britain's motor pioneers. A cycle-repairer at Oxford, W. R. Morris, made his first motorized cycle in 1900.

Like dust, clouds of class-feeling swirled around the early motorist, widely regarded as a rich eccentric who killed hens and frightened humans and (worse) horses. Any notion that motoring would ever be for the millions was so far-fetched that the comedian singing that 'it's all U.P. with the poor gee-gee' got a big laugh with his prediction that 'On Sunday afternoons you'll see the loving spoons riding on a motor-car.' Yet motorized 'spooning' did very soon arrive for the plebs as well as the aristocrats: by 1897 a humble clerk could take his lady friend for a twopenny ride on the first horseless-bus to ply in London, between Charing Cross and Victoria. It was electrically driven and *silent*. Two years later the first petrol-powered bus banged its way through the startled horse-traffic on the Kennington–Victoria route.

Despite the prejudice and jokes surrounding the motor, a few people saw that it must be taken seriously. In 1896 they were discussing its possible effect on the great bicycle boom (annual sales of bicycles £12 millions). The *Illustrated London News* thought that 'Horseless carriages promise to be a great institution for ladies with plenty of pluck to go about alone and steer themselves, but not enough vital force to propel a bicycle.' The *Western Morning News* said: 'The autocar will not greatly displace the horse, but it may do a great deal of harm to the cycle trade.' When the Prince of Wales (later Edward VII) took to bicycling, *Punch* naturally called him 'the Prince of Wheels'; he did not buy a motor-car until 1901.

Highways and lanes had a romance, now lost. The white road stretched quietly before the cyclist, and in the evening yellow smudges of oil-lamps drifted like silent fireflies between the hedgerows. 'The arrival of the motor killed all the old cycling as I knew it, both for pleasure and for racing' – thus MR J. PLATT-BETTS. He won dozens of silver cups on the track. At the Crystal Palace he was paced by a fantastic machine called a quint: 'When there were no

Dunlop Rubber Co

A bicycle made for five, a quint, paces racing cyclist Platt-Betts

IN DORSETSHIRE.

Punch, 1899

The period of bloomers was also the golden age of the pun. Bernard Partridge was a sensitive artist, but this was his style of humour:

Fair cyclist: Is this the way to Wareham, please?

Native of Dorset: Yes, Miss, yew seem to me to ha' got 'em on all right!

24

motor-cycles for pacing we used first the ordinary tandem. Then, to get more power and speed, a third man was added – that was called a triplet, and so on to quads and quintets. After that we had the idea of using a team of several quints, a fresh machine swooping into position ahead of me at regular intervals. When I was breaking records for Dunlop's I had nine quints to pace me, forty-five men in all. They were paid about 35s a week. The team manager had as many as 100 men on his pay-roll.' Commercialism in sport is nothing new.

Another bizarre consequence of the bicycle boom was the controversy about showing a leg. A *Daily Mail* reporter, viewing ladies in Hyde Park riding bicycles instead of chestnuts, commented that their new dress was not as charming as the riding-habit: 'The cycling costume presents a vexed question: skirts or knickerbockers?' Marie Lloyd on the music-halls lustily championed the bloomers, politely known as the Rational Dress:

> *You see I wear the Rational Dress –*
> *Well, how do you like me? eh boys?*
> *It fits me nicely – more or less,*
> *A little bit tasty! eh, boys?*
> *When on my bike I make a stir,*
> *Girls cry 'My word' – Men cry 'Oo-er!'*
> *And in this garb they scarce can tell*
> *Whether I'm a boy or 'gell'.*[1]

A court case in 1899 dealt with the fact that Lady Harburton had been refused admission to a hotel because she was wearing her Rationals. Afterwards she delivered herself of this challenge to posterity: 'I admit that it is probably certain that women will never ordinarily wear knickerbockers. But mark this – short skirts for walking-wear will be a boon that ought to be easily attained, and, once attained, cherished like Magna Carta in the British Constitution.'

★   ★   ★

Queen Victoria, the old lady who was still in mourning nearly forty years after the death of her beloved Albert, invited the Czar Nicholas of Russia and the Czarina to Balmoral in 1896 after their coronation in Moscow. The Queen confided to her diary: 'I said it was so important that Russia and England should go well together, as they were the most powerful Empires, for then the world must be at peace.' This bland assumption drifts sadly down the years; these words belong to the far distances, but then one's eye turns to another diary-entry and in a flash there is a link with today: 'Went down below the terrace and we were all photographed by the new cinematograph process. We were walking up and down, and the children jumping about.'

Monsieur Lumière, who had improved on Edison's Kinetoscope, had just given his first British performance at the London Polytechnic. It was the first public film show to attract wide interest, and was repeated at the Empire music-hall, Leicester Square. His 'French Cinématographe' of 1896 consisted of films running not more than a minute each, under such exciting titles as *Watering the Gardener*. In the same year Robert W. Paul, a London

[1] 'Salute my Bicycle', words by J. P. Harrington, music by G. Le Brunn (reproduced by permission of Francis, Day and Hunter Ltd.).

National Film Archive

The Lumière cinematograph presents *Watering the Gardener:* comedy, brief and broad, is born on the screen. In London the Lumière programme is shown first at the Polytechnic in 1896, then at the Empire music-hall, and in the same year (*see opposite*) . . .

scientific instrument maker, made a film projector he called the Theatregraph. He filmed the Derby. This really stirred the British public. The *Strand Magazine*'s headline was: 'The Prince's Derby as Told by Lightning Photography.' As it was the first time for 100 years that a Prince of Wales had won the Derby (with Persimmon) the crowds gave themselves up to 'an utter and complete abandonment of cheering', in the midst of which Mr Paul stood 'with his hand on the wheel looking anxiously along the vast expanse of green turf. The inventor paid little heed to the appalling uproar that marked the finish of the race. He only turned the handle for dear life, and for the benefit of the public who were not there. The moment the race was over Mr Paul whipped out the film, packed it, and made a dash for Epsom Downs station,' reported the *Strand*, the most alert magazine of the day.

He developed the film in his laboratory at Hatton Garden, and next evening it was shown by his Theatregraph at the Alhambra music-hall in Leicester Square. There were no cinemas yet. 'The great race as depicted by Mr Paul's animatographe is a veritable marvel of modern photography and mechanism', pronounced the *Strand*.

While seeing-at-a-distance was newborn, hearing-at-a-distance was already about twenty years old; by 1896 there were some 140,000 telephone subscribers in the United Kingdom. The controversy surrounding them in the Nineties has a topical ring today: nationalization. The telephone service of this country was an uncoordinated and inefficient hotchpotch, part run by the Post Office, part by the National Telephone Company and other private enterprises, while six municipalities were to venture into it in the early years of the new century: Brighton, Glasgow, Portsmouth, Swansea, Tunbridge Wells, and Hull. Only the last survives with its independent service today. A Select Committee appointed by Lord Salisbury's Conservative

26

Illustrated London News　　　　　　　　　　　　　　　　　*Strand Magazine*
Marconi is sending a wireless signal over a distance of a few yards in the garden of his
father's villa in Italy, before going to England, while (*right*) the far-sighted Mr Paul is
at the wheel of his Lightning Photography machine at the Derby

Government laid the way in 1898 for the nationalization to come in 1912. The last years of
the old century also brought two great technical strides towards the telephone of today. One
was the abolition of the messy battery formerly required in every subscriber's home or office,
and the magneto generator with a little handle which you had to turn furiously when making
a call; the first 'common battery' exchange to obviate all this was opened at Bristol in 1900.
The other major advance was the automatic telephone, first patented by a Mr Strowger in
1889 in America, where various dialling systems appeared during the next few years; the
British Post Office carried out many experiments but did not open its first public auto-exchange
until 1912, at Epsom.

The dial had an origin comic and quaint, as Sir Thomas Eades[1] tells us: 'An undertaker
began it – Almon B. Strowger, of Kansas City, USA. The Chicago engineers who later developed
his system told me that old man Strowger found that calls to his place of business were being
"accidentally" transferred by the local switchboard girl to a rival undertaker. By a very remarkable coincidence, the girl happened to be engaged to the rival's son. Strowger swore he
would stop this by inventing an automatic system, the "girlless, cussless telephone". He began
by building a model switch with pins stuck around a collar box. The present system came from
that elementary start.'

If a wire could transmit speech from office to office, why shouldn't it transmit music into
the home? The thought had occurred long before. As early as 1883 Sir Arthur Sullivan

[1] In a letter to *Scrapbook*. Sir Thomas is a telecommunications pioneer who has played a prominent part in the
development of telephones in this country and overseas.

27

surprised friends at his birthday party by inviting them to listen to *Iolanthe* over a wire fixed from his London house to the Savoy Theatre,[1] and for some years there were a few stunts such as music being sent to the Crystal Palace from concert-rooms as far away as Birmingham, Manchester, and Liverpool, but it was the Electrophone Company which systematically started wire-broadcasting in 1895. This did not catch on like wildfire – in the next twelve years only about 600 subscribers in London were linked to some thirty theatres, churches, and concert halls, and eventually the enterprise fizzled out – but there was one man who had a vision of the possibilities of what he called the Pleasure Telephone: 'One man's voice will be heard simultaneously by the whole six million inhabitants of London. All that is necessary is a central office, from which the whole of England might be supplied with a constant flow of news and pleasure all day long.'

In fact, Broadcasting House – yet this was written as early as 1898 by MR ARTHUR MEE, a rising journalist then twenty-three, later to become the most successful of popular communicators of information for the young; he started the *Children's Encyclopaedia* in 1908, the *Children's Newspaper* in 1919. Later still, when preparing a piece he was to broadcast, he invited the editor of *Scrapbook* to the fine house he had built on a Kent hill-top and with justifiable pride in his prevision he took from the shelves the volume of the *Strand Magazine* for 1898 and turned to the article he had then written on the future of the Pleasure Telephone. How astonishing it is to see how right he was. He foresaw Children's Lectures; news would be 'imparted with strict impartiality' by an announcer 'who must, of course, possess a strong, clear voice'; 'the Budget speech would be known in thousands of homes before the Chancellor of the Exchequer had sat down'; and Mee imagined a 'central hall' (studios) where a twenty-

[1] See *The Gilbert and Sullivan Book*, by Leslie Baily (Spring Books).

THE AFTERNOON CONCERT.

CRICKET NEWS AT THE CLUB.

Strand Magazine, 1898, by permission of George Newnes Ltd

four-hour programme of music would be performed by 'several corps of musicians'. Contrasted programmes would be 'simultaneously performed . . . so that all tastes and moods can be suited'. There would be nightly relays from theatres, and occasional fashionable (royal?) weddings would be on the Pleasure Telephone. Concerning church services, 'It might be objected that religious worship by telephone is not calculated to inspire reverence or inculcate virtue, but at any rate the system will be an inestimable boon to the aged and infirm, the patients in hospitals and the women who are unable to leave their houses.'

Arthur Mee rounded off his vision in 1898 glowingly: 'Patti and Paderewski may yet entertain us in our own drawing-rooms, and the luxuries of princes may be at the command of us all. Who knows but that in time we may sit in our armchairs listening to the speeches of Her Majesty's Ministers?' This amenity would be fitted cheaply into houses 'just like the gas'. And finally: 'It will be so entertaining and useful that it will make life happier all round and bring the pleasures of society to the door of the artisan's cottage. That, indeed, will be the unique feature of the Pleasure Telephone. It will make millions merry who have never been merry before, and will democratize many of the social luxuries of the rich.'

If messages could be sent over a wire, what about doing without the wire? The general public was unaware in 1896 that Guglielmo Marconi had just landed in England; he was virtually unknown. This Italian was aged twenty-two when he took out his first British patent. Though not the sole inventor of wire-*less*, he was one of its most vigorous developers, both technically and commercially. After he had demonstrated his apparatus to British officials a reporter from *McClure's Magazine* called at a house in Westbourne Park, London, where Marconi had lodgings, and asked for details. Marconi said he had installed his transmitter on the roof of the General Post Office, and had put a receiver in a building on the Thames Embankment, 500 yards away.

'Was the message quite clearly received?' asked *McClure's* man.

'Quite clearly.'

'And do these waves really pass through things?'

'I am forced to believe the waves will penetrate anything and everything.'

'Won't fog prevent them?'

'No, sir, nothing prevents them.'

'Do you mean to say, Mr Marconi, I could send my report of this interview from London to New York?'

'Please remember wireless is a new field. With regard to the future, so far as I can see it does not present any impossibilities to signal to New York.'

McClure's interviewer added: 'Such are the astounding statements and views of Mr Marconi. The imagination abandons as a hopeless task the attempt to conceive what, in the use of electric waves, the immediate future holds in store. The air is full of promises, of miracles. The certainty is that strange things are coming.'

Marconi demonstrated wireless to army and navy officers on Salisbury Plain. Its first proof of virtues came in 1899 when the first life was *saved* by wireless: the East Goodwin lightship radioed that a steamer was stranded on the Goodwins, a lifeboat was sent out and the entire crew were saved.

All wireless messages were by the dots and dashes of telegraphy. Telephony through the air, and entertainment – the Pleasure Wireless, shall we call it? – was twenty years yet to come.

The great scientist Lord Kelvin wrote in 1896 that 'I have not the smallest molecule of faith in aerial navigation other than ballooning.'

A newspaper report of that year tells us that 'A series of experiments likely to have an important bearing on the question of the employment of balloons for military purposes took place last week at Shoeburyness. A balloon controlled from the ground by a hawser was sent up to a considerable height. The artillery-men began to fire. The stricken balloon speedily collapsed and fell hopelessly to the ground. The trial proved that no balloon could be expected to pass unscathed by efficient artillery unless at a very great height.'

Since the invention of the balloon in 1783 the idea of aerial warfare had occurred to a few pioneering minds intent on the progress of mankind (the Austrians had actually balloon-bombed Venice in 1849). To the average civilian at the end of the nineteenth century flying other than by balloon was Wellsian science-fiction stuff. One evening H. G. Wells was walking on Woking Common with his brother when they noticed the planet Mars burning in the sky, and Frank Wells said: 'Suppose some beings from another planet were to drop out of the sky suddenly, and began laying about them here!' H. G. went home and wrote a novel, *The War of the Worlds*[1] (1898) telling how a large hot cylinder was found in a crater on the common, its end unscrewed, and out came a Being: 'As it bulged up and caught the light it glistened like wet leather. It was rounded and had, one might say, a face. There were two luminous discs like eyes. There was a mouth, the lipless brim of which quivered and panted and dropped saliva. The body heaved and pulsated convulsively. A lank tentacle appendage gripped the edge of the cylinder, another swayed in the air. Those who have never seen a living Martian can scarcely imagine the strange horror of their appearance.'

Pure fantasy . . . but at the very time of Wells's space-flight dreams an Englishman named Percy Pilcher was making in real life some experiments which could well have made him the first man in the world to fly by aeroplane. He had already built and flown several gliders, and wrote: 'It is my intention to make another machine, but having a small oil engine situated just in front of me on the machine, with a shaft passing over my head, working a screw propeller of about four feet diameter, situated behind me.' It was never made. At Market Harborough in 1899 Pilcher sat in his glider as it was pulled off the ground by a team of horses on the end of a rope; when he was fifty feet high the tail collapsed, the machine dived to the ground and he was killed.

Little attention was ever paid to this pioneer, his experiments, or his end. Aeroplanes, too, were fantasy.

The fascination of the Nineties lies in the fact that below a social scene utterly different from today's we can see nascent forces that have blown it sky high, among them the popular newspaper. A young spark in Fleet Street, Alfred Harmsworth,[2] set off one explosion. He saw that the Education Act of 1870 had produced an enormous new reader-public who, having received a simple education, could read simple things; he had published two weeklies, the chit-chat *Answers* and the schoolboys' *Comic Cuts*, both highly profitable to Harmsworth. Now, in 1896, he foresaw that an increasingly educated and prosperous artisan and middle-class might welcome a halfpenny daily paper, a bright break-away from the pomposity and

[1] His first big success as a writer, when 32. Had a scientific training (B.Sc.), was previously a teacher.

[2] Later Lord Northcliffe. Was only thirty-one when he started the *Daily Mail*; had already bought London *Evening News*. Later proprietor, *The Times*, and powerful propagandist during First World War.

30

Illustrated London News

While Queen Victoria is in her twilight (her youngest daughter Beatrice reads to Mama), the Prince of Wales sets a new pace:

Radio Times Hulton Library

1899: the Prince's first drive in a horseless-carriage. His driver was the Hon. J. W. E. Scott-Montagu, MP (later Lord Montagu of Beaulieu). The car, a 12 horse-power Daimler, was reputed to have attained 40 miles per hour

heavy reporting of Victorian penny papers. The first number of the *Daily Mail* was an instant success, selling 397,215 copies, enormous for that date. It carried concise news, political gossip, women's realm, 'Chat About Books' in snappy paragraphs, and lots of 'human interest'.

'Written by office-boys for office-boys' gibed Lord Salisbury, the paragon of aristocrats (the last Premier to sit in the Lords and the last to sport a beard); but Harmsworth, the first tycoon of pop-journalism, had his ear closer than Salisbury's to the interests of the lower classes. One of the *Daily Mail*'s shrewd perceptions of social change lay in its ample coverage for sport. Only in the last third of the nineteenth century had football, cricket, and tennis begun to show signs of changing from casual pastimes to mass-entertainments. The FA Cup Final of 1896, held in those pre-Wembley days at the Crystal Palace, attracted 48,000 spectators, then a record. County cricket had its special top-class aura with such rich amateur giants as Dr W. G. Grace and 'Ranji', but even here the professionals took time by the forelock in 1896 by demanding more than the traditional £10 for playing in a Test Match against Australia. Two years later a Players' Union was formed for Association Football.

Perhaps the most astounding long-term effect of sport (or so our Victorian forefathers would have thought) has been its influence on women's dress. When the New Woman thrust into tennis, hockey, golf, lacrosse, and cricket in the amazonian Nineties (when there was even a British Ladies Football Club, founded in 1895 and banned by the Football Association in 1902) formal dress made little concession to the gameswoman. Here is MRS C. R. STERRY, one of the most formidable of British tennis champions – five times Singles Champion at Wimbledon between 1895 and 1908 – and yet hardly known at all to the modern public until *Scrapbook* brought her to the microphone, for her triumphs were won before Wimbledon became drenched in publicity. It is pleasant to contemplate the relaxed atmosphere of those days when Mrs Sterry (or Miss Charlotte Cooper as she was until her marriage in 1901) could cycle up to her Ealing home on a summer's evening, and her brother could pause from mowing the lawn and say 'Hullo, where've you been?' and she could reply 'Wimbledon – I've just won the All-England Championship.'

Women players had to cope not only with their opponents but with long skirts and hairpins: 'Nevertheless', asserts the gallant Mrs Sterry, 'we could get across the court at a pace that I think might amaze present-day players. The orthodox length of the skirt was about two inches off the ground, as it would have been outrageous to expose any part of one's limbs above the ankle. We wore dreadful pads in our hair. The hair was brushed over these, which looked awful. All the same, walking on the court in our long white skirts, a blouse with a stiff collar and tie, peppery sand-shoes and black stockings, we thought we were the essence of smartness. Playing in tennis tournaments in those days before there were taxis and motor-cars to take the players to the courts meant a great deal of walking and bicycling, often in sweltering heat. I frequently bicycled ten miles from my home to play in a tournament.'

The worst tyrannies of feminine fashion were not to be relaxed until the First World War brought other social loosenings, but some sporting ladies were already complaining in 1896 that, as one fashion-writer put it, 'If we are steel-bound and whalebone-lined throughout, the free use of our four limbs, which the game demands, is rendered impossible'. An advertisement in an adjoining column offered a better Way of Life, and shows that the soft-sell of the modern TV-advert was not unknown:

'How to be a Beautiful Woman. The lady who would be beautiful keeps her system well regulated, is careful of her diet, sleeps nine hours out of the twenty-four, takes a cold plunge

The long and the short of it: Mrs Sterry at Wimbledon, in her final triumph of 1908; and
Miss Marie Lloyd, the saucy queen of the music-halls

or sponge bath every morning upon rising, and then exercises a little time with her two-pound
dumb-bells. Her stockings are held by suspenders from the shoulders, thus allowing for the
free circulation of the blood, and her corsets are loose. She avoids very strong tea, coffee, and
rich-made dishes. After each meal she takes about ten drops of Vogeler's Curative Compound
in a wine-glass of water.'

The wave of feminine athleticism (in the upper classes – no working-class girl played tennis)
was a small part of a wider movement towards women's emancipation, socially and politically.
The London County Council was considering in 1896 whether there was any clerical work in
its offices suitable for women; John Burns[1] dared to say that women should have equal pay
and that he favoured opening all appointments to them, not only 'the dish and bottle-washing'.

Stubborn centres of discrimination against women were the universities of Oxford and
Cambridge. In 1896 the Senate at Cambridge refused by a huge majority to admit ladies to
degrees, and that day ragging undergraduates celebrated a gallant victory by dressing a female
dummy in pink blouse and blue bloomers, putting her in a hansom-cab, and dragging her to

[1] Left-wing member of LCC and MP; in 1906 was to become the first working-class Cabinet Minister when he
joined the Liberal administration as President of the Local Government Board.

33

the gates of Newnham. At this college and at Girton women already took similar examinations to the men's, yet they were not allowed degrees; at Oxford the girls of Somerville and Lady Margaret colleges were in a similarly ludicrous position, which was to continue until the 1920s.[1] The provincial universities and London were more enlightened; all were giving women degrees by the Nineties.

Suffragettes had not yet blown off the top. Patience was, in the beginning, the virtue of all who called for the vote, since the first society for female suffrage had been formed at Sheffield as early as 1857. A Conservative MP appropriately named Mr Faithfull Begg introduced a Women's Suffrage Bill in 1897, backed by a monster petition bearing over a quarter of a million signatures, which was spread out in Westminster Hall. The Bill was thrown out like all its predecessors, for most men (and the Queen) agreed with Mr Gladstone's dictum that it was unseemly to invite woman 'to trespass upon the delicacy, the purity, the refinement, the elevation of her own nature'.

Under the Victorian code a woman who smoked a cigarette labelled herself a Jezebel, but in 1896 (so goes a legend which is difficult to verify) the brave spirit who first broke the taboo in England was the Duchess de Clermont-Tonnerre, a lady of the French nobility, who performed the feat in – of all places – the genteel public rooms of the Savoy Hotel.

One of the few places where woman worked in equality with man was on the stage. Even there her general acceptance by the public was impeded by a wall of puritanism. The prim section of the public might approve of Ellen Terry in Shakespeare but not Lottie Collins (mother of José, of later *Maid of the Mountains* fame) kicking up scarlet legs to reveal a foam of lace petticoats while she teased every man in the audience with the anthem of the so-called Naughty Nineties:

> *A smart and stylish girl you see,*
> *Belle of good society;*
> *Fond of fun as fond can be –*
> *When it's on the strict Q.T. . . .*[2]

. . . followed by the famous tribal-chant of 'Ta-ra-ra-BOOM-de-ay!' repeated eight times, everybody joining in, for in music-halls the audience was part of the show. Gregariousness was the essence of pop-entertainment seventy years ago. The music-hall was rooted so firmly in towns up and down the land that anyone who forecast its virtual extinction by the Lightning Photography and by Marconi's 'air full of promises' would have been told to have his head examined. Its idols were 'of the people and for the people', stars like Dan Leno, Vesta Tilley, Marie Lloyd, the mistress of *double entendre*, and Albert Chevalier, the master of a Cockney humour which came near to poetry:

> *We've been together now for forty years,*
> *An' it don't seem a day too much,*
> *There ain't a lidy livin' in the land*
> *As I'd swop for me dear old Dutch . . .*[3]

[1] In 1920 Oxford gave women full equality to men. In 1921 Cambridge admitted women to 'titular' degrees, but not to membership of the university until as recently as 1948.

[2] 'Ta-ra-ra-boom-de-ay', words and music by Harry Pleon (Francis, Day, and Hunter Ltd.).

[3] 'My Old Dutch', words by Albert Chevalier, music by Charles Ingle (Reynolds).

34

The Empire Theatre, Leicester Square: the original caption below this picture was rhapsodic: 'You are now looking at one of the most gorgeously appointed and most fashionable variety theatres in Europe, and one in which evening dress is very much in evidence. The interior is upholstered in a palatial manner, and the orchestra is unrivalled. The weekly salary list is simply prodigious. No one can deny the dazzling brilliance of the scene at, say, 10.30 p.m.; no wonder that the Empire lounge should be the favourite resort of the Oriental potentate in London'

Many comedians were as clean as a whistle; some were human trombones, apt to make rude noises. One manager pinned up backstage this notice which I commend today to all owners of television studios: 'The Proprietor will Peremptorily Punish all Performers Playing Putrid Programmes by Promptly Prohibiting their Performance, and Pocketing all Promised Pounds and Pence. Dirty Ditties, Wicked Wheezes, and Gone-wrong Gestures No Go Here. We Want Willing Workers Who Will Work Wholesome Wares Without Wrong 'Uns.'

An entertainment to which Pa and Ma could safely take the children was the nigger minstrel show, with its banjos and blacked-up faces, a style imported from America many years earlier. Surely its most wicked joke (and the most often repeated) was when Bones asked 'Who was that lady I saw you walking with last night?' and Sambo replied 'That am no lady, that's my wife!' These shows had a stereotyped routine, and the audience loved them all the more for that; they were seen at most seaside resorts and reached their peak in London when the Mohawk, Moore, and Burgess Minstrels took up residence in Piccadilly, at St James's Hall (now the site of the Piccadilly Hotel). A vestigial trace today is in BBC TV's *Black and White Minstrels*. But the original minstrel shows had no women, no sex appeal.

All down the changing years popular and even frivolous entertainment can be socially significant. It reflects the temper of the times. When the periodic appearance of the witty Gilbert and Sullivan comic operas ended rather feebly in 1896 with *The Grand Duke* another tide was already rising. Musical comedy's easy-going tunes captured the parlour piano and the Palm Court Hotel, and West End stages were paved with gold. Great hits like *The Geisha* (760 performances in the West End alone, and heaven knows how many elsewhere) and *San Toy* (768) set a rage going.[1] All were English except *The Belle of New York* (697), the first American musical ever to score a success over here. Americanism in British life was not strong a lifetime ago.

Musical comedy was not in the same class of wit and musicianship as Gilbert and Sullivan comic opera; its dramatic construction was flimsy; but there was something of chocolate-box-pretty-prettiness about it, an artless ostentation which matched the mood of Britain in the complacent Victorian and Edwardian years before the First World War. The easy-going assumption that John Bull was living on top of the world was echoed in the cheerful, saucy, simple tunes; and how revealing of the swaggering imperialism of the years running up to the Boer War was Leslie Stuart's marching song 'The Soldiers of the Queen' with its brassy boast that:

> *. . . when we say we've ALWAYS won,*
> *And when they ask us how it's done,*
> *We'll proudly point to every one*
> *Of England's Soldiers of the Queen!*

The composer of this (both words and music) was an eccentric half-Irish Lancashireman, a church organist at Manchester who found that by writing winsome little tunes of the 'Little Dolly Daydream' type he had a big public asking for more. His daughter MISS MAY LESLIE STUART has given us this view, as nostalgic as a picture postcard, of the day in 1896 when Father moved to London: 'Five children, nurse, Aunt Hetty, and a piano pupil who refused to be separated from The Master were packed into a cab trotting up Albert Road to a large house overlooking Battersea Park, and behind came a procession of pantechnicons drawn by heavy carthorses. Father superintended operations as they were unloaded. Among the furniture was a grand piano he'd been given by Paderewski and a harmonium, a relic from his church days and one of his treasures. A surprising thing about Father was that some of his brightest tunes were composed on the old harmonium, in his room with a window facing an ugly brick wall!'

These included 'The Soldiers of the Queen', a martial song first tried out in the musical comedy *An Artist's Model* in 1895. It didn't quite catch on. Two years later Queen Victoria's Diamond Jubilee (Sixty Years a Queen) sent a wave of patriotic fervour through the land. London was decorated and the Queen forsook her purdah to drive in an open carriage to St Paul's, surrounded by prancing horses, plumed helmets, crowds cheering the frail old lady who was in a curious but affecting way the symbol of Britain's imperial might. In this mood the public was ripe for 'Soldiers of the Queen' – to quote again Leslie Stuart's daughter: 'I heard a Guards' band playing it in the Mall; it was the first time I ever heard one of Father's songs out of doors, soon everybody seemed to be singing it, and the birds in the trees seemed to be whistling it. So Father found his first fame.' He went on to the resounding success of *Florodora*, and to make a fortune writing ear-catchers like 'Lily of Laguna'.

---

[1] For details of the chief musical comedy successes throughout this vogue, up to 1912, see Calendar.

36

The Air is Full of Promises

'The Soldiers of the Queen' is now as dated as British imperialism. It is a museum piece in our gallery of tell-tale songs. The Empire in Leicester Square, the most famous of music-halls, celebrated the 1897 Jubilee with a ballet called, inevitably, *Under One Flag*, in which strapping dancers with the fashionable hour-glass figure 'impersonated' the colonies of an ever-wider empire; the bill also included sundry comedians, acrobats, performing dogs, and (says the Empire programme) 'Prof. Jolly's Improved Cinématographe with the latest Jubilee Pictures, the entire Procession; also a Realistic Scene taken at Clapham Junction – two express trains rushing through the station at express speed.'

Now Telstar flashes pictures across space, and the British Empire is no more. The changes in great things and small are immense; often a small personal experience brings them sharply in focus. MR HUNTLEY WRIGHT, comedian in musical comedies, has told *Scrapbook* that he often rode from his house to Daly's Theatre on horseback. After the show he fetched his horse from a mews near Leicester Square and rode away through the streets of London. Imagine a West End star doing that today! Daly's and the Gaiety were for years the meccas of musical comedy, but Huntley Wright reveals a curious double-standard of behaviour at these theatres: '*We* at Daly's were very respectable, no swear words on the stage and strict instructions that on leaving the theatre all chorus girls must go straight home.' (Stage doors were haunted by top-hatted Johnnies.) 'One afternoon George Edwardes, who was the boss both at Daly's and the Gaiety, called one of the girls into his office at Daly's and gravely remarked: "I've been hearing some *dreadful* things about you, having dinner at the Criterion and supper at the Savoy. You know, if this sort of thing goes on, my dear, you will have to be *sent down* to the Gaiety".' This reprimand was hardly terrifying, for every Gaiety girl dreamed of a coronet in her bottom drawer:

> . . . *the millionaires devotedly adore me,*
> *And the peerage in a body kneels before me,*

she had sung in *The Shop Girl* (1894) and this fairy story was to come true in Edwardian times when numbers of musical comedy ladies married either into the peerage or the American dollar aristocracy:

> *And a dancing girl, burlesque or operatic,*
> *May be the mother of a race aristocratic,*
> *Who will have their noble rights*
> *To an ancestress in tights,*
> *For you never, never, never know your luck, luck, luck,*
> *For you never, never, know your luck!*[1]

Sugar and spice and all things nice was the world presented in musical comedy. Like looking into a child's tinsel peep-show, it well served its genial purpose, but real life was something very different. It needed the red-blooded and red-bearded revolutionary Bernard Shaw to mock society's follies and to attack its evils, not by Victorian moralizing but with wit, satire, freshness, and vitality. He was the comedian with a social conscience. 'I find it impossible to take the inhabitants of this world seriously', he said through the mouth of one of his characters,

---

[1] 'You Never Know Your Luck', words by Adrian Ross, music by Ivan Caryll (Ascherberg, Hopwood, and Crew).

but he really took them very seriously. His first play, *Widower's Houses*, attacked slum land-lords, his next, *Arms and the Man*, lampooned the romanticism surrounding the profession of arms. Such subjects were unpopular. His plays were rarely seen in public because playgoers funked the facts of life, and Shaw didn't provide conventional star parts to show off important actor-managers. When the private Stage Society was founded 'to produce on Sundays plays of merit which the commercial theatre hesitates to take up' its first choice was Shaw's *You Never Can Tell*, championing women's freedom. Naturally, *Mrs Warren's Profession* (prostitution) was banned by the Censor. 'To prohibit the play is to protect the evil which the play exposes', said Shaw.

Shaw was part of a wider revolution outside the theatre. Poverty was the great national evil – or rather, complacency towards poverty, and exploitation of it in slums and slave-factories; the Liberals were to get to administrative grips with it later but at the turn of the century the drive came more from the left. A strangely assorted group – many tough trade unionists, a few of the intelligentsia such as Shaw and the Webbs, some magnificent homespun idealists like Keir Hardie – came together against social injustice and lack of representation in Parliament. Their day of decision, one of the most fateful dates in our national calendar, ought to be known to every schoolboy and schoolgirl but possibly isn't (recently a sixth-former told the author she had learnt no modern history beyond 1850). On February 27, 1900, at the Memorial Hall in Farringdon Street, London, 129 delegates set up the Labour Representation Committee: this was the foundation of the Labour Party, though it did not adopt that name until 1906.

Here is a link with that day. A delegate from the Gas Workers' and General Labourers' Union was MR ARTHUR HAYDAY, many years later MP for West Nottingham: 'I'd been born in West Ham in 1869, I left school at nine years of age, and became a labourer at 3s 4d a day. In 1900 it was beyond my wildest dreams that I should ever be an MP. You must realize that almost all MPs came in those days from the upper classes. Some of these men certainly wanted to see the conditions of the working class improved, but the fact remains that they were prac-tically all rich business men, manufacturers, or men of property and leisure, and to that extent they had no real connection with the great masses of the people of this country. I don't suppose any of us went so far as to imagine a Labour Government. But the important thing that hap-pened at the Memorial Hall was that we all got together – all the varieties of working class and Socialist bodies, and by our deciding on a common policy the present-day political set-up was made possible. They elected as secretary J. Ramsay MacDonald, who was to become Prime Minister in 1924.

The meeting attracted little public notice. The burning focus of attention was the war in South Africa between the British and the Boers, and the day of the Labour Party's inaugura-tion happened to be also the day of the relief of Ladysmith, which seemed much more exciting. To what the Press called 'the intense joy of the Queen and all her subjects', our garrison – decimated by dysentry, typhoid fever, semi-starvation, and Boer bullets – was relieved by General Buller's column after being boxed-up for 119 days. War correspondent Winston Churchill rode into Ladysmith, while at Haileybury College in England seventy-two boys rebelled against the headmaster's decision not to give them a festive half-holiday and marched in a cheering procession through Hertford and Ware; they were duly caned, among them young Clement Attlee – forty-five years before he was to become Britain's second Labour Prime Minister.

Good-bye Dolly, I must leave you,
Tho' it breaks my heart to go,
Something tells me I am needed
At the front to fight the foe.

Painting by George Harcourt, shown at the Royal Academy, 1900: Grenadier Guards leaving Waterloo station

Tolsey Museum, Burford

The relief of Mafeking brought a new verb to the English language, to *maffick*: exuberance reigned everywhere from London to small places like Burford in the Cotswolds

Hand-to-hand fighting in South Africa: a drawing by the *Sphere's* war artist Lance Thackeray. War correspondent Winston Churchill saw this battle of Pieter's Hill and wrote, 'It was a frantic scene of blood and fury'. More than half the attacking Inniskilling Fusiliers, out of 1,200, were killed

The Air is Full of Promises

You lose a lot of chances,
And you don't get asked to dances
If you're not dressed all in khaki
Like a military man.[1]

This advice to young men had been hurriedly popped into *Florodora* as a topical song when war began in 1899. Khaki had been tried earlier but in the Boer War it came fully into its own: the old scarlet and gold was out. Nevertheless, it is amusing to see our chameleon-like song-writers suggesting that there was something glamorous in being 'dressed all in khaki'! At first the popular attitude to the war was frivolous. *Punch* encouraged its readers to believe that the Boers were 'shambling oafs who grinned vacuously and fell over their rifles'. Soldiers of the Queen who had 'always won' would have the Boer in the bag almost as soon as fighting began. People like Lloyd George who opposed this war were extremely unpopular. It was to drag on for nearly three years. Long casualty lists appeared. The country's mood sobered. The lady at Windsor made her famous declaration: 'Please understand that there is no one depressed in *this* house; we are not interested in the possibilities of defeat; they do not exist.'

In the year when the Boer War began there was an event which the people didn't take to heart but in the long perspective of history, it may now seem of even greater, if depressing significance. The following words were spoken by the Czar of Russia in 1899 in connection with the first international conference for disarmament in history; they might well be placed on the desk of every prime minister, monarch, and dictator in the modern world:

'*Hundreds of millions are spent to obtain frightful weapons of destruction which, while being regarded today as the latest inventions of science, are destined tomorrow to be rendered obsolete by some new discovery. National culture, economic progress, and the production of wealth are either paralysed or turned into false channels of production. Therefore the more the armaments of each Power increase the less they answer to the purposes and intentions of the Governments.*'

The conference of twenty-five States was called at the invitation of Russia. The Czar asked them to agree to a five-year freeze on armaments. They set up a Court of Arbitration at The Hague, but the proposed standstill in armaments was negatived. The Conference tried to draft rules for 'civilizing' war. It agreed to a five-year ban on explosives thrown from balloons, and it made rules against the use of gas and of dum-dum bullets; but Britain (with Austria and Italy) declined to sign the anti-dum-dum declaration on the grounds that these bullets which expand on impact, producing a terrible wound, were necessary for dealing with 'savages'. Presumably we would not use dum-dum bullets against appropriately 'civilized' opponents.

All war is uncivilized, not only because war's price is suffering and death and sorrow, but because it brings to nations a hardening of heart and conscience. Courageous disarmament decisions by our forefather-statesmen might have saved young men in future wars from the duty to inflict horrors far worse than dum-dum bullets.

Not only statesmen were blind: very few people anywhere were sensitive or worried about the evil possibilities of increasing technological power. As the last months of the nineteenth century ran out and the twentieth approached there was earnest faith in material progress plus spiritual piety. An unconventional journalist, W. T. Stead, editor of *The Review of Reviews*,

[1] 'A Military Man', words by F. A. Clement, music by Leslie Stuart (Francis, Day and Hunter Ltd.), 1899.

41

shocked his sanctimonious friends by writing that, on the contrary, it had been a century of spiritual poverty, and as for material advance: 'The supreme outcome of its labours is the production of a quick-firing gun capable of pumping tons of explosive shell over four or five miles of country at the rate of twelve shots a minute.'[1]

In South Africa, Ladysmith was followed by Mafeking, relieved after 217 days' siege by the Boers, The Queen wrote: 'The people are quite mad with delight.' At Leeds one firm sold 25,000 Union Jacks; at Abergele a man died from excitement; in London young women danced down the Strand on the roofs of cabs, erupting themselves into the crowd 'mafficking' in Trafalgar Square. *The Times* asked: 'Will the verdict of history find London and England guilty of ridiculous exaggeration and a childish lack of the sense of proportion?' The war was to go on two more years.

Victoria did not see its end. She was eighty-one when her death came in 1901, in the first weeks of the twentieth century. Hers was the longest reign in English history (63 years – only aged cronies could remember the last coronation). A sombre reign ended in sombre magnificence, singular even among royal funerals, for the Queen had died at Osborne House in the Isle of Wight and across the Solent they brought her, between ten miles of warships booming a last salute. SIR JOHN FOSTER FRASER (correspondent of the *Yorkshire Post*) has painted that unique picture – the slow, silent passage of the Royal Yacht *Alberta*, an old-fashioned paddle-boat . . . 'the coffin on her deck, covered by a pall of white satin with the Royal Standard thrown across it . . . Boom! go the guns, and the clouds of smoke linger over the waters. Ahead crawl a double file of eight grim torpedo-boat destroyers, painted black from stem to stern. All the sentinel ships are manned, their sailors stand at attention and, while the *Alberta* passes, the band of each takes up Chopin's Funeral March. It is just after three when the *Alberta* leaves Cowes. It is dusk and chill and five o'clock when she reaches Portsmouth. Splash, splash, go her paddles as she sails into the gloom of enfolding night. And what a dusk – the sun setting in a mass of flame, and its last shafts flashing red upon the sparkling crown that lies on the coffin.'

King Edward was already fifty-nine and a grandfather – but a *King!* – what a thrilling novelty, and, rumour had it, a gay king . . . the new century was getting off on a light foot, what with the excitement of a coronation and better spirits concerning the war. By our standards in two later wars the cost now seems trivial. Income tax had risen from a pre-war 8d in the £ to a shilling in 1901 (and was to reach a post-war peak of 1s 3d in 1903). For every one of our men who died in South Africa about fifty were to die in the First World War.[2] The prolonged setbacks of the Boer War had stimulated anti-British derision in Europe, irritating to the Islanders, who felt isolated. But now Kitchener was in command on the veld, the campaign was turning for the better, and before long (1903) the King's passion for visiting the Continent, especially France, was going to earn him the name Edward the Peacemaker.

The first Parliament of the new reign (1901) was opened by the King and Queen in full state, a tradition Queen Victoria had not followed for forty years. King Edward VII's personality demanded a vivacious and ostentatious Court and a return to the full pageantry of public ceremonials. He was to bring pomp and colour back to the monarchy – and the people

---

[1] 'Lest We Forget, a Keepsake from the 19th Century', by W. T. Stead (*The Review of Reviews*), 1900.

[2] In the Boer War 5,774 were killed, plus over 16,000 who died of disease. In the First World War the number of Commonwealth war dead as recorded by the Commonwealth War Graves Commission was 1,114,214.

were to love it. Better still, he was the sporting king. In the previous year he had won the Derby, the Grand National, and the St Leger. Now he bought a 12 horse-power Daimler and *motored* from Sandringham to Newmarket and back. *The Autocar* reported: 'The event is worthy of mention on account of the fact that hitherto he has always had a special train. The roads were extremely dusty, but His Majesty expressed himself as delighted with the drive. At Downham great crowds collected to see him pass down the High Street, which he did at a right regal speed of between 20 and 30 miles per hour.' (The right legal limit was 12 miles per hour.)

So Edward hustled into the twentieth century. The great question was whether victory in South Africa would come in time to crown his coronation. One music-hall song-writer took a chance on it in 1901 with one of the worst event-songs ever written:

There's a good time coming, boys –
  Later on – yes, in the future;
What a day of Jubilation
  When the King is crowned.
What with war and price of sugar,
Trade's been awful for the nation,

But we're going to do our level best to pull it round.
For then we'll march along with flags and banners
  With our Sunday manners,
  We will spend our tanners.
Then on concertinas and pianos,
We will play 'God Save the King!'

  Oh! on Coronation Day, on Coronation Day,
    We'll have a spree, a Jubilee,
    And shout 'Hip, hip, hooray!'
  For we'll all be merry, drinking whisky, wine and sherry,
    All be merry on Coronation Day.[1]

[1] 'Coronation Day', words by A. J. Mills, music by George Everard (reproduced by permission of Francis, Day and Hunter Ltd.).

CALENDAR OF SIGNIFICANT DATES

1896

Emancipation of the motor-car: 'Red Flag Act' repealed, celebrated by run to Brighton (November 14).

Marconi demonstrated wireless to British Post Office.

Queen's reign became longest in English history.

Czar and Czarina of Russia visited the Queen at Balmoral.

Prince of Wales's 'Persimmon' won the Derby, which was filmed by R. W. Paul.

Lumière gave film performance at London Polytechnic.

Royal College of Art established.

The *Daily Mail* founded (May 4).

National Portrait Gallery opened.

Will Catlin's pierrots started at Scarborough, one of the first parties.

The Great Wheel at Earl's Court got stuck for fifteen hours; each of sixty 'prisoners' received £5 compensation.

British naval expansion; estimates increased from £26.8 million in 1896 to £27.5 million in 1900.

Matabele rising in Rhodesia.

1896–8: British expedition under Kitchener reconquered the Sudan.

STAGE: *The Grand Duke*, the last Gilbert and Sullivan opera; *The Geisha* began its run of 760 performances.

BOOKS: *An Outcast of the Islands* (Joseph Conrad); *Many Cargoes* (W. W. Jacobs); *The Wheels of Chance* (H. G. Wells); *A Shropshire Lad* (A. E. Housman); *Jude the Obscure* (Thomas Hardy); *The Exploits of Brigadier Gerard* and *Rodney Stone* (Conan Doyle).

SONGS: 'Algy, or the Piccadilly Johnny'; 'All through the Motor-car'; 'A Hot Time in the Old Town'; 'In a Persian Garden'; 'Sweet Rosie O'Grady'; 'The Amorous Goldfish' (*The Geisha*).

1897

Queen Victoria's Diamond Jubilee.

Kipling's *Recessional*.

Colonial Conference, attended by eleven colonies.

Lord Lister the first medical man ever raised to peerage.

Ronald Ross discovered malarial parasite.

J. J. Thomson disclosed his discovery of the electron.

Wallace Collection bequeathed to nation.

First transmission of wireless signals over water by Marconi, to Flat Holm, Bristol Channel, $3\frac{1}{2}$ miles.

First horseless-bus in London, an electrically driven vehicle between Charing Cross and Victoria.

Royal Automobile Club founded.

National Union of Women's Suffrage Societies founded (President, Mrs Millicent Fawcett).

Workmen's Compensation Act, providing for compensation for injuries received in course of employment.

STAGE: *The Liars* (Henry Arthur Jones); *John Gabriel Borkman* (Ibsen).

BOOKS: *The Invisible Man* (H. G. Wells); *Liza of Lambeth* (Somerset Maugham); *The Christian* (Hall Caine); *Captains Courageous* (Rudyard Kipling); *The Skipper's Wooing* (W. W. Jacobs).

SONGS: 'Asleep in the Deep'; 'On the Banks of the Wabash Far Away'; 'Sons of the Sea'.

1898

Marconi established wireless telegraph between Poole and Isle of Wight.

British and Egyptian flags hoisted at Khartoum after defeat of dervishes at Omdurman.

Players Union formed for Association Football.

English Folk-Song Society founded.

STAGE. *Trelawny of the Wells* (A. W. Pinero); *The Belle of New York* began its run of 697 performances.

BOOKS: *The Turn of the Screw* (Henry James); *Rupert of Hentzau* (Anthony Hope); *Elizabeth and her German Garden* ('Elizabeth'); *The War of the Worlds* (H. G. Wells); Thomas Hardy published his first volume of verse.

SONGS: 'Lily of Laguna'; 'She is the Belle of New York' (*Belle of New York*); 'Soldiers in the Park'; 'The Rosary'.

1899

Boer War began (October 10).

Mr Winston Churchill taken prisoner by Boers and escaped.

Percy Pilcher, English aviation pioneer, killed at Market Harborough.

Glasgow School of Art, in revolutionary 'modern' style, designed by C. R. Mackintosh.

Ruskin College, Oxford, opened.

First petrol-driven motor-bus in London, between Kennington and Victoria.

First wireless transmission across English Channel, from Wimereux to South Foreland.

First life saved by wireless message from East Goodwin lightship.

First pony show ever held in England, at Crystal Palace.

Hague Conference set up international Court of Arbitration.

Board of Education established.

Cecil Sharp's first encounter with Morris dancers, Headington.

'Enigma Variations' (Elgar).

STAGE: *Florodora* began its run of 455 performances; *San Toy* 768; *You Never Can Tell* and *The Devil's Disciple* (Bernard Shaw).

BOOKS: *Stalky & Co.* (Rudyard Kipling); *The Story of the Treasure Seekers* (E. Nesbit).

45

SONGS: 'Always'; 'Bobbing Up and Down Like This'; 'Chinee Soger Man' (*San Toy*); 'Son of Mine'; 'Tell Me, Pretty Maiden' and 'The Shade of the Palm' (*Florodora*); 'What Ho! She Bumps'; 'The Absent-Minded Beggar'.

1900

Labour Representation Committee established; the birth of the Labour Party (February 27–28).
Relief of Ladysmith (February 28).
General Election: Conservatives returned with 402 seats out of 670.
Relief of Mafeking (May 17).
University of Birmingham established.
The Wallace Collection opened.
First common-battery telephone exchange in Britain opened at Bristol.
House of Keys (Isle of Man) passed bill legalizing marriage to deceased wife's sister.
Prince of Wales's horses won the Derby, St Leger, and Grand National.
Daily Express founded.
Central London electric railway (the 'Tuppenny Tube') opened by the Prince of Wales.
'The Dream of Gerontius' (Elgar); 'Hiawatha's Wedding Feast' (Coleridge-Taylor).

STAGE: *The Gay Lord Quex* (A. W. Pinero); *Candida* (Bernard Shaw); *Mrs Dane's Defence* (Henry Arthur Jones); Pélissier's *Follies* first appeared in music-hall, at the Alhambra.

BOOKS: *Lord Jim* (Joseph Conrad); *The Brass Bottle* (F. Anstey); *Love and Mr Lewisham* (H. G. Wells); *Dictionary of National Biography* first published.

SONGS: 'A Bird in a Gilded Cage'; 'Beer, Beer, Glorious Beer'; 'Good-bye, Dolly Gray'; 'I'll Sing Thee Songs of Araby'; 'To-night'.

The Calendar is continued on page 68

OPPOSITE:

Drawing by Fell, *The Bournemouth Graphic*, 1902
The electrical twentieth century arrives. Tramcar No. 1 bursts into peaceful Bournemouth; nanny and horse bolt as mechanisation sets in

Punch, 1900

'Life had beauty and gaiety and charm'—the German band played beside the Thames lock on a summer's evening. Everyone wore a hat and a tie, including the lady with the punt-pole whose dress was the essence of style; but what a far extreme from the appearance of the river-girl of today!—yet this scene was only a lifetime ago

2 TURN OF THE CENTURY

The Fun and the Hardness of Life

'I do believe this was a time when life had a great deal of beauty and gaiety and charm. *People were not in such a hurry to rush on from one thing to another.*'

This was the observation of DAME IRENE VANBRUGH when asked in a *Scrapbook* to put her finger on the quality which most irradiated the period at the turn of the century when she was the reigning young queen of the London and New York theatre, triumphing on both sides of the Atlantic in A. W. Pinero's comedy *The Gay Lord Quex*. She did not reply with any stage nostalgia. She preferred to remember the River Thames on a summer's evening: 'when bicycles were piled outside the old Star and Garter Hotel at Richmond and the strains of a waltz tinkled across the darkening river, when chinese lanterns caught the gleam of bright dresses and bright faces as Cockney clerks and their girls drifted by in punts and rowing-boats. It was a gentle scene. There was a sort of unconscious acceptance of a beautiful world – and it *was* a beautiful world in many ways.'

Some of it has vanished, but in one of the most tranquil corners of England lived a magician who was able to lock beauty into a form that will endure as long as there are ears to hear: as Edward Elgar walked over the Malvern Hills and looked down upon the noble valley of Severn he was a man to whom (in his own words) '. . . there is music in the air, music all around us; the world is full of it, and you simply take it as you require.' At the turn of the century, when two very different giants – Elgar and Shaw – were showing their paces, England was being lifted to new levels of creativeness and sensitivity; in the ensuing years others in all the arts were to join in this renaissance, and it was a blessed coincidence that at this very time Marconi was developing the medium which has since made the riches available to everyone. The twentieth century has been black as hell in some directions; we have much to be grateful for in others.

One of Elgar's endearing qualities was his many-sided love of life: he would push aside his work on the sublime 'Dream of Gerontius' to take a day at the races; he would give his friends a series of portraits of themselves in the form of the musical joke he called 'The Enigma Variations'. MRS RICHARD POWELL, the 'Dorabella' of the 'Enigma Variation' so named, gives us this picture of him at work:

'It was a lovely hot day at Birchwood, a little house which the Elgars had taken in the woods to the north of Malvern, and I went to see them there, cycling from Wolverhampton, forty miles. When I got near the house I heard the piano. I saw Mrs Elgar sitting on a seat below the studio window; she had a red parasol. I leant my bicycle against a tree and went and sat down beside her without speaking. He was playing something that I had never heard before, something perfectly lovely. I found afterwards that it was the orchestral opening to Part Two of "Gerontius". The music stopped and a voice behind us remarked "Are you two going to have your photographs taken or what?" We spent that afternoon in the woods. Elgar was devoted to birds and animals, and we used to sit watching on the hills and in the woods and by the river. After tea we settled down to some more music. He played me part of "Praise to the Holiest". I was thrilled by it. He came to the end of a section, sat back in his chair and felt in a pocket for his pipe. I couldn't speak. I just had no words and there was silence.'

Elgar wrote at the top of the score of 'The Dream of Gerontius' these words from Ruskin: 'This is the best of me. This, if anything of mine, is worth your memory.' The range of his lifetime's music is wide: here it is mystical, elsewhere it marches with pomp and frolics with gaiety, often it is imbued with the unhurried beauty of the world around him in the Malverns. To anyone who loves music and loves England it is fitting that her greatest music of the last years before the full blast of modern life hit us was written in a countryside which could not be more English or more serene.

No aeroplane disturbed the sky over Elgar's hills. No transistor squawked. But the new century was already showing small occasional signs of being the century in a hurry. MR JOSHUA LAMB, farmer, of the then remote village of Sibford Ferris, in Oxfordshire, has told how the first signs came to his part of the country, the northern spur of the Cotswolds: 'My diary records that the first telephone wire connecting Sibford with the outside world was fixed in 1896, and even then I only heard of the relief of Ladysmith in 1900 by the ringing of the Banbury bells as I rode in to market early that morning. When the first motor-cycle appeared in our village I was on a reaping machine and my horses took fright and bolted.'

Museum of Rural English Life, Reading

Haymaking when the sun-bonneted women helped to load the great horse-drawn farm-waggons: picture taken at Lockinge, Berks, 1906

The Fun and the Hardness of Life

Sibford is only eight miles from Banbury but eight miles meant something near isolation to this and thousands of other villages. MRS ALICE GREEN, who was Sibford's postmistress for many years, says: 'During the Boer War the news used to come by telephone to the Post Office on Sunday mornings, and it was written down and posted up where people in the village could see it.[1] News of Queen Victoria's death came the same way. Not many people in the village took newspapers. The postman came out from Banbury with a pony and trap.' Carrier carts trundling two or three times a week between market towns and the villages were the only public transport (private enterprise), carrying papers, paraffin, parcels, poultry, and people.

When Joshua Lamb spoke to our microphone in his cottage as long ago as 1938 he was over eighty so his recorded voice is now a link with 'the greatest rural change of all, the introduction of farm machinery', nearly a century ago. This lies beyond the general span of years covered by the present book but it is worth quoting as one of the most delightful pieces of description *Scrapbook* has ever recorded, with its measured countryman's rhythm: 'Up to the year 1872 there were neither reaping nor mowing machines on our farm of over 600 acres, and I remember during haytime I used to love to watch the string of mowers with their scythes following each other across a field of grass or clover, often six together, and their song I can still recall:

> *Eat before you're hungry,*
> *Drink before you're dry,*
> *Whet your scythe before it wants,*
> *And you'll mow as well as I.*

'The thud of the flail on the barn floor, the blind horse pacing round and round attached by a pole to an old threshing machine, the patient oxen plodding before the wooden plough, the

[1] Mrs Green provided the same service in the First World War.

Dan Albone, publican of Biggleswade, invented the first successful internal-combustion-engined farm tractor; 900 were made before the firm went to the wall around 1921

harsh cry of the corncrake and the call of the quail, these, together with many other sights and sounds of my childhood, have passed away.'

He was questioned about the corncrake and quail: 'Yes,' he said, 'in this district they've gone almost entirely, and I believe we must lay the blame on the mowing machine. Another sad change is the disappearance of our village industries. At one time we had our baker, tinker, barber, tailor, shoemaker, cooper, and so on. Today only the carpenter and blacksmith remain.' These, too, have vanished since the recording was made.

In country as in town, the century of mechanization was at hand. Dan Albone, of Biggleswade, little knew what he was doing when in 1902 he produced the first successful agricultural tractor with an internal combustion engine. Great improvements in efficiency and labour-saving have come on the farm and in the village, but it is a pity so many of the simple, genial customs of rural life have gone or are going. Of the Harvest Home celebration old Joshua Lamb said:

'Extra beer was taken to the field before the last load was picked up. From the top of the waggon the words "Up, up, up, up, harvest home!" were shouted again and again, between liberal potations from the bottle. Afterwards, all the farm hands would sit down to supper, with plum pudding, and rounds of beef, accompanied with songs and stories.'

Turning to another ancient and picturesque scene still remembered all over Britain, Mr Lamb said: 'Farm hands were hired for a year at a time at the Michaelmas Fair at Banbury. It was called the Hiring Fair. Parson's Street used to be crowded with young men and maidens seeking situations, and with masters and mistresses in quest of shepherds, carters, and dairymaids. Intending shepherds wore a piece of wool in their hats so that they could be recognized, and similarly the carters wore a twist of whipcord.' He added that ten days or so later they held the Runaway Fair, so-called because it was attended by workers who had left their recently acquired jobs precipitately.

The Hiring Fairs (in some places known as Mops, as at Stratford-on-Avon) continued in many parts of the land well into the twentieth century. Why and when did they vanish? Joshua Lamb's description prompted *Scrapbook* to inquire further on this point, for the disappearance of a custom that began in medieval times (at Banbury the earliest charter reference is dated 1155) is one of the many drastic social changes of this century. Our research was supplemented when the BBC programme *On Your Farm* re-broadcast Mr Lamb's recording recently (1965) and as a result a large number of people connected with farming wrote in with personal memories of Hiring Fairs. From these and other sources[1] it is possible to give a picture of a custom which is described by some with nostalgia ('We have lost many good things in the countryside in the name of progress') and by others as a good riddance ('The hirings reminded me of slave markets', says one; and another, remembering being hired in Northern Ireland, 'What a humiliating experience it was').

Up to the First World War this was the scene in hundreds of towns. Wearing their Sunday best, perhaps with a nice clean smock, the workers would congregate in the street, each usually wearing his insignia of wool, whipcord, etc., while in some towns it was customary for a servant girl to carry a broom, but symbols of trade were not everywhere shown: at Ulverston a matchstick stuck in a man's hat meant he was for hire. In some Scottish towns the hirings were called Feeing Markets; in Yorkshire and Lancashire they were the 'Statices', a corruption of

---

[1] See Acknowledgements, p. 5.

Statute Fair (likewise, 'Statchets' at Burton-on-Trent, 'the Status' at Chesterfield, etc.). The custom at Monmouth, where a bridge crosses the river, was for the men to gather on one side and the girls on the other, waiting for the farmers and farmers' wives to look them over.

The choice at Hiring Fairs was not all on one side: the workers discussed among themselves the merits of farmers and their wives. They all sought what they called in Yorkshire 'a good meat house', for the nation-wide custom was for unmarried farmhands to get board and lodging, and sometimes married men got meals. A lot depended on the farmer's wife. A Scarborough listener writes: 'A man left one farmer to go to another who asked him why he had not wanted to "stop-on". The reply was: "Oh, t'boss was all right. An' it was a good me'at house. But Ah care nowt about missus".'

From Ripley in Derbyshire comes this recollection: 'While the labourers at the Hiring Fair paraded up and down, the farmers stood around and if they saw anyone worth hiring they

Radio Times Hulton Library

A Hiring Fair, as drawn by an artist towards the end of the nineteenth century: farmer engages man and maid while labourers look on. The recruiting sergeant is there, too, to give any man the Queen's shilling who prefers it to the farmer's 'fastening penny'

would start conversation with him. I was fifteen when I was first hired in 1906. As a bond of the agreement, the farmer gave you a shilling and you were expected to work twelve months, then you got your pay.' (In some places the term was six months.) 'I received £8 for my first year, had to live in, do my own washing and buy my clothes, and be in the house at nine p.m. when the doors were locked. Then up at five a.m. and work until six p.m. The last time I hired out I stayed four years then got fed up with the money and hours, and went down the pits.'

The shilling mentioned was widely and very anciently called a 'fest' or a 'fastening penny'. A listener at Ledbury writes: 'Only the mean type of employer gave a shilling, the good boss offered half-a-crown. One farmer took the labourer into a near-by pastrycook's and supplied him with tea and a strictly limited number of cakes while they discussed terms.' Pay rates varied from region to region and also according to the individual bargaining-power of master and man. An Irishman writes: 'I remember my father coming home and saying he had hired the two best men in Coleraine – in that year, 1900, men were getting £8 to £10 for six months, with food, and girls £6, with every other Sunday off.'

There were occasional scrimshankers who strolled round the fair hiring themselves to several farmers. A Warwick farmer remembers 'a young man who hired himself to three or four, accepted their shillings, then he joined the army, taking the King's shilling from a recruiting sergeant who was also at the Fair' – but breaking of the verbal hiring contract could be, and sometimes was, brought to court.

'At Lancaster,' says another listener, 'the Hiring Fair was on Whit Saturday and Martinmas Saturday. Any worker not successful went on to Ulverston Fair the following weekend.' All over the country the hirings were at different dates, so that there was a constant drift of labour from area to area. A man hired at Lincoln in 1900 says there were between 200 and 300 people there seeking engagements. Once hired, the hand tramped to the farm unless the farmer gave him a lift in his gig, and the life there was very different from farm life today; a letter addressed from a seventeenth-century farmhouse near Bedford tells us that 'This house has four attic rooms under the thatch, approached *only* from the big corn barn which is built on to the farmhouse. In the old days these attics were the "bothy", sleeping quarters for the men. For meals they went into the house – and it's a marvel to me that the farmer's wives and the maids accepted a system which brought perhaps eight pairs of muddy boots and dirty hands four times a day into the kitchen.'

Up to the end of the nineteenth century the hired hands could be mere children: a correspondent now in her eighties remembers 'a farmer's wife going to Witney and hiring a little servant girl, eleven years old, with all her belongings tied up in a red handkerchief. Having parted from her parents, she walked seven miles to her new farm-home, crying her eyes out.'

But there was a merry, bucolic side to the Hiring Fairs: some of those giving us their memories speak of flirtations with the servant girls ('many a match was made at the hiring fair') and of the fastening penny being spent at boxing booths, coconut-shies and roundabouts by tipsy men of the soil – 'market merry' they called it in Devon – while folk-songs hiccupped on the evening air. (It is worth noting today when moralists often despair of pop-songs that as long ago as 1796 a writer[1] after visiting the fairs wrote that ballad singers 'disseminated sentiments in dissipation'. Songs, he remarked, had much influence in forming the morality

---

[1] William Marshall in *Rural Economy of the Midlands*.

of the agricultural population, and if only the singers would praise conjugal happiness and country life wholesome results would accrue.)

From the start of the present century the Hiring Fairs slowly diminished; a number still existed in the 1920s and 1930s, but today only in two or three isolated spots is there a small trace of the old tradition.[1] Reasons for the decline were many: as the twentieth century came in more people could read and answer advertisements, and rural transportation improved; in times of depression farmers preferred to engage men by the week, so that they could be laid off at will, then when the First World War brought shortage of labour the farmer held on to a man by renewing the contract before the Fair; another reason was the growing reluctance of farm-wives to provide board and lodgings; most of all, there was the coming of labour exchanges and agricultural wages boards (the first in 1917), and the work of unions and governments to establish a national minimum weekly pay packet.

Today the ancient bargaining in the street has gone with the fastening penny; all that is left is the fun-fair, in many towns held on the same spot and at the same date as the old Hiring Fair, and in some still called the Mop Fair. At Banbury, remembered by Joshua Lamb in *Scrapbook* as a place where Master looked for 'young men and maidens', the leather-jackets now look for a 'bird' amid the raucous pandemonium of booths, bingo, and pop. The ghosts are all around them.

In radio we have more than ghosts; we have voices, deathless links with the beginning of this century and beyond. Listen to MR FRED GREEN, Cotswold gardener, husband of the former Sibford postmistress, telling how a fellow had his own subtle way of catching a bird on nights when all the village got together to have their own pre-bingo pranks: 'Ar. Used to collect round the village and have quite a *do*, you see. In a barn. Or schoolroom. Ham and beef and all things good to eat, cider and beer and lemonade and tea and coffee, quite a good feast it were. Then after it were all cleared away they had a sing-song, and the country dancing – used to keep it up till perhaps one o'clock in the morning. They had candles and hurricane lamps all about the barn to light it up. Looked very comfortable and cosy. Had some *lovely* times. We had one country dance which was *very familiar*. Cushion Dance. A gentleman walks round with this cushion and when the music stops he drops it down before a lady, and she's got to kneel on it and kiss the young man. Ar! If she didn't she had to pay a penny. That went to the fiddler. He got a lot of pennies: girls was very *shy* in them days.'

Fred's father was the fiddler at one time, and his grandfather before him played the fife and fiddle. Such musicians in the villages of this country could rarely read music. The tunes had been passed on by ear for centuries. When the BBC met Fred Green he was at his fireside playing his violin: 'My dad taught me this tune. Used to be played for a dance called "Leadings Through". Up to the First World War time.' We recorded it. It was a merry little air and, surprisingly enough, had not been collected previously.[2] Here are the first few bars of it:

---

[1] Details will be given in Volume 2 concerning Hiring Fairs since 1918. Letters from listeners tell of them continuing during the years between the wars at Stockton-on-Tees, Cockermouth, Carlisle, Penrith, Berwick-on-Tweed, Scarborough, Driffield, Durham, Lancaster, Settle, Blairgowrie, Pembroke, Newark, Newcastle, Hexham, Rhayader, Malton, Morpeth, Alnwick, Brecon, Carmarthen, York, Selby, Lincoln, Bedale, Brigg, Kendal, Ulverston, Glasgow, Pickering, Sleaford, Darlington, Hull, Hay-on-Wye, Knighton, Goole, Ballynahinch and other towns in Northern Ireland.

[2] Later it was used as the signature tune for a radio series called *Leslie Baily's Log Book*, and published in a song arrangement by Max Saunders, words by Leslie Baily (Keith Prowse Ltd.).

Britain's heritage of folk-tunes for dancing and singing would have perished under the pressures of modern society but for the collectors who combed the villages in the Nineties and especially in the early years of this century. The golden harvest came after a dramatic experience of Cecil Sharp's on Boxing Day 1899 which made this London musician into an enthusiast. He was staying with relatives at Headington, Oxford, when he saw a procession of young men dressed in white, decorated with gay ribbons, accompanied by a concertina-player and a man dressed as a 'fool'. Through the snow they sprang and capered with gusto, the bells at their shins marking the rhythm of their heavy boots. The Headington morris 'side' normally earned their living in the local quarries but bad weather had brought three weeks without a pay packet so they decided to dance through the district, carrying round a bag for contributions. Their concertina-player, a dashing young bricklayer, William ('Merry') Kimber, so captivated Sharp that he wrote down the notes then and there, and next day played them back to Kimber, who said: 'I thought that only my dad and I knew those tunes!'

The revival of folk-music became nation-wide. Cecil Sharp started collecting folk-songs (as distinct from dance tunes) in 1904 when he heard a gardener at Hambridge in Somerset singing while mowing the vicar's lawn. It was that charming song, 'The Seeds of Love', the first of hundreds saved for posterity.

A recent and happy sequel to all this has been the new wave of enthusiasm for these old songs by guitar-equipped young men and women who sing and dance and televise tunes which sixty years or so ago were only on the lips and in the fingers of village musicians like 'Merry' Kimber and Fred Green.[1] But the moderns don't favour the expurgated versions published in the Cecil Sharp period. Rural song often had a rural earthiness. After some folk-songs had been included in *Scrapbook* a listener[2] wrote to the BBC: 'The programme reminded me of a ditty I heard as a lad when I lived in a Buckinghamshire village. My parents were members of what was called a "singing class" which performed the part-songs and glees of the period. Visits were paid to near-by towns and villages and of course the journeys were made in a horse-drawn conveyance, and I was often taken. The driver of the brake had as a helper an old chap who rode on the step at the rear and on homeward journeys would frequently amuse himself by singing songs in a rather thin quavery voice. His versions were not always very respectable but he refused to be silenced by any protests. One song in particular drew forth many exclamations of "Stop it, Charlie – do behave yourself" and so forth from indignant matrons but there

---

[1] Soaring numbers of clubs have been reported in the last two or three years. There are now (1966) some 800 country dance societies and 600 folk song clubs affiliated to the English Folk Dance and Song Society, plus about 90 morris dance clubs; and the Royal Scottish Country Dance Society has a membership of 18,000 in Britain and abroad. The new upsurge of interest is due undoubtedly to television which seemed some years ago to be killing such clubs, until it took up folk song and dance itself.   [2] Mr W. J. Gwynn, of Dunstable.

were also giggles from the younger members of the party who joined very heartily in the *bang-bang-bang* at the appropriate places. I send you what I remember of the words and music.' Here it is:

According to Mr Douglas Kennedy (formerly Director of the English Folk Dance and Song Society) this song has never been published. He points out that the melody is reminiscent of several traditional airs such as 'Villikins and his Dinah' and 'The Wearing of the Green'. This relationship of tunes is frequent in folk–music, arising from days when they drifted across country from mouth to mouth and were varied *en route*.

Not only were many of the old tunes well worth rescuing on their own merits but they were an inspiration to creative composers such as Elgar, Vaughan Williams, and Delius. Elgar was walking in the Wye Valley in 1906 when he heard snatches of a song across the valley, a tune which he threaded into his 'Introduction and Allegro for Strings'. Percy Grainger in 1905 anticipated BBC tape-recording methods by carrying a phonograph recorder with him when collecting tunes; he recorded a Lincolnshireman singing 'Brigg Fair', and played it later to Delius who developed it into the orchestral rhapsody of the same name.

It is easy to be romantic about Merrie England. It is realistic to remember that alongside the fun was the hardness of many lives when agriculture was in a slump at the turn of the century. The bottom had fallen out of prices. Between 1870 and 1900 the acreage of English wheat had shrunk by nearly half and it continued shrinking up to 1914. Unemployment meant hard living for the villagers, sickness, malnutrition, massive migration from the land. Thatched cottages with roses round the door, so beloved of almanacs and magazine illustrations, were often rural slums.

MR FRED GREEN is again an eye-witness: 'Had some hard times all the wintertime when half the men in the village got no work on the farms. I've known the time when there's been as many as thirty or forty lads on the village crossroads in the winter nights playing a game called Stag – they'd nothing else to do. A lot of them very poorly shod and clothed. Out-of-work farm labourers would try to earn a few pennies by digging up tree stumps and chopping them for firewood. Lot of poverty in them days. And no unemployment pay.'

The scene is reflected bitterly in a song collected by Lucy Broadwood at Dunsfold, Surrey, in 1898:

> *The labouring man will plough the deep,*
> *Till the ground and sow the wheat,*
> *Fight the battles when afar,*
> *Fear no danger nor a scar;*
> *But still they're looked upon like thieves*
> *By them they keep at home at ease,*
> *And every day throughout the land*
> *They try to starve the labouring man.*

Hereford Public Library   *Imperial War Museum*
The makers of song: a pedlar of ballads tramping round the villages in the Nineties, and a group photographed in the trenches during the First World War

The Fun and the Hardness of Life

This ballad dated back to Napoleonic times but labourers were still singing it early in this century. And it was prophetic:

> *Now if the wars should rise again,*
> *And England be in want of men,*
> *They'll have to search the country round*
> *For the lads that plough the ground.*
> *Then to some foreign land they'll go,*
> *To fight and drub the daring foe;*
> *Do what they will, do what they can,*
> *They can't do without the labouring man.*

They sang it to a tune with a defiant gusto. The labouring class in country and town faced hardship with a wonderful combination of stolidity and humour. Later in this book some link will be suggested between such songs as the above, home-made by peasants close to the earth of England, and the wry ballads sung by their descendants close to the mud of France, 1914–18:

> *Send out the Army and the Navy,*
> *Send out the rank and file,*
> *Send out the brave Territorials,*
> *They'll face the danger with a smile*
> *(I don't think!).*
> *Send out mother,*
> *Send out my sister and my brother,*
> *But for Gawd's sake don't send me!*

> *　　　　*　　　　*

At the end of Queen Victoria's century a finger was probing at a cancer within town life. 'I decided to try to obtain information concerning the housing, occupation, and earnings of every wage-earning family in York,' wrote Seebohm Rowntree, sociologist, Quaker, and cocoa industrialist, in his historic book published in 1901, *Poverty, a Study of Town Life*. 'These particulars extended to 11,560 families living in 388 streets and comprising a population of 46,754.' He found that 27.8 per cent of the city's population were living below the poverty line. 'No civilization,' he said, very truly, 'can be sound or stable which has at its base this mass of stunted life.'

Such researchers as Rowntree were digging the footings on which the foundations of the Welfare State were to be laid later. A check in other towns satisfied him that York was not exceptional. He described what life meant for over a quarter of Britain's townspeople: 'A family living upon the scale allowed for in this estimate must never spend a penny on railway fare or omnibus. They must never go into the country unless they walk. They must never purchase a halfpenny newspaper or spend a penny to buy a ticket for a popular concert. They must write no letters to absent children, for they cannot afford to pay the postage. They must never contribute anything to their church or chapel, or give any help to a neighbour which costs them money. They cannot save, nor can they join sick club or trade union, because they cannot pay the necessary subscriptions. Their children must have no pocket money for dolls, marbles, or sweets. The father must smoke no tobacco, and must drink no beer.'

59

THE MERRY MEN:

Headington Quarry Morris side, about 1900

William Kimber (*left*) in 1946 at a Stratford-on-Avon Festival

Fred Green in 1953 at Sibford Ferris
Photos by English Folk Song and Dance Society, and Leslie Baily

60

Many did, of course, but at dire cost: 'If any of these conditions are broken, the extra expenditure involved is met, *and can only be met*, by limiting the diet; or, in other words, by sacrificing physical efficiency.'

A macabre sidelight on the state of the nation was that when British troops sailed away to war in South Africa the *Daily Mail* launched an 'Absent Minded Beggar Fund', raising £100,000 for families left behind, the charity gaining its title from words written by Kipling to a tune by Sullivan which 'was guaranteed to pull teeth out of barrel-organs', said Kipling:

> *Cook's son, Duke's son, son of a belted Earl –*
> *Fifty thousand Horse and Foot ordered to Table Bay,*
> *Each of 'em doing his country's work –*
> *And who's to look after the girl?*
> *Pass the hat for your credit's sake, and Pay, Pay, Pay!*

The 1899 background of this song was a London where the infantile death-rate reached the unprecedented figure of 279 per 1,000; the counties of Durham and Northumberland had 34 and 38 per cent respectively of their population living in grossly overcrowded conditions, and parts of Glasgow, Liverpool, South Wales, and London were as bad.

Sub-human conditions had horrible side-effects. Sexual prostitution by women was often *solely* because they were among the 27.8 per cent living below the poverty line. Drunkenness was a common sight in the streets. The first ten years of the twentieth century had the highest murder rate of any decade recorded so far.[1] After the Boer War public opinion was shocked by publication of the enormous number of volunteers medically rejected.[2] This spurred a movement towards better child-welfare measures, enacted later among the many social reforms of the Liberal Governments of 1905 onwards.

Such was the stratification of society early in the century, and the built-in blinkers of class, that many good, kind-hearted souls living in comfort had no notion of the lot of the lower orders. Today all this may seem unbelievable to younger readers but come in the 1960s with *Scrapbook*'s tape-recorder to an elderly lady who lives quietly in a country cottage, and suddenly that dim, distant, disgraceful England will focus sharply into the realism of personal experience. She tells us first that she was brought up in a comfortable middle-class home:

'Everything in the house was kept shining and spotless by well-trained servants, who looked so decorative in their morning print-dresses, caps, and aprons, and positively theatrical in the afternoon with their lace-trimmed best aprons and caps with long streamers at the back!' This affluent household fell in a family disaster, so that at twenty our lady had to fend for herself in London: 'I knew how to do *nothing at all*. I was fond of painting and drawing, and at last I was offered a job at a factory where they made those romantic picture postcards of stage stars which were so popular. I had to colour them, by hand. They offered me eight shillings a week. I was living in a little attic room at five shillings a week, but I knew that eight was more than five, so I took the job and scraped along somehow. . . . Holidays? – well, you could take

---

[1] The number of men and women sentenced to death (with the numbers executed in brackets) was: 1900–9, 284 (159); 1910–19, 233 (123); 1920–9, 234 (138); 1930–9, 197 (85); 1940–9, 262 (127); 1950–9, 225 (104). These figures were for England and Wales. During the period 1901 to 1951 the population rose from approximately 32½ millions to 43¾ millions, which has to be remembered to keep the murder rate in correct perspective.

[2] Memorandum by Director-General, Army Medical Corps, published 1903, stated that in 1893–1902, 34.6 per cent were rejected on medical examination.

a summer holiday if you liked to chance whether you'd get your job back when it was over. I stayed on. I shouldn't have had my rent. So it was fifty-two weeks work in a year.'

Radicals like Rowntree tore off the nation's blinkers. It is one of the finest achievements of this century that a host of crusaders down the years have striven to end this sort of thing; thanks to them and thanks to the advance of medicine we live in an utterly different Britain. The picture postcard girl's story is human evidence of that; statisticians can provide plenty of facts. These are sufficient:

In 1900 *the number of deaths* per thousand of population was 18.4; in 1965 it was 11.5.

Expectation of life for men in 1900 was 46 years, for women 50. In 1965 it was 68 for men, 74 for women.

Infantile mortality: in 1900, 153 babies died out of every 1,000 born. By 1965 this figure had dropped to 19.

The old stratification of society is well shown in three memories side by side in *Scrapbook for* 1902; we might call them a Symphony of the Bath, in three movements. LADY DIANA COOPER first tells how as a small child she went to stay at Belvoir Castle in Leicestershire, the seat of her grandfather, the Duke of Rutland. First movement, *con grazioso:* 'Belvoir Castle was a great rambling house with hundreds of rooms and an army of servants. Some of the old retainers made an almost overpowering impression on the mind of a child. There were, for instance, the watermen. They had stubbly beards and a Bill Sykes appearance, and wore green baize aprons from chin to knee. On his shoulders the waterman carried a wooden yoke from which hung two gigantic cans of water. He moved on a perpetual round of the southern bedrooms in Belvoir Castle. Above the ground floor there was not a drop of hot water and not one bath, so the waterman's job was to fill all jugs and kettles in the bedrooms, and morning and evening to bring the hot water for the hip-baths, in which one bathed in front of a wonderful roaring fire.'

Second movement, *con coal dust*, from an old collier, MR LEWIS WILLIAMS, of Treharris, South Wales: 'The old tub was one of the greatest hardships a miner's wife ever had to bear. She had to carry heavy buckets of water; I really believe that the women at that time had many miscarriages and other evils because of the hard, heavy work that they had to do. We had to bath in the kitchen. There was no privacy. We had to dry our clothes there, too. The fumes arising from the pit clothes were in the air, and you could grind the dust that was coming from them; you could feel it grinding between your teeth.'

Third movement, from the comfortable middle-class – but not *too* comfortable, for MRS FLORENCE INGILLSON, a Leeds housewife, says: 'When I got married I was considered very lucky indeed to have a bathroom. Over the bath was a geyser that roared and steamed like fury. The house was gas-lit, and we had a great coal-fuelled Yorkshire range in the kitchen. On Thursday or Friday you'd see eighteen loaves and two dozen teacakes on the table, fresh from the oven – and how delicious the smell! Food was different from today in many ways. Grapefruit was unknown to me, tomatoes were rare and said to be bad for you, and bananas a novelty.' (The first big cargo of bananas arrived in 1901.)

On this young woman, when attiring herself for the theatre or a ball, fashion imposed a fiendish form of eroticism: merciless corsets thrust the bust enticingly forward and the bottom

In the dark age before pithead baths: the collier at the kitchen hearth

In the golden age of armies of servants: Belvoir Castle, where Lady Diana Cooper bathed before the fire

Dressing the lady: to the corset ('real whalebone', 21s from Peter Robinson's) add various layers of frillies, and you achieve the apparition on right, as drawn in *Pictorial Comedy*, 1899

boldly backward. This grotesque shape was built on the theory that to distort is to attract attention. Concealment of legs was elaborate: 'When I was dressed in my finery I wore three petticoats, the under one of white flannel beautifully embroidered, then a *moiré* one, and the third of silk with five or six rows of frills – and didn't they take some ironing! The frills had to be goffered with a special iron, like a pair of curling tongs, but when you walked they sounded lovely, they went *frou-frou*. Underclothes were of silk or wool or cotton. Most girls wore black cotton stockings at sixpence or a shilling a pair; real silk were anything from 10s 6d to £5.'

There was no artificial silk, no nylon, none of the cheap and charming garments which nowadays make it difficult to distinguish between a duchess and a typist. Scientists have brought in marvels to ease and brighten a woman's way of living, but few of them were yet in sight at the turn of the century. Everywhere household chores were manual, housewives laundered with dolly-tub and wringer, cooks perspired over coal-ranges. We must pay a tribute to Mr H. C. Booth, whose name should be enshrined in gratitude by every housewife. His experiments with An Invention had an absurdity that is comic to us but must have been unpleasant to him. This Englishman aspired to improve the nineteenth century hand-pushed carpet-sweeper (motion over the floor causing brushes to rotate against the carpet); he had seen an American carpet-sweeper which *blew* air into a carpet in order to shift the dust, but he had the brainwave of reversing the process: 'I tried the experiment of sucking with my mouth against the back of a plush seat in a restaurant in Victoria Street, with the result that I was choked.' Undaunted, Booth patented in 1901 his mechanical sucker-out. This Heath Robinsonish device was mounted on a push-cart and sent on hire to hotels and swell houses into which its snakey pipes were taken; the machine outdoors was hand-operated by contracting and opening a huge bellows and its noise was atrocious: 'I was frequently sued for damages for alleged frightening of cab-horses in the street.' So began the now indispensable vacuum-cleaner. Electric models came after 1910.

At the century's dawn, signs of an electrical revolution in the home were hardly discernible. The great Gas Age reigned. Millions of citizens trotted off to bed carrying the centuries-old candle. It was in public transport that electricity got a move on. The 'Tuppenny Tube', as the Central London underground was dubbed by Cockneys, was opened in 1900 from the Bank to Shepherd's Bush, with a uniform fare of 2d any distance. For nearly forty years Londoners had known underground railways but they were just below ground-level, steam-driven and unpleasantly smoky; the first electrification had come in 1890 (the City and South London), but the Tuppenny Tube, bored deep under the metropolis, was the first to be planned on modern lines.

Provincial towns were ahead of London with that clanging, lurching challenger to the horse, the electric tram. Some towns had had them ten years and more when London's first came in 1901. It was a threat to the 'poor G.G.' because it was both faster and cleaner (the crossing-sweeper shovelling up horse-droppings is one of the 'picturesque' sights of old times for which no nostalgia need be spared). Leeds was trying a tramcar pulled by a steam-engine; coupled together, this double-monster came snorting through the streets with smoke floating from its high funnel, a sight to thrill every schoolboy and to put the breeze-up every horse. But horses weren't easily run off the roads. London still had nearly 4,000 horse-buses in 1902 but only twenty-eight motor-buses and one thirty-six-seater steam-bus, burning coke. It puffed briefly between Hammersmith and Oxford Circus, then vanished into the elysium for brainwaves that don't work.

Electric trams quickly caught on. By 1902 there were getting on for 200 in London.[1] In-evitably, there was a tramcar song, sung by George Lashwood who advised young couples to:

> . . . *go, go, go for a ride on the car, car, car,*
> *For we know how cosy the tops of the tram-cars are,*
> *The seats are so small, and there's not much to pay,*
> *You sit close together and 'spoon' all the way.*
> *There's many a Miss will be Missis some day*
> *For riding on top of the car.*[2]

The telephone was regarded almost entirely as for office use. In 1901 the metropolitan area was carved up between the National Telephone Company and the Post Office, which opened its first London exchange, the Central. One of the original ladies of that switchboard, MISS E. R. JOHNSTONE, directs our attention to the fact that the telephone was not only an electrical engineering development but it stirred a small eddy in the deep waters of sex-relationship: 'People seemed to think it rather saucy to be a switchboard girl. I don't know whether this was because our job required us to speak to a great number of strange men, but we were very strictly supervised. My pay as a telephone girl was seventeen shillings a week. When we started the Central Exchange it had only 200 subscribers, but so great was public interest that within three months the number had increased to 3,000. Six other Post Office exchanges were

---

[1] Most run by London United Tramways Company, a number by East Ham municipality. The big LCC fleet did not come until 1903.

[2] 'Riding on Top of the Car', words by F. W. Leigh and V. P. Bryan, music by Harry von Tilzer (reproduced by permission of Francis, Day and Hunter Ltd.), 1902.

opened in London in 1902. They were Western, Victoria, Putney, Kingston, Wimbledon, and Richmond.'

It was to be a noisy as well as an electrical new century, but there was little extra noise yet. A very few homes possessed the gramophone, more usually known as the phonograph. This was *non*-electric. You turned a handle to wind up its clockwork motor. The needle scratched; a strangulated voice came from the tin trumpet; it was a surprise at parties, nothing more than a toy until the great singers began to record – first, Caruso. The young Italian who was to become the most famous tenor of his time made something of a stir, though not a sensation, in his 1902 London debut at Covent Garden ('The higher he sings, the more easy it seems to him,' said Melba after singing with him in *La Bohème*). MR F. W. GAISBERG, of HMV, has told *Scrapbook* how he went to Milan before Caruso's Covent Garden debut, taking a recording machine. He heard Caruso at the Opera and immediately invited him to make records. Caruso boldly asked for £100 for ten songs, all to be recorded in one afternoon. Gaisberg wired his London office. They replied: 'Fee exorbitant. Forbid you to record.'

Chancing his arm, Gaisberg went ahead. The records were cut one hot afternoon at the the Hotel Milan, in a room over the apartment where Verdi had died the previous year. It was a good bet by Gaisberg: the technical quality of those discs was astonishing at that time (though the great breakthrough, electrical recording, was to wait twenty-three years) and the publicity surrounding Caruso's appearance at Covent Garden gave his first records a splendid send-off. Gaisberg was forgiven. The phonograph began to be taken seriously. Caruso's £100 was also a good bet for himself: by the end of his life in 1921 he had made £600,000 by recording. The original Milan records are now rare museum pieces (the BBC library has them) but in modern times they have been reissued, the recording engineers having given Caruso a voice-lift by electrically re-recording the old voice with a new orchestral accompaniment.[1]

Today we are fully conscious of a rapidly changing world around us. This was not so at the dawn of the century. It needed a sharp eye to read the signs. Our oracle, H. G. Wells, wrote a book of *Anticipations*, not fiction this time, but a serious pre-view of life in the 20th century: 'There will be roads upon which motor-vehicles will be free to travel up to the limit of their very highest possible speed. These roads will be very wide, made probably of asphalt sloped to drain, and traffic in opposite directions will be strictly separated.' He thought that private vehicles would be capable of a day's journey of 300 miles or more, and that there would be motor-trucks for freight. For soldiers he anticipated trench-warfare, and for housewives 'a neat little range, heated by electricity and provided with thermometers'. But he was surprisingly imperceptive on aeroplanes, as we shall see later, and his imagination refused to see 'any sort of submarine doing anything but suffocate its crew'.

In the very same year (1901) the first British submarine was launched at Barrow without calamity. At Belfast the White Star's *Celtic*[2] was launched amid whoops of pride at her being the largest liner in the world (20,880 tons). An intense Anglo-German maritime rivalry was to develop during the first thirteen years of the new century, the *Dreadnought* and *Titanic* era. Alongside this was the industrial feud, Britain losing her old place as the 'workshop of the world', Germany pulling ahead in steel, iron, and cotton; but right up to 1914 the British remained

---

[1] Many inquiries were received from listeners about a re-recorded Caruso disc broadcast in *Scrapbook for 1902*: its number is HMV COLH 119; we used an excerpt from *Tosca* among other arias.

[2] I saw this liner beached off Peel, Isle of Man, after being torpedoed in the First World War. – L.B.

by far the greatest seafarers, nearly half the world's ships flying the Union Jack. Everyone took it for granted that Britannia would always rule the waves.

Ruling the air was not even thought of. Aviation had no part in the Boer War, not even a balloon for observation. MR GEOFFREY DORMAN tells us of an invention which seemed to have military possibilities: 'As a boy of eight I used to walk to school every morning through the Crystal Palace grounds where the great S. F. Cody was experimenting with his great man-lifting kites. I used to watch him flying them up to 1,000 feet or more. From the wire cable he suspended a basket in which a man stood; this was pulled up by a pilot kite. One morning in 1902 Cody asked me if I'd like a kite ride, and up I went. And was I thrilled! It made me late for school, but I gave a plausible excuse and got away with it for the time being, but in the break I boasted to my mates what I'd been doing, and my form-master overheard, and when we returned to class I was sternly lectured and told to bend down and touch my toes for six strokes of the cane. The master said he hoped this would be a lesson to me not to be such a silly reckless little boy, but all it did was teach me the danger of careless talk.' (The Cody kite was adopted by the War Office in 1904.)

We see that small boy gazing down on the little people far below; does he wonder what the future will bring them, and himself, and the sprawling city with its glistening peaceful ribbon of Thames? Over there is Putney where Irene Vanbrugh watches the Cockneys in their punts, and is so impressed by 'a sort of unconscious acceptance of a beautiful world' that many years later she is to tell another world that once 'People were not in such a hurry to rush on from one thing to another.' Down there in Baker Street Sherlock Holmes is unravelling the mystery of the *Hound of the Baskervilles*, and across there at Lords a ghostly batsman plays to the bowling of a ghost – C. B. Fry is it? – and if the schoolboy is allowed another kite ride as darkness falls he will see the city touched with a special magic, spurts of light dancing through the streets as the lamplighter passes along with his wand, the distant bell of muffin man calling small boys to firesides, and for older boys:

> *Like dragonflies the hansoms hover,*
> *With jewelled eyes to catch the lover . . .*

. . . and under London's roof a hundred simple tunes spin cheerfully into the new century with their Arabian Nights dream of you being my honeysuckle and I your bee.

1901

Queen Victoria died (January 22), 'surrounded by her children and grandchildren, including the German Emperor'.

Commonwealth of Australia inaugurated.

Lloyd George after giving anti-Boer-war speech at Birmingham had to escape from rioters, dressed as policeman.

107,539 persons in London receiving poor relief, highest since 1872.

British Navy's first submarine launched.

Marconi's first wireless signal across Atlantic (December 12).

Scott's first Antarctic expedition in *Discovery*.

First British ocean-going vessel to be fitted with Marconi wireless apparatus, *Lake Champlain*.

Cody's man-lifting box-kite patented.

Aero Club founded in London.

First electric trams in London.

University College, Exeter, established.

Factories Act.

Garden City Association met at Birmingham to promote building of new towns in country districts.

H. C. Booth patented the vacuum cleaner.

STAGE: *A Chinese Honeymoon*, musical play, started run of 1,075 performances; *The Toreador*, 675.

BOOKS: *Poverty, a Study of Town Life*, by Seebohm Rowntree; *Anticipations* and *The First Men in the Moon* (H. G. Wells); *Kim* (Rudyard Kipling); *Monsieur Beaucaire* (Booth Tarkington); *The Eternal City* (Hall Caine); *Life of the Bee* (Maeterlinck).

SONGS: 'Absent'; 'After the Ball'; 'Coronation Day'; 'Louisiana Lou'; 'Mighty Lak' a Rose'; 'O Dry Those Tears'; 'O Lovely Night'; 'The Absent-minded Beggar'.

1902

Coronation of King Edward (August 9), after postponement from June 26 due to appendicitis.

King gave dinner to 500,000 of the poor.

Queen gave medals and tea to 12,500 maids-of-all-work in London to celebrate coronation.

Treaty of Vereeniging ends Boer War (May 31).

Anglo-Japanese alliance.

Arthur Balfour became Prime Minister succeeding Lord Salisbury.

Education Act abolished School Boards and transferred control of elementary, secondary, and technical education to local authority.

Hartley University College, Southampton, founded.
Round-the-world Imperial cable completed.
Opening of National Physical Laboratory.
First flight across London by Spencer airship.
First agricultural tractor with internal combustion engine.
First Sturmey-Archer three-speed gear for bicycles.
First steam-driven omnibus in London, between Hammersmith and Oxford Circus.
W. R. Morris makes his first motor vehicle, with de Dion engine.
First Post Office motor-mail vans.
Sir Ronald Ross awarded Nobel Prize in medicine for work on malaria.
Cancer research scheme inaugurated by Royal Colleges of Physicians and Surgeons.
Caruso's debut at Covent Garden.
'Land of Hope and Glory' first sung in 'Coronation Ode' (Elgar)

STAGE: *Merrie England* (Edward German); *A Country Girl* began its run of 729 performances; *Mrs Warren's Profession* (Bernard Shaw); *The Admirable Crichton* and *Quality Street* (J. M. Barrie); *Cathleen ni Houlihan* (W. B. Yeats).

BOOKS: *The Grand Babylon Hotel* (Arnold Bennett); *Just-So Stories* (Rudyard Kipling); *The Hound of the Baskervilles* (Conan Doyle); *The Four Feathers* (A. E. W. Mason); *Path to Rome* (Hilaire Belloc).

SONGS: 'Because'; 'Bill Bailey, Won't You Please Come Home'; 'Honeysuckle and the Bee'; 'I May Be Crazy'; 'Just Like the Ivy'; 'Land of Hope and Glory'; 'Riding On Top of the Car'; 'Under the Deodar' (*Country Girl*); 'Yeomen of England' and 'O Peaceful England' (*Merrie England*).

1903

King Edward VII's visit to Paris and French President's visit to London paved the way to the *entente cordiale*.
King exchanged wireless greetings with President Theodore Roosevelt in USA.
Joseph Chamberlain declared for imperial preference, seceding from free trade.
Income tax reached highest level since before Boer War, 1s 3d (it fell to 11d in 1904).
First garden city, Letchworth.
First aeroplane flights by Wright brothers in USA.
Poor Prisoners' Defence Act, first law for giving legal aid.
Motor-car Act: speed limit raised to 20 miles per hour.
Auto-cycle Union founded to control motor-cycle sport.
First country motor-bus service, Helston-Lizard.
Headquarters of army at Aldershot brought into wireless contact with Channel Squadron.
Tribunal of judges refused to admit Miss Bertha Cave to the Bar on ground that there was no precedent.
Women's Social and Political Union (suffragettes) founded at Manchester.
Daily Mirror launched as 'the first daily paper for gentlewomen'; it failed.
Workers' Education Association founded.
Scottish Women's Golf Championship instituted.

Sir William R. Cremar awarded Nobel Prize for peace.
University of Liverpool founded.

STAGE: *The Orchid* began its run of 559 performances; *Princess of Kensington* (Edward German).

BOOKS: *The Riddle of the Sands* (Erskine Childers); *The Way of All Flesh* (Samuel Butler); *Typhoon* (Joseph Conrad); *The Call of The Wild* (Jack London); *Principles of Mathematics* (Bertrand Russell).

SONGS: 'Bedelia' (*The Orchid*); 'Down at the Old Bull and Bush'; 'Mother o' Mine'; 'Stop yer Tickling, Jock'; 'Two Eyes of Grey'.

1904

Fleming invented the thermionic valve.
First British permanent cinema, the Daily Bioscope.
Motor registration started (January 1) under 1903 Act.
Cody's man-lifting kites adopted by British Army.
Anglo-French agreement signed.
Dogger Bank incident, Russian battleships fired on Hull fishing boats.
First Empire Day celebrated (May 24).
Sir William Ramsay awarded Nobel Prize in chemistry for discovery of gaseous basic materials in atmosphere.
Lord Rayleigh awarded Nobel Prize in physics for discovery of argon.
At Rhayader King and Queen inaugurated new water-supply for Birmingham from Elan Valley.
King laid foundation-stone of Liverpool Cathedral.
Ritz Hotel, first steel-framed building in London.
W. G. Grace made his 126th century, at Crystal Palace (record until 1925).
Cecil Sharp started collecting English folk-songs.
Victorian (12,000 tons), built for Allan Line, first large ocean-going vessel with steam turbines.
First covered-top tramcar in London.
Steam trains abolished from District and Inner Circle Lines, London.
Ladies' Automobile Club held first meeting.
Daily Mirror re-launched as the first halfpenny daily illustrated publication; big success.
University of Leeds founded.
Elgar Festival at Covent Garden with Hallé Orchestra conducted by Richter.
London Symphony Orchestra founded.
Abbey Theatre, Dublin, opened.

STAGE: *Peter Pan* (J. M. Barrie); *The Walls of Jericho* (Sutro); *Riders to the Sea* (J. M. Synge); *Véronique* (Messager); *The Catch of the Season* began its run of 621 performances.

BOOKS: *Radioactivity* (Rutherford); *Napoleon of Notting Hill* (G. K. Chesterton); *Green Mansions* (W. H. Hudson); *The New Treasure Seekers* (E. Nesbit).

SONGS: 'My Ain Folk'; 'Swing Song' (*Véronique*); 'The Church Parade' (*The Catch of the Season*); 'Tobermory'.

1905

Sir H. Campbell-Bannerman became Prime Minister, heading Liberal Government.
First suffragette interruption of political meeting, at Manchester.
Unemployed demonstrations in London; Queen Alexandra launched charity appeal.
Automobile Association founded.
First RAC motor-car TT race, Isle of Man.
First Rolls-Royce car.
First £1,000 transfer of football player.
Welsh women's golf championships instituted.
Prince of Wales inaugurated LCC 'river bus' service.
King opened Aldwych and Kingsway.
British and French fleets exchanged courtesy visits.
University of Sheffield founded.
Foundation of British Red Cross Society.
Sinn Fein Party founded in Dublin.
Rescued by Rover film produced by Cecil Hepworth.
'Introduction and Allegro' (Elgar).

STAGE: *Man and Superman* and *Major Barbara* (Bernard Shaw); *The Voysey Inheritance* (Granville Barker).

BOOKS: *Kipps* (H. G. Wells); *The Scarlet Pimpernel* (Baroness Orczy); *The Return of Sherlock Holmes* (Conan Doyle); *The Four Just Men* (Edgar Wallace); *The Mayor of Troy* (Quiller-Couch).

SONGS: 'I Love a Lassie'; 'In the Shade of the Old Apple Tree'; 'I Wouldn't Leave My Little Wooden Hut For You'.

The Calendar is continued on page 86

TRENDS OF THE NEW CENTURY

A man of destiny is on his way: Winston Churchill wins Northwest Manchester for the Liberals in 1906. Election results are flashed by lantern-slides

*Illustrated
London News*

The launching of Britain's first submarine at Barrow in 1901 seems to have attracted no crowd and hardly an arm's wave, if the *Illustrated London News* artist is to be believed

The first great star to record: Caruso caricatures himself singing into the phonograph machine

HMV

A superlative era for English cricket: when Tom Webster drew this cartoon in 1946 he firmly believed there had not since been such giants as those of the early years of the century

Empire News

News of victory in South Africa, 'broadcast' by the Lord Mayor of London reading a telegram from Kitchener

Illustrated London News

The crowd waiting outside Buckingham Palace for news bulletins of King Edward's illness in 1902 (incidentally, this picture shows the palace before its façade was rebuilt in 1913)

3 THE STORY BEHIND
LAND OF HOPE AND GLORY

In the absence of radio and of evening newspapers on a Sunday afternoon in June 1902 a banner was slung across the portico of the London Mansion House: *Peace is Proclaimed*. The Boers had capitulated at last.

SIR COMPTON MACKENZIE was an undergraduate at Oxford: 'We had the news in the early morning, and the whole city and university were full of jubilation. I remember we burnt a cab shelter in the Broad, among other things. We had £90 worth of fireworks to let off the next evening and we didn't get back till about three in the morning, when we had a supper (dressed crab, I remember). At four o'clock the sun was shining brightly, a glorious, glorious morning, and I said, "Well now we must let off the fireworks", and everybody said, "Don't be silly, we can't let off fireworks *now*". But with that logic one has when one has had a good deal of champagne and an exhilarating evening, I demonstrated that it was absolutely necessary. We started letting off catherine wheels and rockets and everything else, and among the fireworks were two Chinese crackers, each about two feet tall. I tied these to the Dean's oak. The oak is a second door which both undergraduates and dons have, which they shut when they don't want to be disturbed. Suddenly the Dean put his head out of the window and said "Mr Mackenzie and the rest of you gentlemen, if you don't go to bed at once, you'll be sent down tomorrow". And at that moment the two Chinese crackers went off and his oak fell with a crash.'

The penalty was a 'varsity fine of £5 each.

Throughout the land the outlook was now jubilant for King Edward VII's coronation. All was well: the troopships were coming home in triumph, Kitchener was rewarded with a victory viscountcy plus £50,000 *and* membership of the newly formed Order of Merit, and the Flag flew from the Cape to the Zambesi. 'Wider still and wider shall thy bounds be set' – A. C. Benson's words to Edward Elgar's tune come rolling down the years from this period when a song was born which may be called the biggest of all the pop-songs; it became the theme of the Edwardian era, and is still sung lustily like a tribal rite at the last of the Promenade Concerts each year. To young promenaders some of the words are just a joke; 'Land of Hope and Glory' seems on the face of it to be highly charged with a jingo spirit now largely departed and discredited. Conservative Party meetings chant it, but not unblushingly: one member has asked the party 'to make more realistic political life by replacing the wretched anthem of ours with something more in keeping with the times. "Wider still and wider, etc." is an insolent and arrogant prayer and a futile suggestion.'[1] So it is, if its prayer to 'Make us mightier yet' is

---

[1] Letter to *The Observer* from Mr L. Garnham-Fisher, of Weybourne, November 21, 1965.

assumed to be the text of old-fashioned militarist colonialism, but *Scrapbook* research brought to light correspondence between Benson and Elgar and this led us to consult their old friends, all of which suggests that this jingo interpretation needs qualifying.

It would be difficult to imagine a man more unlike Colonel Blimp than the scholar, A. C. Benson. A diffident housemaster at Eton, he spent much of his time retired in his study writing biographies, essays, and verses. When Edward VII came to the throne and Britain was still at war Benson wrote a sequence of five poems linking the two things: 'Peace, gentle peace . . . when comest thou? Our brethren long for thee', he wrote. Another verse, 'Crown the King with life' (i.e. with an end to war), he visualized as a great chorus, for he had the idea of getting a composer to set the verses to music. Rather shyly he ventured to wonder whether they might be sung in the Coronation service at Westminster Abbey. He showed them to the Master of the King's Musick, Sir Walter Parratt, who sent them on to Elgar, now living at Plas Gwyn, Hereford, asking would they be of any interest to him?

Elgar was smarting under a rejection by the Covent Garden Opera Syndicate of his 'Caractacus': 'in its present form . . . unsuitable for dramatic representation on the stage', but their letter added these honeyed words: 'There will be undoubtedly a gala performance at Covent Garden in honour of the Coronation: would you be prepared to undertake the composition of a 'Coronation Ode'?' Rather. Elgar certainly would, but what about the words? He looked again at those Benson verses lying on his desk. Then he wrote to Covent Garden outlining a Benson–Elgar collaboration. A telegram soon came back: 'The King approves of our plan. Proceed.'

The housemaster at Eton was delighted. His dream about the Coronation service had already been pricked by a bishop-friend's remark that Benson's verses were 'not sufficiently liturgical', but the prospect of his work being performed at Covent Garden in a setting by Elgar more than mollified him. They set to work consulting about those five poems, Benson revising them as Elgar set them to music. The King also had a suggestion. Could the programme at Covent Garden include Elgar's new orchestral march 'Pomp and Circumstance' (No. 1)? It had been first performed at Liverpool in 1901, then had taken by storm a Prom Concert in London with Henry Wood conducting. The composer responded to the royal request with a stroke of Elgarian showmanship: he decided to have the main marching tune sung as the finale of the 'Coronation Ode'. He asked Benson for a sixth poem, fitting words to the march. Benson replied: 'The metre is a hard one. If you could string together a few nonsense words, just to show me how you would wish them to run, I could construct it, following the air closely.' Alas, we don't know what nonsense Elgar posted to Benson, but a few days later Benson replied from his study at Eton:

> '*Land of Hope and Glory*
> *Mother of the free,*
> *How shall we extol thee,*
> *Who are born of thee?* –

You will criticize frankly anything I send you, will you not? I don't think I have quite the popular ring.'

The popular ring! . . . Elgar approved. Benson wrote the rest of the now-familiar anthem but it did *not* contain the wider-still-and-wider bit. Instead was this (after the above four lines);

Cambridge Studios

Dr A. C. Benson

Radio Times Hulton Library

Sir Edward Elgar

Truth and right and freedom,
Each a holy gem,
Stars of solemn brightness
Weave thy diadem.

Benson, who sang of 'truth and right and freedom' as every Briton's birthright, was not conventionally Establishment-minded: at Eton he often met Lords and Ladies visiting their sons, and of one Peer he wrote to Elgar: 'He is one of the most simple and delightful people I know, exactly the opposite of all that men of his type would be expected to be.' And when Elgar suggested introducing some references to the King in the 'Coronation Ode' Benson declined: 'There is so little that is romantic and distinguished about the King personally that one cannot linger on the personal side.' This was the unBlimp man with hopeful and glorious sentiments.

His brother, the novelist E. F. Benson, has written[1] that A.C.B., while 'a hugely successful master at Eton for nearly twenty years' was a rebel against the barrenness of a strictly classical education, and 'he also detested, as a mischievous idolatry, the worship of athleticism'. In fact, he was a bit off-beat for Eton and the conventional upper crust, yet he wrote a song lyric which seems at first sight to be distinctly on-beat for jingo Britain.

[1] In the autobiography *Final Edition* by E. F. Benson (Longmans Green). E. F. and A. C. Benson were sons of Archbishop Benson of Canterbury.

As to the composer, for the 'Coronation Ode' Elgar brought up all the big guns – soloists of Melba's calibre were booked for the Covent Garden performance along with massed battalions of orchestra, military band, and the Sheffield Festival Choir, all to be conducted by Elgar himself. The news of peace in South Africa came just over three weeks before the coronation. 'Crown the King with life!' was apt. Foreign royalties, great and small, arrived in London. Troops came from every corner of the Empire. Towns and villages bedecked themselves with flags. At Covent Garden seats were selling like hot cakes at ten guineas. At Sheffield the Festival Choir were 'in a seventh heaven of anticipation', said the Chorus Master, as they rehearsed the 'Coronation Ode' for their London confrontation with 'a gathering of emperors, kings, queens, princes, potentates, powers, diamonds, tiaras, pendants, bracelets, rings, flowers, £5,000 spent in floral decorations alone – and our worthy selves would be there to see this regal splendour, surpassing anything in the Arabian Nights.'[1]

In Westminster Abbey rehearsals of the Coronation service were simultaneously in full swing. Three days before the great occasion an orchestra there was playing Saint-Saens' 'Coronation March' in the morning when it was interrupted by a Church dignitary who announced that the King was to undergo an operation for appendicitis that very day. The orchestra broke up and left the Abbey. The news was not known outside, and a State trumpeter from the Abbey, MR W. A. FEATHERSTONE,[2] has told of walking home, still in uniform, through decorated streets full of sightseers: 'As I turned down York Road I saw a clergyman and his wife festooning a balcony with bunting. I said, "I wouldn't put any more of that up." He asked why. "The coronation's off," I said. "The King is very seriously ill" – for at that time an operation for appendicitis was a dangerous thing. The padre looked at me. "I can't believe it", he said.' The same afternoon a bulletin on the railings of Buckingham Palace and in the Press announced that the operation had been performed. Services of intercession were held. Faces were long. Flags came down. Foreign royalties went home.

Benson, writing to Elgar, remarked that the King had only an outside chance of recovery and referred to general disappointment at the cancellation of festivities: 'Your account of your consolation is highly philosophical – Bach and tricycling! We poor professionals, who had expected a five days holiday diversified by historical ceremonials, had to turn feebly to our most ordinary tale of work, correcting exercises! It was singularly flat.'

The Coronation was postponed only six weeks – the King's quick recovery put appendectomy into surgical fashion – but many royal functions were cancelled altogether to spare the King, including the Covent Garden gala; instead, Elgar's 'Coronation Ode' had its first London performance at the Queen's Hall.

'I was there in 1902 as a schoolboy, sitting in the gallery,' says SIR ADRIAN BOULT.[3] 'Elgar was my hero, the greatest composer Britain had produced for 200 years. His "Enigma Variations" and "Dream of Gerontius" had recently shown his genius. Now came the "Coronation Ode", soaked with the spirit of the Edwardian era; and "Land of Hope and Glory"! When we first heard that Finale the effect on the audience was electric. We called Elgar back five times. Someone near me shouted, "Let's have the last part again, sir!" – and Elgar, looking like a

---

[1] *Reminiscences*, by Dr Henry Coward (Curwen).

[2] Years later conductor of the BBC Orchestra at Bournemouth.

[3] Born 1889, Adrian Boult was Musical Director, Birmingham City Orchestra, 1924–30 and 1959–60; BBC Director of Music, 1930–42; conductor, BBC Symphony Orchestra, 1930–50; London Philharmonic, 1950–7.

Number Five in Elgar's score of the 'Coronation Ode': here, in his own hand, is the song
that was to sweep an Empire

cavalry colonel, with his great moustache and his back as straight as a ramrod, raised his baton again. "Land of Hope and Glory" has since become hackneyed, but it remains a noble tune. When, later on, high-brows scoffed at its popularity, Elgar himself gave them the retort courteous. "Every composer," he said, "ought to unbend and write a popular tune occasionally".'

Very soon after the war ended in South Africa, Elgar's publisher printed the Finale of the 'Ode' as a separate vocal solo with piano accompaniment but before it went to press Benson crossed out the four lines quoted earlier ('Truth and right and freedom . . .') and inserted:

> *Wider still and wider*
> *Shall thy bounds be set;*
> *God, who made thee mighty,*
> *Make thee mightier yet.*

Easy as it is to assume that Benson was carried away on the wave of victory-emotion, a study of the man suggests strongly that these lines were not inspired by the popular mood of arrogant imperialism. It is not in character; significantly, at the time of Mafeking he had severely deprecated the hysterics, and one of his friends has said that he abhorred the 'popular taste for vulgar excitement'.[1]

Benson represents a sector of public opinion during the high days of Empire which gets less credit than its due nowadays, and 'Land of Hope and Glory' has a value different from common assumptions. There were on one hand fiery imperialists; there were also the mild liberal Bensons. 'There was nothing of the jingoist about him,' says another of his friends.[2] 'But like many people of that time his imagination was stirred by what seemed to be the majesty and splendour of the British Empire. I don't think "wider still and wider" had any literal meaning.'

It was possible to see our world-wide hope and glory in the practice of good administration, medicine and the conquest of tropical diseases, exploration, and the pursuit of the arts and sciences wider still and wider, in which Benson had a clear interest as a scholar; if the modern promenaders can sing that song today with this meaning let them roar it as lustily as they please, for then it will not be a joke but a dedication. What the Edwardian Bensons were often blind to, as the majesty of Empire dazzled their eyes, was that colonialism in practice could fall short of their ideal and become what Lord Courtney of Penwith condemned in 1906 as 'the imperialism which aims at domination and aggrandizement'. Later both Benson and Elgar realized that the phrase 'wider still and wider' was aggressively construed by the public, and when the First World War came they wished to cut these words, as we shall see later.

In Elgar's career the 'Coronation Ode' was a fleeting piece for the occasion; he was to climb soon to the towering heights of his 'First Symphony' (1908). 'No English composition of later date,' Mr Neville Cardus has said, 'has so much turned the tide of music in this country.' Today the 'Ode' is forgotten, excepting that song from its Finale, but in 1902 the complete work had triumphant performances up and down the country, and after attending one Benson wrote to Mrs Elgar: 'I felt like the fly on the engine who said "How fast I run, and how everything gets out of the way for me" – only, unlike the fly, I know I was not the motive power.'

---

[1] *Arthur Christopher Benson*, as seen by some of his friends (Bell), 1925.

[2] Mr Francis Turner, of Chichester, in a letter to *Scrapbook*.

The Story Behind Land of Hope and Glory

A. C. Benson was appointed in 1904 Fellow of Magdalene College, Cambridge, and Master in 1915; there he remained until his death in 1925. He left his copyrights to the College, so every time 'Land of Hope and Glory' is sung at the Proms, or anywhere else in public, royalties are paid to the College coffers. We have this nice situation: an academic recluse who doesn't think he has 'the popular ring' writes the words of a pop-song which profits a learned college and will do so until expiry of the copyright in 1975.

*   *   *

The 1902 coronation was not seen or heard outside the Abbey. The new-fangled film camera was prohibited. 'It is a pity,' remarked the *Illustrated London News*, 'that the populace cannot have their imagination touched by direct vision of this imposing scene', but forty-nine years were to go before a coronation was to reach the people by 'direct vision' (television). In 1902 an ancient method was used to signal the news of the crowning from the capital to the farthest hamlet. MISS RACHEL MACLEOD, ex-teacher on the Hebridean island of Barra, remembers it: 'We saw the distant bonfires on the hills. When the King was crowned at last the celebrations began all over again and the school-children had a picnic on the sands and were presented with mugs with pictures of the King and Queen on them.'

That night on Barra the people held a ceilidh, the Gaelic informal gathering of friends: 'You're not invited to a ceilidh, you just go. There is sometimes a ceilidh house in the village, a house that's noted for its ceilidhs. The man of the house knows the tales of long ago, the stories of the bards, and there's the singing of Gaelic songs.'

When at last they went home they lit their way over the hills by a burning peat skewered on a garden fork: 'There weren't any electric torches in Barra in those days, but we had the burning peat, which was better, and it blew sparks in the wind; one of the visiting teachers thought it was a procession of ghosts, she'd heard so much about ghosts in Barra. We were a bit afraid, but we knew all the haunts of the ghosts, and we just held this torch and watched the flame.'

*   *   *

Gone now was the gloom of the Victorian Court. King Edward enjoyed the worldly pleasures. The doors of his Court were thrown open to American beauties and British captains of industry. When the King went yachting at Cowes with Sir Thomas Lipton the German Kaiser gibed, 'My uncle has gone boating with his grocer.'

BARONESS ASQUITH OF YARNBURY (Lady Violet Bonham-Carter) says: 'What first struck me as a girl about his appearance was his immense girth – his waistline was like the equator. He was the gay prince who became a wise King, dearly loved by all sorts and conditions of men – partly because, unlike most Kings, he had lived and moved amongst them. The fact that in his youth he had sought his friends outside Court circles had given him a wide (though perhaps not deep) experience of his fellow men. He was gregarious, tolerant, cosmopolitan, a seasoned citizen of the world.'

Edward the Peacemaker was the nickname bestowed on him because of his support for the Anglo–French *entente* of 1903–4, when hatchets a century old were buried. In relation to what was to happen ten years later, this was of greatest importance. Along with the Anglo–Japanese treaty of 1902, it marked the emergence of Britain from her Victorian political isolation.

Blue-blooded London took its cue from an ostentatious monarch. The houses of the aristocracy blazed like palaces. They were second only to the King's, with their champagne suppers, their gold plate, the rows of powdered flunkeys. Peace enabled income tax to fall back to 11d in the £ (and no surtax) by 1904. Trade reached new peaks. Riches piled up. The aristocracy has never since had it so good. Life in the great houses had the panache of a fastidiously produced play, a play which seemed to its actors, stars and minions alike, certain to run for ever. Longleat House, one of the stately homes of England where today the public pays half-a-crown to stroll and stare, was then the very private palace of Lord and Lady Bath. MR CHARLES DAVIS, who worked there as a groom from 1907, give us this 'below stairs' view of extravagantly formalized palace-life:

'The indoor servants had to go to prayers in the private chapel at 9 o'clock in the morning. Sometimes Lord Bath would read the prayers, sometimes the curate would come down from the village. On Sunday morning there was a service: the butler would lead the menservants in to the chapel, then came the housekeeper, then the maids. All the women were in their best Sunday dresses, and the footmen in their livery. The head coachman used to lead us in from the stables. We sat in pews on the ground floor, and the gentry were in the gallery.

Punch, 1908

The Tenants' Ball at the Big House: the groom is saying to Her Ladyship: 'I'm sorry I'm dancin' so bad, ma'am, but this 'ere floor's that slippery, an' I aren't got no nails in my boots'

'The indoor staff in those days was one butler, an under butler, a groom of the chamber, three footmen, a steward's room footman, one odd man, a pantry boy, the housekeeper, two lady's maids, a nurse, a nursery maid, eight housemaids, two sewing maids, three still-room maids, and six laundry maids. Then in the kitchen were a cook, two kitchen maids, a vegetable maid, a scullery maid, and a daily woman.

'In the stables at Longleat were about ten stablemen looking after twenty horses and a victoria, a landau, a big barouche, a dog cart, a shooting brake, and a big wagonette.

'At Christmas we had a big ball for the staff. Lord Bath used to start the dance with the housekeeper while the butler danced with Lady Bath, then everybody else would join in, and we had a very good evening. We had an orchestra of eight to ten, and the room was all decorated up. The lighting was oil lamps and candles. When we had our Christmas dinner all the understaff had to go in and stand up round the table until the butler and the housekeeper came in, and the butler would say "Be seated".

'For the London season we used to go up to Town about the end of February. We took about nine horses and two carriages which went by rail to Paddington, and then we used to drive to his Lordship's house in Grosvenor Square. Lord Bath kept his State coach in London; it was used for State occasions, the opening of Parliament, Courts, and levees. We came back to Longleat at the end of July.'

MR REGINALD ROBBINS was shepherd on the estate at Longleat: 'I worked from six in the morning till six at night, for six days, and about six hours on a Sunday. As well as the usual work of a shepherd I did the killing for the house – often in a week we killed three sheep for the kitchen, to be consumed by the gentry and the servants. I was paid eleven shillings a week, but I must say I was happy in my work; people today, the more they have the more they want, that's the trouble. In the old days we were satisfied with simple things. We had the reading room in the village where we had papers and magazines, billiards, card playing, and draughts. And practically everybody was musical, even if it was only a comb and a bit of paper, or a jew's harp; and the village also had a good brass band.'

This zest in the *simple* things is recalled by MR LEWIS WILLIAMS who was a youth coal-mining in South Wales when the going was tough and the pay poor: 'Our entertainment we made ourselves, the Band of Hope, penny readings, and debating societies. We got a lot out of them because we made them ourselves. Then the Sunday School! – man, it was a veritable forum, a university!'

All through industrial Britain was this passionate working-class urge for self-improvement: 'I read everything avidly, although my father rather frowned at my reading anything in English! But reading things made me *think*; it was a time when reform and revolution were pushed into the consciousness of the workman. We could see the affluence in the manager's house, and the squalor in our own. The motto of the coal-owners had always been "safety with economy", but the emphasis was on economy. Safety measures which cost money were neglected.'

It wasn't a land of glory in these terms, but it had a measure of hope. This old miner, like so many, remembers Keir Hardie as the apostle of the Promised Land: 'To me he was one of the greatest men that ever lived. Early in the century he was the only socialist in Parliament. I had the honour of shaking hands with him at a May Day demonstration in Merthyr. There was a warmth in his handshake which I can vividly recall now, and a pat on the shoulder: "My boy", he said, "keep on to the end of the road!" It was what we thought of as the beginning of a new vista, a new era. We thought that Keir Hardie could, and did, emphasize those great ideals that were found in the Sermon on the Mount.'

There was a long row to hoe yet. The Conservative Government's Factories Act of 1901 prohibited the employment of children under twelve. MR BEN JEFFERY, of Mousehole, Cornwall, was twelve years old in 1902 when he first went to sea: 'We boys used to go fishing all night long, and then come home and catch a bit of sleep and get to school for a few hours, then the master would let you out early to work the next night – boys of twelve, going to sea perhaps for half-a-crown a week. It was very, very hard in them days, lifting the great sails about.'

A Newlyn fisherman, MR JOSEPH MADRON, spoke to our microphone of being cook in a drifter at fourteen, for five shillings a week: 'We boys had to try to help things out because fish prices were very, very bad in them days, and ours was a large family, and every penny helped.' Then his memory turned to a sight that has vanished – anything from 100 to 150 craft sailing out into Mounts Bay; and MRS MADRON, seated beside him in their quayside cottage, joined in with eloquence: 'I can remember coming home from school at Mousehole – my father was a fisherman – and seeing the fishing fleet lazily going out of the harbour, just taking their time slowly, but beautifully and gracefully. It seemed to me in my childhood days a lovely sight. It was poor days, if you know what I mean, but there was a great deal of contentment in peoples hearts.'

Distance makes the heart grow fonder, of course; the joy found in simple pleasures was true enough, but it would be false to give an impression of general contentment, more especially in the dark satanic centres of industry. A few lines from a *Times* report from Belfast are a reminder of the roughness of Edwardian discontents: 'There was desperate fighting here yesterday between a howling crowd and strong forces of police, cavalry, and infantry. A child was killed and twenty policemen were seriously injured.' This was in 1907 when Big Jim Larkin led the Belfast dockers and carters on strike. Rioting, during which the police suffered from wild attacks by mill-girls whirling tea-cans tied in shawls, caused the government to send in 7,000 troops. Industrial strife took a form it never does now, thank God: 'The military were ordered to fire a volley into a frenzied mob of roughs who had subjected both military and police to a fusillade of stones, bricks, and broken bottles,' says *The Times* later. 'Four people were killed.'

In the East End of London at that time lived Herbert Morrison, the Cockney lad who was to become LORD MORRISON OF LAMBETH. Like many working-class memories, his embraced both the hardness and the happiness of life: 'In my boyhood we could rarely afford the theatre, and then only the gallery, and the music-hall was not considered respectable, so we entertained ourselves with singsongs at home, my brothers playing the mandoline and jew's harp, while I was the drummer with a saucepan, and jolly good it was. Mind you, there were no frills on life. My mother's housekeeping must have been on about fifteen shillings; my father earned as a policeman thirty bob a week. I started as an errand boy, then shop assistant, then telephonist at a brewery. I was very familiar with the sights of the gin-shops and pubs discharging their drunks at midnight, and with other sordid conditions, but I don't know whether I would have done anything about it but for a phrenologist. This was a chap on a street stall – he read bumps. He told me I had a good head and asked what books I read.

'"*Deadwood Dick*", I told him.

'"It's better to read rubbish than nothing," he said, "but why not try history and economics?"

'I took his advice. I read Macaulay and Marx and Engels in a cheap restaurant at Victoria while drinking ha'penny cups of cocoa. I came to the conclusion that if anything was to be

'It seemed to me in my childhood days a lovely sight.' The fishing harbour in the age of sail; oil painting, *Between the Tides* by Walter Langley, R. I., shown at the 1901 Royal Academy

done to improve social conditions for the masses, it must be done by the acquisition of political and economic power. That's why in 1910 I became the honorary secretary of the South London Federation of the Independent Labour Party, and so embarked on political life.'

By that year Labour MPs in the Commons had increased to forty-two, but only 28 per cent of the adult population had the vote.[1] Britain was not a democracy as understood today. Herbert Morrison's career is a measure of the changes in our times. This errand boy became an MP and leader of the LCC; as Minister of Transport (1929–31) he put in motion the vast scheme for setting up the London Passenger Transport Board, and as Minister of Home Security was a member of Churchill's War Cabinet (1942–5). This breaking of the bounds of class was beyond anyone's dreams in the first decade of the century.

CALENDAR OF SIGNIFICANT DATES

1906

General election, Liberals returned with 400 seats, twenty-nine Labour members elected.
Labour Representation Committee became Labour Party.
King Edward launched HMS *Dreadnought*, biggest battleship in world.
Liner *Lusitania* launched (32,500 tons) on Clyde.
Bakerloo and Piccadilly tubes opened.
Sir J. J. Thomson awarded Nobel Prize in Physics for work on conductivity of electricity through gases.
First cross-Channel flight by a woman, Mrs Griffith Brewer, in a balloon.
Legislation for provision of school meals for children whose education was suffering through lack of food.
Big unemployed demonstrations and march on London.
George A. Smith, of Brighton, patented Kinemacolour film.
First British production of ballet *Coppélia*, Empire Theatre.
Patti's farewell concert at Albert Hall.

STAGE: *The Doctor's Dilemma* (Bernard Shaw); *The Silver Box* (Galsworthy); *His House in Order* (Pinero); *The Belle of Mayfair* (Leslie Stuart).

BOOKS: *Puck of Pook's Hill* (Rudyard Kipling); *The Man of Property* (Galsworthy); *The Beloved Vagabond* (W. J. Locke); *The Railway Children* (E. Nesbit).

SONGS: 'By the Side of the Zuyder Zee'; 'If Those Lips Could Only Speak'; 'Mr Chamberlain'; 'The Galloping Major'; 'Waiting at the Church'.

---

[1] All women were barred, and also 42 per cent of adult males. Their enfranchisement came in stages, by Acts of Parliament of 1918, 1928, and 1948.

1907

First flight in Britain by a man-carrying aeroplane, by Horatio Phillips.

Anglo-Russian Convention.

Government announced its opposition to Channel Tunnel.

First recognition of taxi-cabs, in draft of proposed cab regulations for London.

Baden-Powell's first camp for boys, Brownsea Island.

Parliament provided for medical inspection in elementary schools, and organised games.

First 'School for Mothers', St Pancras (child welfare centre).

Qualification of Women Act enabled women to sit as councillors, aldermen, mayors, or chairmen on County and Borough Councils.

Marriage to deceased wife's sister enacted.

Colonial Conference decided in future to use the term 'Dominion'.

Haldane's Territorial and Reserve Forces Act, established territorials, reformed army, and set up a general staff.

Imperial College of Science founded.

Dock strike and rioting, Belfast.

Photograph of King Edward telegraphed from Paris to London *Daily Mirror*.

Order of Merit conferred on Miss Florence Nightingale.

Rudyard Kipling awarded Nobel Prize for literature.

Northern Tube Line opened; passengers carried free first afternoon and evening (127,500 travelled).

Theft of the Ascot Gold Cup.

Theft of jewels of Order of St Patrick, Dublin.

First TT motor-cycle race, Isle of Man.

Opening of Brooklands motor racecourse.

Turbine steamer *Victoria* made record passage, Dover–Calais, forty-six minutes.

British military airship *Nulli Secundus* flew over London from Farnborough.

Tetrazzini's phenomenal debut at Covent Garden.

STAGE: *Caesar and Cleopatra* (Bernard Shaw); *Waste* (Granville Barker); *Tom Jones* (Edward German); *The Merry Widow* began its run of 778 performances; *When Knights Were Bold* (C. Marlowe), 579; *The Girls of Gottenburg*; *The Mollusc* (H. H. Davies); Pélissier's *Follies* first appeared regularly in a London theatre, the Royalty; *The Playboy of the Western World* (J. M. Synge).

BOOKS: *Three Weeks* (Elinor Glyn); *The Passing of the Third Floor Back* (Jerome K. Jerome); *White Fang* (Jack London).

SONGS: 'I Love You So' and 'Vilia' (*The Merry Widow*); 'In the Twi-Twi-Twilight'; 'Jolly Good Luck to the Girl Who Loves a Soldier'; 'Put Me Amongst the Girls'; 'Red Wing'; 'She's a Lassie from Lancashire'; 'The New Taxi-meter Car'.

1908

Mr H. Asquith became Prime Minister.

King and Queen attended Requiem Mass in London for murdered King and Crown Prince of Portugal: no English king had attended Roman Catholic service since Reformation.

Electrical ticket issuing machines introduced on London Underground.

'Hunger marchers' (unemployed) demonstrated.

Children Act, for protection of children against negligence; imprisonment of children abolished; remand homes set up.

First woman mayor in the UK elected at Aldeburgh, Dr Garrett Anderson.

Women suffragettes first chained themselves to railing of 10 Downing Street.

Boy Scouts founded.

Franco–British Exhibition at Shepherd's Bush; King and Queen opened the Olympic Games.

Sir Ernest Rutherford awarded Nobel Prize in Chemistry for work on radioactive substances.

Port of London authority set up.

Queen's University, Belfast, and National University of Ireland, Dublin, founded.

Scandal over Epstein statuary in the Strand.

First cinema organ, at Tamworth Picture Palace.

First pre-selector epicyclic gearbox, on Lanchester car.

Arthur Mee started *The Children's Encyclopaedia*.

Miss Horniman opened Gaiety Theatre, Manchester.

'First Symphony' (Elgar); 'Brigg Fair' (Delius).

STAGE: *Getting Married* (Bernard Shaw); *What Every Woman Knows* (J. M. Barrie); *Passing of the Third Floor Back* (Jerome K. Jerome); *The Flag Lieutenant* (Drury and Trevor).

BOOKS: *The War in the Air* (H. G. Wells); *The Old Wives' Tale* (Arnold Bennett); *The Wind in the Willows* (Kenneth Grahame); *The Blue Lagoon* (H. de Vere Stacpoole); *The Man Who Was Thursday* (G. K. Chesterton).

SONGS: 'If I Should Plant a Tiny Seed of Love'; 'I Hear You Calling Me'; 'I'm Afraid to Go Home In the Dark'; 'My Girl's a Yorkshire Girl'; 'Oh! Oh! Antonio!'; 'She Sells Sea Shells'; 'Take Me on the Flip-flap'.

The Calendar is continued on page 116

The international spleen during King Edward's reign is shown in this unflattering German cartoon, 1907. On a visit to Britain by Prince Fushimi of Japan the censor's licence for all stage presentations of *The Mikado* by Gilbert and Sullivan was withdrawn for fear of offending the Prince. This absurd ban was so widely ridiculed that the Lord Chamberlain quickly rescinded it. The cartoonist of the magazine *Kladderadatsch* shows Edward's Britain giving servile attention to the rising power of Japan (which had beaten Russia at war in 1905); kowtowing beyond are the USA and Russia, and the original German caption below the cartoon may be translated: 'Perhaps even proud Japan will be satisfied with *this* cast for the Mikado'

Punch, 1909
This sketch by Lewis Baumer neatly hits off characteristics of the Edwardian seaside resort: the bathing machines, the pierrots, the band on the prom, the young man with binoculars, the rise of advertising (Winkle's Pills). And the universality of *hats*

The Kaiser had dreams of maritime might: as an amateur artist of some proficiency, he painted this sea battle

EDWARDIAN

There'll be no Wo-ar!

'In the winter we had skating parties on the ponds. By moonlight the skaters gathered round glowing braziers for hot drinks and potatoes roasted in their jackets. Indoors at home we had ping-pong, we never called it table tennis. And our much-loved musical evenings: I was the accompanist and everyone joined in. They were very simple pleasures, but I think that creating and doing things oneself was much more interesting than having everything ready-made in the way of entertainment. It wasn't at all *dull*. Croquet, for instance, in the summer – it wasn't the dull game people nowadays suppose. It was even more popular than tennis or golf. It needed great skill, and the tournaments on the lawn at my parents' house were exciting events. There was always a break for a strawberry cream-tea. Then in the cool of the evening we played to the finish, sometimes until 10 o'clock, aided by candles.'

This enchanting glimpse of middle-class life in King Edward's time was recorded for *Scrapbook* by MRS VICTORIA TRETHOWAN of Truro. The Edwardian period is so near and yet so far: close enough for many of its people to be lively commentators at our microphone, yet what they describe as they look back across the chasms of two world wars is immensely different from life today, both in outward appearances and inward values. The greatest difference is that the people of Edward the Peacemaker *felt safe*. To be sure, there was dreadful insecurity for the working class, internally in this country, but externally the Edwardians of all classes felt secure on their islands bounded by the sea and a great navy. It was an illusion. In these very years the Great Powers were lining up preparatory to their plunge into the chasm of 1914, but the panorama as we look beyond that intervening darkness is bathed in Edwardian sunshine, a golden sovereign is worth twenty shillings,[1] and the tunes of the time jingle with light-heartedness:

> *I do like to stroll along the prom, prom, prom,*
> *Where the brassbands play Tiddly-om-pom-pom!*[2]

A visit to the Edwardian seaside takes us straight into great differences, compared with today, of manners and appearances. MISS MADGE POSNETT gives us a child's-eye-view from Broadstairs: 'The bathing-van horses spent their off time in a field belonging to my father.

[1] The internal purchasing power of the £ has fallen from 20s in 1914 to less than 4s now (1966).

[2] 'I do like to be Beside the Seaside', words and music by John A. Glover-Kind (Feldman), 1909.

The bathing machines were very high contraptions on huge wheels, in which we undressed before getting into the sea. They were smelly old things divided into two by a partition, and always full of sand, and very often with earwigs and other things in them as well. They were dragged out by the horses into fairly deep water so that you could descend four or five steps into the sea, for reasons of modesty. There was an old lady in a sun-bonnet, fully dressed, standing in the water, and she would take hold of us children and give us a good duck. She was known as The Bathing Woman.'

How fascinating to find a Bathing Woman within living memory! – *Scrapbook*'s compiler had associated such buxom naiads with John Leech's mid-nineteenth-century *Punch* drawings of the seaside, but here she was still going strong in the twentieth century. It is now something like 200 years since the good Benjamin Beale of Margate invented the bathing machine so that sea-bathing might be enjoyed in a manner 'consistent with the most refined delicacy' at a time when naked bathing was common, though with the sexes segregated (see Rowlandson's cartoons of Margate beaches around 1800). The Victorians enforced bathing machines and elaborated bathing-dress. In the Edwardian era all seaside resorts had a lawyer's delight of complicated bye-laws in action. It is astonishing how long some have remained technically in force. As recently as 1952 Margate, according to the letter of the law, required your bathing machine to be 'moved into such a depth of water as will prevent any indecent exposure of the bather', and in 1966 Castletown (Isle of Man) revoked its 1900 prohibition of mixed bathing; a blind official eye had long been turned to such improprieties.

Typical of the old code round our coasts is Bournemouth's, dating from 1900. The regulations divide the entire beach into 'stands' or sections, some for male use of bathing machines, some for female ditto, and the sexes must not swim within 20 yards of each other or the law will be after them. But Edwardian Bournemouth is broadminded: it also has 'stands' for mixed bathing. There are even 'stands' where you need not use a bathing machine at all, instead a screen at least 6 feet in height is permitted; and on a few stretches of sand you may actually change without this shelter before 8 a.m. and after 9 p.m. but only if you are male.

'From the neck to the knee' is the male costume required on mixed bathing 'stands' where the ladies must wear 'a tunic or blouse reaching from the neck to the knees, with belt or knickerbocker drawers', *but* (note the subtle difference) females dipping in female-only stretches of the ocean may omit the fal-lal about belts or knickerbockers as long as they wear 'sufficient dress or covering to prevent indecent exposure of the person'. Page after page of regulations reveal the Victorian-cum-Edwardian mind; thus, no male over ten years of age may use a bathing machine occupied by a female, but no female of any age at all may set foot inside a machine used by a male over ten. Pleasure boats must not approach closer than fifty yards to any bather. And so on, forty-three rules in all – and officially they only lapsed in 1948.

An attempt today to apply such a blitz of regulations would make the beaches of Britain run with revolution – bikinis to the barricades! – but the Edwardians took it all in their stride. Such a code seemed all right. It is a matter of relativity. To each age its standards. As Mark Sheridan sang on the music-halls in 1910, 'You can do a lot of things at the seaside that you can't do in town':

> *Fancy seeing Mother with her legs all bare*
> *Paddling in the fountains in Trafalgar Square!*[1]

[1] Words and music by Charles Ridgewell and George Stevens (Francis, Day and Hunter Ltd.).

There'll Be No WO-AR!

An eye could be winked at 'a lot of things' – in fact, overdressing for a bathe began slowly to disappear, the ladies who thought it seemly to wear bathing stockings became few, and from about 1910 a few daring girls wore one-piece costumes, sometimes even unskirted but still long-legged like 'combs'. And who would feel constricted by the bye-laws at a time when any seaside holiday at all was sheer adventure for millions? This was what mattered. In Edwardian times holidays with pay were slowly spreading (but were not enforced by law) so that many working people saw the sea for the first time. The railway companies enticed them with, for example, the Great Northern's offer of a day excursion between King's Cross and Skegness for *three shillings* return, exploited from 1908 onwards by Hassall's famous poster 'Skegness is so Bracing'.

For children of all classes 'the seaside' meant first the thrilling adventure of a train journey, then perhaps a horse-cab to your digs, then the simple things that were your delight. As MISS MADGE POSNETT remembers: 'A black-faced minstrel, Uncle Mac, was my first sweetheart at Broadstairs, though he knew nothing about it. Uncle Mac would move along the beach, singing to a banjo, and the children would move along with him. We wore sun-bonnets to keep the *very evil* rays of the sun off us, and we had several stiffly-starched petticoats which had to be tucked into our drawers if we wanted to paddle.'

Punch, 1908

'Hadn't we better go home, Nurse?' says this sophisticated little Edwardian girl. 'I don't think these pierrot songs are quite suitable for baby'—a satirical touch from the cartoonist, for the songs were as innocuous as pop-songs ever were

The blacked-up minstrels of nineteenth-century origin had given pride of place in the twentieth century to the pierrots. Of all the waxing and waning in entertainments the pierrot craze is one of the most interesting as an index to popular taste. It had a short life, comparatively, but a gay one. It was what used to be called a 'family' show, good for all ages. We have to turn back the pages for a moment to the Nineties to hear of its origin from MR CLIFFORD ESSEX: 'In 1891 I introduced the Clifford Essex Pierrots at Henley Regatta, and as a result we were commanded to appear at Cowes on the royal yacht before the Prince of Wales. We stayed on in the Isle of Wight, performing a show at all the resorts. We wore the pierrot costume, white with black pompoms, which soon became so familiar at the seaside.' This simple idea – a few songs round a piano, some gay, some sentimental, with unpretentious sketches and monologues to raise the laughs from holidaymakers in rows of deckchairs – quickly sent its ripples all round our coasts. Will Catlin started his party on Scarborough sands in 1896. Many others followed. Banjoist Will C. Pepper left Clifford Essex and formed his own *White Coons* (in later years perpetuated on the radio by his son Harry). The pierrot craze was at its height in the years up to the First World War; with clean fun on the sands and merry jingles at the end of the pier, many a London star of the future was making a nervous debut – Stanley Holloway at Walton-on-the-Naze, Bobby Howes at Margate, Tom Walls at Brighton, Leslie Henson and W. H. Berry at Yarmouth . . . and at Scarborough the famous *Fol-de-Rols* started in 1911.

Why does hardly anything of such a great vogue survive today? Would it seem too naïve, too clean, for modern audiences? Perhaps the basic answer is that the pierrots were tuned-in to the tempo of their times, unhurried, uncomplicated, unthreatened (it seemed) by war. Their setting at every resort had the same placid quality – no roaring torrent of motors on the prom, no neon signs flashing, no loudspeakers; walk along the dark shadow of the pier with its mellow gas lamps, look landward into the Edwardian twilight, and:

From inland
Leaps a gay fragment of some mocking tune
That tinkles and laughs and fades along the sand,
And dies between the sea wall and the sea . . .

A Cambridge undergraduate, Rupert Brooke, wrote this in 1908. It was a gentle scene.

Out of the seaside pierrots sprang the more sophisticated *Follies* in the West End, and later *The Co-Optimists*, the fashionable show of the Twenties. After the First World War the seaside pierrots tinkled on, still a training ground for stars (Elsie and Doris Waters at Clacton, Max Miller at Brighton, Arthur Askey at Ventnor) but this type of entertainment virtually failed to survive the Hitler War. Many of us cherish a memory of half-a-dozen white figures singing under the seaside moon. The pierrots were pure Edwardiana, gay fragments of the last years when the peoples of these islands could feel secure behind the sea that washed the long-uninvaded beaches.

The Follies, at various London theatres between 1907 and 1913 scored an immense success under Harry Pélissier, their genius, compere, and writer of most of their sketches and songs:

Moon, moon, serenely shining,
Don't go in too soon . . .

Such moony sentiment always captured the audience's heart, but the prime Pélissier *pièce de résistance* was burlesque, says a member of the party, MISS DOLLIS BROOKE: 'Burlesque of every-

94

thing topical, of politics, plays, people, from Lloyd George's budget, to the Edwardian Music Hall, with Dan Everard (my husband) dressed up as Mister Alf Gag-pincher – grey bowler hat, check trousers, cane under his arm – singing:

> *There'll be no WO-AR*
> *As long as we've a king*
> *Like good King Ed-EW-ARD!'*

This cod-Cockney song took off Harry Champion of 'Boiled Beef and Carrots' fame. *The Follies* likewise had a go at Bransby Williams when his Dickensian character studies were top-of-the-bill on the halls. The curtain rose to show a music-hall gallery where a row of unimpressed galleryites looked down at an imposing thespian bathed in a spotlight:

GRANDSBY BILLIOUS: Ladies and gentlemen – a few character impersonations from the works of Charles Dickens . . . will any lady or gentleman –
GALLERYITE: I'll 'ave a small lemon.
BILLIOUS: Will any lady or gentleman or other person in the audience –
GALLERYITE: Archie, 'e's speakin' to you.
BILLIOUS: . . . kindly select their favourite character from Charles Dickens?
GALLERYITE: Winston Churchill.
BILLIOUS: Thank you, madam. Ladies and gentlemen, my first impression this evening will be that of little Nellie's grandfather, from *The Old Curiosity Shop*.
GALLERYITE: Wot's 'e going to do, sitting at that table?
GALLERYITE: Makin' 'is fice up.
GALLERYITE: Coo! Look – Robinson Crusoe!
BILLIOUS (*turning to footlights*): Where's little Nellie?
GALLERYITE: Gorn to the 'Ippodrome.
BILLIOUS (*emotionally*): They tell me little Nellie's dead!
GALLERYITE: So's Queen Anne.
BILLIOUS (*more emotionally*): The angels have taken little Nellie!
GALLERYITE: Well, *you're* perfectly sife.
BILLIOUS: *Angels, don't take little Nellie!*
GALLERYITES (*all together*): WE DON'T WANT 'ER!

★   ★   ★

Some corners of London were still Dickensian. MR L. R. WILLDRIDGE has given us these memories of a clerk in an old-established bank in the City: 'No one hurried or worried or got cross, and indeed why should they? The bank was a quiet, homely, and friendly place. The first thing you would be struck by if you could be taken back to it today is the quietness – no machines, no typewriters, no *women*. No sound save the scratchings of a pen or the clink of gold sovereigns being weighed. On the counter there were even ink-wells made of pewter, with quill pens. The older people were really still Victorian in their ways. I looked through the windows and saw a horse-bus pass with the people huddled up on the open top, and I thought that there were worse places than the warmth and quietness of this old bank, with an assured future and £50 a year. Being fond of anything in the theatrical line, I went to all the shows I possibly could. At the Oxford, Tivoli, or Metropolitan music-halls one got twenty turns, all the way from Marie Lloyd to Harry Lauder. The main thing that impressed me was the air of jollity everywhere; this may have had something to do with the cheapness of beer. At Collins's Music Hall the waiters dashed up and down the aisles with trays of mugs of beer, handing them to customers in their seats.

'The great West End musical comedies were very expensive – it cost me a shilling to go to those. There was *The Girls of Gottenburg* at the Gaiety, in 1908, and of course the famous *Merry Widow* at Daly's. There were Lily Elsie, Joseph Coyne, George Graves, W. H. Berry, and heaps of other stars, and of course glorious music – you could hear it hummed, whistled, and played all over London. It was a wonderful sight when the theatres emptied, the hansoms dashing up outside, the streets so full of people and bustle and general gaiety that I felt I never wanted to go home. So I strolled along, drifted with the crowds, watching the fashionably-dressed people, and the lovely soft lighting from the gas street-lamps, so much kinder than the harsh electric light of today. There was a kind of golden glow over the streets then.'

It would be more accurate to call it a golden façade. When the Gaiety Theatre, so aptly named, was pulled down in 1903 in a clearance operation to make way for Aldwych and Kingsway, acres of London's most stinking slums were revealed, and when Kind Edward opened the fine new thoroughfares two years later he was shocked by a petition from the unemployed of Poplar being shoved into his hands; they immediately marched with their wives and children to 10 Downing Street where their leaders were admitted, including George Lansbury and Margaret Bondfield, in later years to enter the same house as ministers. They were bitterly disappointed by Prime Minister Balfour's non-committal response, and a few days later when Queen Alexandra issued an appeal to 'all charitably disposed people' to 'assist her in alleviating the sufferings of the poor starving unemployed' (she put herself down for £2,000) the reaction of the workless was a march of thousands to Hyde Park with a slogan on their banners: *Work, not charity.*

Just as those banners were symptoms of the dark side of Edwardian life, the 'golden glow' of musical comedy reflected another side, carefree, gay, intoxicated with its own frivolity. Today we have screaming teenagers, but consider these words by the Queen of the Gaiety, MISS GERTIE MILLAR (the Countess of Dudley), recalling an earlier hysteria: 'On the last night before they pulled down the theatre "Auld Lang Syne" was sung, people on both sides of the footlights were in tears, and when the curtain came down pandemonium broke loose. Soon there was not a door-knob or an electric fitting left. They were all taken as souvenirs. I had a glove box made from a piece of the stage itself.' Soon a new Gaiety opened near by.

When the *Scrapbooks* began in the Thirties, Gertie Millar was in her fifties but had retired from the stage; we sounded her about singing one of her old songs to an audience far larger than all the Gaieties put together. In her forthright Yorkshire way (she had begun her show-life as an infant prodigy at Bradford Mechanics' Institute) the Countess of Dudley said 'Nothing doing'. A few days later she rang up: 'That song . . . I've been having a go at it where nobody can hear me, in my bath, with the water running all the time just to make sure, and you know I think it's *not at all bad*!' – the upshot of which came one evening when the legendary lady of *The Quaker Girl* and *Our Miss Gibbs* entered a Broadcasting House studio for rehearsal. This was a testing moment for her. She knew that making a come-back can be desperately risky. Before her she saw our chorus . . . the orchestra . . . conductor, producer . . . everyone watching her, and wondering. We needn't have worried – the noble lady who planted herself before the

96

Radio Times Hulton Library   *Strand Magazine* (George Newnes Ltd.)

The Queen of the Gaiety, Gertie Millar, the quintessence of Edwardian beauty; and (*right*) George Graves, the clown of musical comedy, caricatured by H. M. Bateman

(*Below*) One of many protest marches similar to the one staged after the old Gaiety Theatre had been demolished; not for these unemployed were gaiety or fun, but the bitterness written in their banners

Radio Times Hulton Library

BBC chorus was Gertie from Bradford, with a cheeky sparkle in her eye, and in her singing that mixture of art and personal magnetism which makes star-quality. A recording of her performance has been kept: a good example of the value of BBC Archives in holding for the future not only what the stars sang but *how* they sang – in Gertie Millar's case, with what the *Daily Mail* called after her *Scrapbook* appearance 'her impeccable articulation and the enchanting lilt of her voice'. The lilt was inborn but the articulation and the entire art of projecting star-quality over to the audience had been learnt by years in the hard school of live theatre, where every note, every gesture, all personality had to reach the top of the gallery without electronic aids.

Another great star, SIR SEYMOUR HICKS, drew attention in a *Scrapbook* to a song he sang in 1904 about a remarkable social rite:

> *The Church Parade beats everything,*
> *The Church Parade when in full swing*
> > *Is a thing to see and wonder at,*
> > *For, oh, the wealth displayed,*
> > *Of the millinery art,*
> > *And costumes smart,*
> > *In the Church Parade.*[1]

In that day 'the best people' paraded on Sundays in the best parks and along the best sidewalks, top-hatting each other with formal gesticulations like toreadors in the arena. 'I think the church parade was invented to make the world believe that everybody in Society went to church,' said Sir Seymour.

It was in *The Catch of the Season* at the Vaudeville Theatre that Seymour Hicks, on a crowded stage, cried 'Look, here she comes!' – and pointed to an immense staircase where

---

[1] 'The Church Parade', lyric by C. H. Taylor, music by Herbert E. Haines, in musical comedy *The Catch of the Season* (reproduced by permission of Francis, Day and Hunter Ltd.).

Punch, 1908

appeared the Gibson Girl. An appropriate thrill ran round the house, for she was a new epitome of what we now call sex-appeal and (even more singular and significant) she was an American invention. In the States an artist, Charles Dana Gibson, had created on his drawing-board a Circe with an eighteen-inch waist, masses of golden hair, and a *décolleté* gown in black velvet. Mr Gibson's magazine drawings enraptured men and disturbed women on both sides of the Atlantic; then, like Pygmalion, the Girl came to life. MISS CAMILLE CLIFFORD tells us how: 'I was playing small parts on the stage in the United States when one night I had to deputise for an actress who was ill. All I had to do was walk across the stage, but they encored me again and again, and the manager said: "You've made your name; the Gibson Girl has come to life!" I thought, if that's so I will *be* the Gibson Girl; so I dressed like the Gibson pictures and came to England, where I appeared in *The Catch of the Season* at the Vaudeville, as Miss Enid Gibson.'

Sex appeal goes through fantastic permutations. The Nineties had had their 'Ta-ra-ra-boom-de-ay' rowdy naughtiness, the 1920s were to have their zippy 'It'-girls, the Sixties their sex-kittens; the Gibson Girl was absolutely unlike any of these. In another West End show *The Belle of Mayfair* (1906) she sidled on, her gown reaching chastely to the floor at one end while it almost fell off her shoulders at the other, singing a curiously *slow* chant by Leslie Stuart:

> *Wear a blank expression*
> *And a monumental curl,*
> *And walk with a bend in your back,*
> *Then they call you the Gibson Girl!*[1]

This aloof eroticism across the footlights sums up an Edwardian attitude to women – the 'allure', the 'mystery' – though it is hard to believe that Leslie Stuart didn't write the song with his tongue in his cheek. His bizarre sense of humour shows in this story told by his daughter, MISS MAY LESLIE STUART: 'There was one never-to-be-forgotten evening when I was present as a small girl at a private party in London when the great operatic tenor Caruso sang "Celeste Aida" to us. He was a little podgy man with a divine voice, and I can see my father sitting there with his head in his hands as Caruso sang. All father's Irish romanticism responded to that lovely tenor voice. And then came a completely ludicrous sequel. My father had a stubborn objection to playing his own compositions at parties, and when, after Caruso had sung, he was asked to play he declined; then someone led him over to the piano. Mother and I waited, breathless, for we knew anything might happen. A few musical fireworks and then, heaven help us, he began to *sing*:

> *Blackwall Tunnel,*
> *A cure for melancholy,*
> *Blackwall Tunnel,*
> *Is ever gay and jolly.*
> *The only game for me*
> *Is a sail upon the sea,*
> *Happy, gay and free –*
> *In Blackwall Tunnel!*

---

[1] 'Why Do They Call Me a Gibson Girl?', words by Leslie Stiles, music by Leslie Stuart (Francis, Day and Hunter Ltd.).

Aloof eroticism: Camille Clifford who (as the song said) walked with a bend in her back, not to mention other places, as the Gibson Girl

There'll Be No WO-AR!

'I saw Caruso's face. He was quite plainly thinking "the mad English"! The explanation is quite simple. Father had been lost in the beauty of the great operatic music; the musician in him fought shy of putting his own work in the same shop-window; improvising both words and music, he went off into the ridiculous as an escape.'

Gushing a shower of golden sovereigns, the musical comedy boom which had started in the Nineties continued through King Edward's reign, a fabulous oil-strike for theatrical potentates, composers, and stars. Every year in the West End a show knocked up over 500 performances, and some a great many more: *A Chinese Honeymoon* with 1,075, *The Arcadians* with 809, etc.[1] and all through the land the frivolous tunes were pumped out by stolid brass bands in parks and murdered gaily on Edwardian pianos. Best of all was *The Merry Widow* (778 performances), composer Franz Lehár. This is light opera rather than musical comedy, and it was for this reason that George Edwardes, the impresario who brought it to London, had little faith in it at the outset. So its author, Victor Léon, has told *Scrapbook*. He writes in his delightfully Viennese English: 'Mr George Edwardes, the manager of the Daly Theatre, came to Vienna to see *The Merry Widow*. In his company was, among other English actors, a young girl named Lily Elsie. She told me that she had only an insignificant position and was languishing for a great roll (*sic*). But Mr Edwardes had no confidence. She told me that she believed to be very able to represent this great roll (*sic*) and I should ask Mr Edwardes that he might let her have this part only as a trial. It had not been so easy to induce Mr Edwardes to do so. But finally she had the greatest success. Miss Elsie became now The Elsie.'

Lily Elsie as the 'Widow' in London sang like a nightingale and danced like a nymph, but as an insurance against operatic perils the down-to-earth George Edwardes hired MR GEORGE GRAVES to play Baron Popoff to the gallery: 'The author had provided me with practically no part so I had to agitate the grey matter. I invented Hetty the Hen. Hetty was an unfortunate bird, for to her life-long shame she laid a bent egg.' Graves built up Hetty week by week as a mythical addition to the cast of *The Merry Widow* until one day some trickster mixed brass filings with her food and 'Horror upon *horror*, *degradation* upon DEGRADATION, she laid a doorknob'.

This was hardly what Lehár and Léon expected of the London production. The English loved it. But they loved The Elsie more – and still today they delight in Lehár's music. It is a commentary on the changed artistic values of our times that in the Sadler's Wells Opera's immensely successful modern production of *The Merry Widow* there is no place for Hetty the Hen.

★   ★   ★

Who could have guessed that the cinemas would ever become a rival to the theatre? Since Lumière's *Watering the Gardener* in 1896 hundreds of smudgy, jerky little films had been made for showing in music-halls and fairground booths. The 'chase' was a staple formula: the policeman chasing the burglar while the dog was after the copper. Many of these were made in the back streets of Camberwell, as recalled by MR HARRY DE METZ: 'Working in the open-air, we had to depend upon the sun and a very fine day. A film actor's pay was three and sixpence for the day, with a break at lunchtime for a twopenny pint of beer and a crust of

---

[1] For details of others, see Calendar.

A shot from *Rescued by Rover*, featuring film producer Cecil Hepworth, his wife, their daughter, and canine star. With baby-and-dog interest this was guaranteed to be a smash-hit. No sound, but who cared?—it *moved*

bread and cheese. I also got a bonus of a few shillings because the producer could not read or write, so he employed me as his secretary. He used to make sketches, similar to cave-drawings, which he would afterwards explain to me and I would make them up into a rudimentary script.'

Rudimentary indeed! – nothing more than thumbnail sketches . . . but the startling idea of telling a rounded story on film began to dawn: in 1901 the British producer Cecil Hepworth made himself up as a burglar and appeared in his own story-film, and in 1903 *The Great Train Robbery* came from America. Next year Hepworth made *Rescued by Rover*, featuring his wife and baby daughter, two hired actors, and his dog Rover, all on a budget of £7 13s 9d – running time, seven minutes. Animals, slapstick comedy, and melodrama were seen to be the way to the public's heart. And crime: *The Life of Charles Peace* was made by the Sheffield Photo. Co. in 1905, the notorious murderer of thirty years earlier having been Sheffield's most inglorious citizen.

The star system had not yet begun, unless Rover may be said to have been the first British star; fifteen-year-old Charlie Chaplin was on the London stage, one of the wolves in the original *Peter Pan*, when in 1904 an astute English businessman saw the possibility of film entertainment standing on its own feet, not as a brief item in the music-halls or a stunt in a fairground booth. In 1904 he opened Britain's first regular cinema, the Daily Bioscope, in Bishopsgate, London, where for an admission fee of threepence or sixpence he offered a programme of fifty minutes. He was COLONEL A. C. BROMHEAD: 'The Daily Bioscope opened before lunch to catch the city clerk, and went on into the evening. The films were chiefly news, science, novelties – not more than five minutes each. Great was the excitement when we rushed down

When sound could not be recorded electrically: Henry Wood and his Queen's Hall Orchestra crowded in the HMV studio, cutting a wax disc acoustically by trying to direct their sounds down the funnel on the right.

to Bishopsgate a shot of the Russo-Japanese War in 1904, taken by Joe Rosenthal, who was, I think, the cinema's first genuine professional war-cameraman. He had taken films during the South African campaign. But I'm afraid some other "war" films weren't so genuine: stirring conflicts between Boer and Briton were fought out on the Yorkshire moors. My company showed a film of the signing of the peace with the Boers at Vereeniging, actually filmed at Loughborough Junction. We had actors impersonating Kitchener, Botha, and others, including Lord Roberts, only to find afterwards that Roberts was not present at Vereeniging.

'At the Daily Bioscope we were very modern – *we* had electricity, and the projector was inside a fireproof cubicle, whereas limelight was generally used in those days, and the film often unrolled into an open box on the floor; the only fire regulations were that there must be a bucket of sand, a bucket of water, and a wet blanket handy. I remember one ingenious operator who suspended an old lavatory cistern over his projector so that when fire broke out all he had to do was to pull the chain.'

Hints came already of the cinema's future growing-up into sound and colour. Kinemacolour, patented by George Albert Smith of Brighton in 1906, was a two-colour system, alternate red and green filters being rotated in front of the camera lens. *The British Journal of Photography* said that 'whilst there is yet room for considerable improvement the progress made is extremely satisfactory.' The rotating discs and the imperfections of colour-range due to the two-colour process were severe limitations; the real breakthrough of the modern three-colour system had to wait until the 1930s. Talkies were even more in their Edwardian infancy. Inventors devised methods for coupling a gramophone and a film projector, rivalling one

103

another in the extravagance of their trade names – the Replicaphone, the Chronophone, the Apollogramophone, the Filmaphone, the Animatophone – and ludicrous in their behaviour, for while the face on the screen was enormous the voice from the gramophone was tiny and strangulated, and synchronization was clumsy, the voice jerking absurdly ahead of or behind the vision.

An early talkie experiment at the London Hippodrome music-hall was in 1907 (twenty-one years before the famous landmark of Al Jolson in *The Jazz Singer*) and the bioscope operator, MR EDWIN PATTERSON, describes it: 'On the screen appeared three darkies with banjoes, and from behind the screen blared voices singing a coon song. This came from an ordinary gramophone record, and I more or less synchronized it by the simple process of speeding-up or slowing-down the record. This altered the pitch of the singing, but what did that matter? – the figures on the screen had found their tongues. The gramophone had an amplifier, not electrical as today but worked by compressed air, and the sound of the air-pump added to the voices made such a row that a newsvendor outside the stage-door said, "Seems as 'ow those lions are restless today!" – for we also had some circus lions on the bill that week.'[1]

All this seems antediluvian now, but it is worth noting that in the same year as Colonel Bromhead's first cinema, 1904, Professor J. A. Fleming was experimenting in the electrical engineering department of University College, London, with his 'oscillation valve', ultimately (when much improved) to be the key to the electronic age, to talkies, to broadcasting.

The primitive pre-electrical marriage of film sight and gramophone sound being unhappy, the cinema pianist and the sound-effects man carried on as described by MISS MAY LANGSTON – she toured corn exchanges and village halls: 'There was the lecturer, the lantern operator, the effects man and myself. In the morning the lecturer donned his top-hat and frock coat and went out billposting. In the evening he announced the films and walked about the hall in evening dress to give the place tone. Sometimes he made up dialogue to fit the films, and cross-talked with the effects man who sat at a table with two half-coconuts for horses, a piece of sandpaper for water, and other sound-making devices. I played sobstuff or dramatic music as the film required. I also sang and entertained the audience with recitations during the intervals.'

The projector was usually worked by limelight. We have observed earlier that at the turn of the century the only direction where electricity really showed its paces was in municipal transport; now the development of steam-turbines by Sir Charles Parsons permitted power-stations (and ships) to grow to great size, and electrical engineers were ready for immense expansion schemes, but Parliament itself 'unwisely saddled the country', Sir Robert Ensor says,[2] with a 'rabble of small inefficient electrical undertakings', whereas they could have planned boldly, nation-wide. Even in London gas lighting was good enough for our legislators within the Houses of Parliament until 1913.

For lack of electricity, domestic labour-saving devices caught on hardly at all. An electric iron had been invented in the early 1900s but few were to be seen in homes before the First World War. Little progress was made with electric ovens and refrigerators. One of the first patents for an electric razor (by G. P. Appleyard, of Halifax) was filed in 1913. A hand-driven

---

[1] The machine, the Stentorphone, was invented by Mr Will Day, of London. Many years later I got him to demonstrate it on BBC Television – a curious meeting of ancient and modern. – L.B.

[2] *England, 1870–1914*, by R. C. K. Ensor (Oxford University Press), the best social history of this period.

dish-washer was marketed in 1910 and one with electric drive came in 1914, but few bought it.

Public transport continued to do better. The last steam trains ran on the London underground in 1905; tunnels were bored for the new Bakerloo, Piccadilly, and Northern Lines; Lots Road electricity station, the largest in the country, was built to provide them with power. Electric tramcars were in their clanging heyday in every go-ahead town, though some parts of London remained faithful to the horse-tram until 1915.

Since Emancipation Day in 1896 the internal combustion engine had made progress. The Post Office first tried motor vans in 1902 (London–Redhill, Liverpool–Manchester, Altrincham–Manchester). The first rural motor-bus service started in 1903; the Great Western Railway opened it between Helston and the Lizard. The driver was MR CHARLES BOLTON: 'The bus had an open body like a charabanc. The passengers had no protection at all from the weather. It was touch and go whether we should make the Cornish hills, so the conductor had to be ready to jump off and shove a chock under the wheel. The brakes were just wooden blocks which rubbed on solid rubber tyres.'

Nobody saw what a harbinger that country motor-bus was of immense social changes a quarter of a century or so later. Normal rural life in Edwardian times is illustrated by a Cornish story from MRS TRETHOWAN: 'Two-horse buses brought the country people into the market town to do their shopping. Those who weren't able to come gave their lists to the driver and he would shop for them, 2d a parcel, and deliver on his return journey in the evening. As a young woman I used to delight in sitting on top with the driver. The bus was piled high with his purchases, large and small. I remember one evening driving down to St Just-in-Roseland. The driver stopped at a cottage, and slung a bedstead over the garden hedge, then we drove on a considerable distance, and stopped again, and he handed a paper bag to an astonished-looking cottager.

'"Here's your hat, ma'am", he said.

'"Hat, I don't want no hat," said the lady. "It's my bedstead I'm waiting for."

'"Your bedstead, was it? – oh, I left he three mile back in Mrs Tregunna's garden"; and without more ado the driver whipped up his horses and left the poor soul helpless.'

★ ★ ★

A horsey Sam Weller type walked shyly into a Broadcasting House studio one day and introduced himself as MISTER ARNOLD. This little Cockney, strange to say, was a direct link with the great days of stage-coaches, for after the railways knocked out that method of long-distance transport for passengers in the nineteenth century the Post Office continued to use the coach-and-four on half-a-dozen long-distance routes out of London, and Mister Arnold was a driver on the Brighton route until 1905. He told us how every night his red-and-black coach set out from London Bridge parcels office to a rousing blast: 'We used a fifty-two-inch horn, sir, and blowed it frew the tahns.'

The crew was the driver and a guard whose job was to attend to the mail inside, then climb up and sit beside the driver, blow the horn as a warning to sleepy drivers of market-garden wagons, and chat to Mr Arnold to keep him awake: 'I once turned the coach over at Norbury. Annover of me mates, 'e was asleep one night when 'e drives clean into the middle of the pond at Thornton 'Eaf. Woke 'im up!'

'How many horses were needed to take the coach from London to Brighton?'

Photo by courtesy H. M. Postmaster General

The Royal Mail long-distance coach turns out smartly, complete with coach-horn.

(*Below*) The new electric trams made *Punch* perpetrate a famous joke: The Old Lady says, 'Would it be dangerous, conductor, if I was to put my foot on the rail?' The conductor answers, 'No, Mum, not unless you put the other one on the overhead wire'

'Sixteen, sir. Three changes.'

'What speed did you do?'

'Twelve an 'our, up to sixteen or twenty at a gallop.'

'It must have been very quiet on the road at night?'

'Oh, it was, sir. Oh, it was *beautiful*. On a moonlight night when the snow was on the grahnd it was *somethink beautiful*.'

The Brighton coach left London at 9.45 p.m. and reached its destination fifty-three miles later at 4.45 a.m. A motor-van replaced it in 1905, knocking an hour-and-a-quarter off the time: no need to stop three times to change horses. The London–Oxford and London–Portsmouth horse coaches continued until 1909.

Very slowly the number of private motorists increased. No reliable figures are available until after the Highways Act of 1903 which first required registration of motor vehicles, and imposed a speed limit everywhere of 20 miles per hour. This is the growth since (private cars only):

1904	1914	1924	1934	1944	1954
8,465	132,015	473,528	1,308,425	755,400	3,099,547

and so to 8,247,000 in 1964, about 1,000 cars for every one in 1904.

That year Mr Royce made a car (10 horse-power, two cylinders). First to appreciate Royce quality was the Hon. C. S. Rolls, already famed as a racing driver abroad, who had set up business in London as a car dealer and who joined with Royce to found a famous line of champions. (Incidentally, Rolls was one of the first squires to install electric light in his country house.) British makes were pushing French cars from the primacy they had established in the Nineties and in this same year 1904 the intrepid Mr Harvey du Cros, son of the founder of Dunlop's, drove his Ariel car to the top of Snowdon. He bumpty-bumped upwards astride the track of the mountain railway, and *The Times* tells us that 'Several stoppages occurred along the five mile route for watering and for cooling purposes. The severe mile-and-a-half stretch with a gradient of one in five-and-a-half was grandly taken. The Ariel was cinematographed at several points on the trip, and the summit was reached in three-and-three-quarter hours.' There the car stood for a time, rampant symbol of the future petrol age; then Mr du Cros bumpty-bumped it back to the bottom again.

In London the turning-point for the horse may be pin-pointed as 1905. This was its zenith: over 7,000 hansom-cabs and 4,000 four-wheelers were plying for hire in the metropolis, and horses pulled nearly 3,500 buses. Never again would there be so many. There were 241 motor-buses: never again would there be so few. The first London taxi-cab (1903) was derided as an absurdity, but presently it had earned an affectionate place in the balladry of music-halls:

> *Oh, the car! the taximeter car!*
> *It's better than taking a trip to Spain,*
> *Or having your honeymoon over again;*
> *If you're out with your sweetheart,*
> *Your mater or papa,*
> *Do it in style for eightpence a mile*
> *In the taximeter car.*[1]

---

[1] 'The New Taximeter Car', by Harry Heath and Will Hyde (reproduced by permission of Francis, Day and Hunter Ltd.), 1907.

Most private cars were still either luxuries or the playthings of sporting types; their first utilitarian use was by doctors, one of whom figures amusingly in the 1910 recollections of an Oxfordshire farmer, MR OLIVER DYER: 'I'd been a plough-boy ever since I was thirteen, and I was very fond of horses. We generally had four horses on the double plough; they'd got bright shiny hames[1] and the brasses were generally shone up nice and bright, whereas a tractor today – well, there's nothing o' that! Thenadays there was only one motor-car as I can remember in our village, and that was Doctor Routh's. It made a tidy row, it frightened the horses tidy! Doctor got stuck several times. Had to be drawed home with a horse.'

When the Brooklands motor-racing track was opened in 1907 the newspapers called its garages 'motor stables'. S. F. Edge immediately made average speeds there of over 65 miles per hour with his six-cylinder Napier. Believe it or not, the world land-speed record was 127 miles per hour, made in America by a Stanley steam-car. Next came a Great Western Railway train at 102 miles per hour.

A steam-car for everyday use was owned by the actor-manager, SIR SEYMOUR HICKS: 'The boiler was under the front seat, and steam could be raised from cold in six or seven minutes, a petrol burner providing heat at threepence a gallon. And a jolly good machine it was. We thought it was superior to the petrol-motor-car because it didn't smell.'

The open road was still the cyclist's paradise, and almost anywhere in Britain you might meet a man on a bicycle to which was strapped several huge leather boxes – a commercial photographer, MR W. J. BRUNELL, who did a thriving business in the picture postcard trade in those days when every self-respecting home had its postcard album: 'I trundled round the country photographing beauty spots, abbeys, lakes, old inns, the Thames from source to sea – the lot – and all on my bike! There were no films, only glass plates, so you can imagine what it was like carrying a huge, heavy camera with a stock of $8\frac{1}{2}$ by $6\frac{1}{2}$ inch plates. When I got to a subject I thought worth photographing, such as a ruined castle, I had to take the case off the front of my bike, the stand off the back-stays where it was strapped, put the camera on the stand and stick my head under the black cloth to focus the subject: the image was thrown on the ground-glass screen upside down.' Comparison between Mr Brunell's ponderous equipment and the modern midget camera is as great as between the rural England he toured and the same countryside today. In his opinion, 'The country was far nicer than it is now. I don't like these big wide modern roads.'

The greatest difference of all is that a townsman seen in any village in this land was a stranger among the aborigines, he looked different, he spoke his townish lingo, he even thought differently; and the same applied to the villager who visited a big town. Many a countryman had never travelled further than the nearest market town. To go to London was an adventure. Easy transport, plus radio and television, have largely wiped out these divisions.

★   ★   ★

'Take me on the Flip-Flap! – do, dear, do!' they sang in 1908. It means nothing now, but was then the latest of recreational stunts in London, two huge metal arms in the sky which flip-flapped to and fro as the passengers in cars on the ends looked down on the Anglo-French Exhibition at Shepherd's Bush and tried not to be sick. Down there below was the White

---

[1] Hames: dialect word for two curved pieces of metal resting on horse's collar, to which traces were attached.

1907: The ladies play diabolo while their men mend the motor-car, a rather obviously 'staged' incident by the photographer of the *Illustrated London News*. How much more lively the black-and-white artist could be (*see below*):

Tom Browne's drawing in *Punch* reminds us how clumsy a business photography was in the days before midget cameras and fast films: a glass plate is in the camera, and the lady must freeze her posture for several seconds

Poor physique and widespread malnutrition in the British working class was shown up by the Boer War, when many would-be recruits were rejected unfit; a wave of reform followed. A 1907 Act legislated for 'attending to the health and physical condition of children in elementary schools'. These London boys drilling in 1908 now look absurdly dressed for physical jerks, but it was a step in the right direction. And . . .

'There is no doubt that these cookery classes are doing a very valuable work, and testimony to the practical utility of the teaching given is constantly forthcoming from parents: for example, a mother is taught by her daughter to make bread, and saves 1s 6d a week in consequence. A higher standard of living is gradually being set up amongst the working classes.' So wrote Ailsa Craig in 1913, in her *History of the Teaching of Domestic Economy*

City stadium, built for the first Olympic Games ever held in this country. Here was the scene of the Dorando affair. Conflicting reports of this sport sensation have been published, so *Scrapbook* was glad to record LORD DESBOROUGH who as President of the British Olympic Council had a close-up of the event: 'These Olympic Games, opened in London by King Edward in 1908, were the most important held up to then. For the first time codes of rules were laid down which have been of the greatest value in succeeding Olympiads. Three thousand competitors came from twenty-one different countries, and previous records went by the board. The Marathon Race, which was started from the East Terrace of Windsor Castle, went through Eton and Harrow to the Stadium. The day was one of those windless sultry days we get sometimes in the English summer. Dense crowds lined the whole course of the route, which added to the trials of the fifty-five runners. The collapse of many of the competitors was due to the heat and to the presence of the crowds – twenty-six miles of them along the route, culminating in 80,000 in the Stadium – the number, according to the police, exceeding anything seen in this country before, at the Boat Race, or the Derby, or any of the great reviews. The Stadium was packed, and at last a figure tottered into it, almost unconscious. It was Dorando Pietri, an Italian. He staggered round the track, his legs sometimes moving up and down without making progress, as in a dream. He fell more than once, and the crowds shouted that he should not be left there, perhaps to expire in front of them all. Finally he was assisted past the post and carried off, but on objections being raised there was no alternative but to disqualify him on the report of the doctors that unaided he could not have reached the post, and on account of the infringement of other regulations. Rumours spread that night that Dorando had succumbed, but they proved fortunately untrue. Queen Alexandra, who was a much moved spectator, announced that she would present Dorando with a special gold cup.'

Britain scored by far the largest number of points in the 1908 Olympic Games. Sport was playing an increasing part in this country's life, with a variety of consequences. Games and 'gym' were penetrating from posh schools to humbler levels, with good effect on health. Among adults a more agile spirit brought a liberating influence on everyday clothing and fashion: such things as starched shirts for men were on the wane, while women were actually beginning to divest themselves of those layers of petticoats essential at the turn of the century.[1]

Sport as a spectacle was taking the turn towards its present-day commercialized form: in 1905 came the first £1,000 transfer for a footballer (A. Common, from Sunderland to Middlesbrough). As an increasingly 'popular' Press increased its sports coverage such rising young stars as Charlie Buchan at football and Jack Hobbs at cricket became national heroes, while the Grand Old Men of sport were built as legendary figures, notably the grandest, Dr W. G. Grace, whose 126th century in first-class cricket in 1904 (166 for London County v. M.C.C.) was to remain a world record until Hobbs beat it twenty-one years later.

To boys there was one supreme hero who in 1907–8 did something highly imaginative in terms of youth-leadership, General Baden-Powell, formerly famed as defender of Mafeking. He invited twenty boys, some from the working class, some from public schools, to join him in a camp on Brownsea Island, in Poole Harbour, Dorset. One of the campers in 1907 was MR REGINALD GILES: 'B-P put us into four patrols – there were the Wolves, the Ravens, Curlews, and Bulls. We had all kinds of exercises, like fire drill and boat drill, and we had a game called

---

[1] The de-petticoating process was to be pushed further by the hobble skirt later on.

"harpooning the whale" which was fine fun, we had to throw the harpoon from our boat into a floating log. B-P sent us out on patrol at night round the island; we were given our rations for the night and B-P told us the way to make our own bread. We had to mix the flour on the lining of our jacket and bake the bread in the embers of the fire. At night we would sit round the camp fire and have a chat and sing songs. B-P would tell us all about the South African campaigns. He was a wonderful hero. We had at the camp the same Union Jack, riddled with bullets, that he flew at Mafeking.'

Encouraged by the camp, B-P. founded the Boy Scouts in 1908. Thus began a great social experiment, the biggest youth movement in the world.

Boys of that generation were destined for the slaughter of over 8,500,000 of the world's young men by other young men (or more truly, by old men). Great armies and navies were building up, and most of the common people of Europe happily trusted that 'the balance of power' meant security: Germany, Austria–Hungary, and Italy on one side, France, Russia, Britain on the other. Little did the boys of the young brigade guess that the long fuse leading to the great explosion was already spluttering underneath them. In 1906 one of the old men, Schlieffen, the German Chief of Staff, was secretly urging on the Kaiser 'the fundamental clearing up of relations with France by a prompt war'. The Schlieffen Plan, practised on paper over and over again, was for a swift drive through Belgium to the Channel ports, then a swing west of Paris.

Secret military conversations were afoot between British and French generals. The Liberal Government in power from 1905 onwards carried out massive Army reforms. The launching in 1906 of HMS *Dreadnought*, the world's colossus (17,950 tons), the most heavily armed battle-ship (eight 12-inch guns) and the first with turbine engines, caught the Germans by surprise, but they soon followed suit with their own dreadnoughts. Up to 1908 Germany was building ships faster than Britain. The Kaiser had a nightmare of Germany being 'encircled' by France, Russia, and Britain. 'Taken all round, it is aimed at us,' he said. He told his people that 'Every German warship launched is a new guarantee for peace on earth.' Our statesmen gave similar assurances as bigger and better British dreadnoughts slid into the sea. The Kaiser's bombast – he called himself 'The Admiral of the Atlantic' – became a joke in England:

> *Who is the man who's working for a universal peace?*
> *Who is the man who by his tact will soon make wars to cease?*
> *Who wants to sink all selfish aims, give up his private ends,*
> *Who says to every foreign power, 'Let's kiss and all be friends'?*
>
> *It's the Emperor, the German Emperor,*
>   *His friends assert he wouldn't hurt a fly.*
> *But he's building ships of war, what does he want them for?*
>   *They'll all be ours by and by.*[1]

Alongside this braggart flippancy a few voices were trying to make themselves heard seriously. Lord Roberts, another Boer War hero, stumped the country urging immediate conscription. A play called *An Englishman's Home* showed Mr Brown's villa being rudely

---

[1] This song, 'Mr Chamberlain', sung by Seymour Hicks in *The Beauty of Bath*, 1906, was written by two young men yet to find fame, the music by Jerome Kern, the words by P. G. Wodehouse (reproduced by permission of the publishers, Ascherberg, Hopwood and Crew Ltd.).

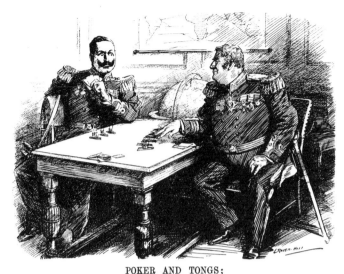

Punch takes a look at the game of power, 1908

POKER AND TONGS;
OR, HOW WE'VE GOT TO PLAY THE GAME.

Kaiser. "I GO THREE *DREADNOUGHTS*."
John Bull. "WELL, JUST TO SHOW THERE'S NO ILL-FEELING, I RAISE YOU THREE."

invaded by the soldiers of a Foreign Power ('Please let me know the meaning of this, sir'). Erskine Childers' *The Riddle of the Sands* wrapped up propaganda for war-preparedness in an exciting novel which John Buchan later declared the best story of adventure published in the first quarter of the century; certainly, this salty yarn of the little sailing craft *Dulcibella*'s adventures off the North German coast captivated a generation, but more by the story than the 'message'.

Sir Edward Grey, the Foreign Secretary, warned in 1909 that rising expenditure an armaments could 'submerge our civilization', and the next year Norman Angell in *The Great Illusion* was arguing that future war would be *economically* disastrous to victor as well as vanquished – a most unusual point of view – but among the masses few read it, or understood it, or bothered. 'There'll be no war as long as we've a king like good King Ed-EW-ARD.'

Few worried about the invisible factors, the jealousies of kings and governments, their ambitions in trade and power, their fears, pride, old scores to be settled. Fewer believed, as Erskine Childers did in later years when he reversed his ideas, that 'preparedness led to international armament rivalries, and bred in the minds of the nations concerned fears, antagonisms, and ambitions that were destructive to peace'.[1]

The supreme tragedy of the Edwardian years was the uninformed, insensitive, unalert attitude of people towards these things. H. G. Wells has been quoted in *Scrapbooks* time and again because he was the most discerning journalist-novelist of his time: in 1908 we find him unfolding another unusual theory (in *The War in the Air*), that science was creating a new Europe which needed some sort of 'league of the nations'. This was his offbeat analysis of the situation: 'The development of science had altered the scale of human affairs. By means of rapid mechanical traction it had brought men nearer together, so much nearer socially, economically, physically, that the old separations into nations and kingdoms were no longer possible;

[1] Foreword by his widow to later editions of *The Riddle of the Sands*.

113

a newer, wider synthesis was not only needed but imperatively demanded. Just as the once independent dukedoms of France had to fuse into a nation, so now the nations had to adapt themselves to a wider coalescence, they had to keep what was precious and practicable, and concede what was obsolete and dangerous. A saner world would have perceived this patent need for a reasonable synthesis, would have discussed it temperately, achieved and gone on to organize the great civilization that was manifestly possible to mankind.'

King Edward died suddenly in 1910. That year the Government decided to lay the keels of eight dreadnoughts in answer to redoubled efforts by Germany; a political slogan was 'We want eight and we won't wait'. It was the year when (a few months after Bleriot's first Channel flight) the Hon. C. S. Rolls flew his aeroplane across to France *and back*, and *Punch* made the pertinent comment:

> *What boots it that the fleet's so whopping*
> *And Dreadnought types the ocean gird*
> *If aviators keep on popping*
> *Across the Channel like a bird?*
> *This is the second time the thing's occurred.*

So the years of Edward the Peacemaker ended in rising tensions, mostly concealed by great illusions. During the King's funeral a broadsheet was sold in the London streets:

> *Greatest sorrow England ever had*
> *When death took away our dear Dad;*
> *A king was he from head to sole,*
> *Loved by his people one and all.*
> *His mighty work for the Nation,*
> *Making peace and strengthening union –*
> *Always at it since on the throne:*
> *Saved the country more than one billion.*

... but this typical German lampoon of Edward VII, in *Kladderadatsch*, 1909, shows him flirting with Austria-Hungary during one of his tours on the Continent.

THE BEGINNING OF THE BOY SCOUTS

On Brownsea Island a lesson in artificial respiration for boys, at the camp which gave an inspiration to Baden-Powell; *right*, B-P at Brownsea; *below*, one of his 1907 campers, Reginald Giles, interviewed in 1964 by Leslie Baily

Photos, *Poole & Dorset Herald* and Boy Scouts Association

1909

First aeroplane flight across English Channel, by Bleriot (July 25).

At Brooklands Moore–Brabazon won *Daily Mail* prize for flight of a mile with all-British plane.

Old age pensions began (January 1), at 70.

Housing and Town Planning Act.

Lloyd George's 'People's Budget' rejected by Lords; Parliament dissolved.

Recorded electioneering speeches played by gramophone in streets during by-elections at Glasgow and Croydon.

Greatest rainfall on record in UK for a month: 56.5 inches at Lyn Llydaw, Caernarvonshire.

Peary (USA) reached North Pole.

Shackleton returned from Antarctic; a party from his expedition had reached the Magnetic Pole, and he had reached within 97 miles of Geographical Pole.

Queen's University, Belfast, founded; also Bristol University.

Experimental trolley bus tried in London.

Liner *Republic* sank: first great saving of life at sea by wireless.

Last long-distance Royal Mail horse-coaches.

STAGE: *Our Miss Gibbs* began its run of 636 performances; *The Arcadians*, 809; *The Dollar Princess*, 428; *Strife* (Galsworthy); *An Englishman's Home* (du Maurier); *The Blue Bird* (Maeterlinck).

BOOKS: *Ann Veronica* and *Tono Bungay* (H. G. Wells); *The Street of Adventure* (Philip Gibbs); *Bella Donna* (Robert Hichens).

SONGS: 'Arcady is Ever Young'; 'The Pipes of Pan' and 'My Motter' (*The Arcadians*); 'Archibald, Certainly Not!'; 'Boiled Beef and Carrots'; 'By the Light of the Silvery Moon'; 'Has Anybody Here Seen Kelly?'; 'I Do Like to be Beside the Seaside'; 'Let's All Go Down the Strand'; 'Moonstruck' and 'Yip-i-addy-i-ay' (*Our Miss Gibbs*).

1910

King Edward VII died (May 6); funeral (May 20).

First General Election of year; Liberals returned (January 14–February 14) with majority of 2.

Second General Election (December 2–20); Liberals and Conservatives each returned with 272 seats out of 670, Liberals' power again depending on support of minorities.

Post-Impressionist Exhibition, London.

First eighty Labour Exchanges opened (February 1).

Hon. C. S. Rolls killed at Bournemouth aviation meeting.

First night flight (Grahame-White); Paulhan won £10,000 for London–Manchester flight.

Calendar, 1909 to 1910

French airship *Clement-Bayard 2* flew from Paris to London in five and a half hours, and Pierre Prier made first aeroplane flight, London–Paris, in under four hours non-stop.
Captain Scott left London in *Terra Nova* for Antarctic.
First two women members of LCC elected.
8,000,000 visited Japan–British exhibition, Shepherd's Bush.
Crippen and Ethel le Neve arrested on liner *Montrose*.
New Great Western Railway Line, London–Birmingham via High Wycombe and Aynho.
Girl Guides founded.
Rayon first commercially marketed in Britain by Courtauld's.
Vaughan William's 'Sea Symphony' and 'Fantasia on a Theme by Thomas Tallis'; Kreisler played first performance of 'Violin Concerto' (Elgar).

STAGE: *Justice* (Galsworthy); *The Madras House* (Granville Barker); *The Quaker Girl* began run of 536 performances, *The Chocolate Soldier*, 500; *The Speckled Band* (Conan Doyle).

BOOKS: *History of Mr Polly* (H. G. Wells); *Literary Lapses* (Leacock); *Prester John* (Buchan); *Clayhanger* (Arnold Bennett); *The Brassbounder* (David Bone); *Howard's End* (E. M. Forster); *Carnival* (Compton Mackenzie); *At the Villa Rose* (A. E. W. Mason), *The Great Illusion* (Norman Angell).

SONGS: 'A Perfect Day'; 'Come to the Ball' (*Quaker Girl*); 'Don't Go Down the Mine, Daddy'; 'Drake Goes West'; 'Flanagan'; 'Ginger, You're Balmy'; 'I Want to Sing in Opera'; 'My Hero' (*Chocolate Soldier*); 'You Can Do a Lot of Things at the Seaside'.

The Calendar is continued on page 153

Punch, 1909

Famous flying men in a famous car, a 1909 Silver Ghost Rolls-Royce. (*From left*), Horace Short, C. S. Rolls, Orville Wright, Griffith Brewer, Wilbur Wright

(*Below*) Not a bird-cage but the first heavier-than-air machine to fly in Britain: Horatio Phillips's fantastic device of 1907

5 THE GREAT BREAKTHROUGHS

(a) THE AEROPLANE

'I do not think it at all probable that aeronautics will ever come into play as a serious modification of transport and communication,' wrote H. G. Wells in his *Anticipations* (1901), misreading for once the crystal-ball, though he conceded that 'very probably by 1950 a successful aeroplane will have soared and come home safely'.

Flying was one of several revolutionary developments in the pre-1914 years. In this chapter we shall look at the beginning of things that have immensely changed our lives right down to the present time. Of all the centuries-old dreams of men none was more daring and magnificent than that of flight in a heavier-than-air machine. Balloons had drifted around since 1783, but having no engine or method of steering the balloon was at the mercy of the winds. Then in 1900 the first Zeppelin flew in Germany. The next year brought news from Paris of Santos Dumont's several attempts to cajole his 12 horse-power airship round the Eiffel Tower from a base three miles away; this attracted world interest because he was risking his neck for big money (100,000 francs) and because his failures were comical ('My capricious motor stopped and the airship, bereft of its power, fell on the tallest chestnut tree in the park of Monsieur de Rothschild'). His eventual success increased the faith of such prophets as H. G. Wells in airships, as distinct from aeroplanes.

In America the Wright brothers were flying only gliders. Wilbur Wright wrote to a friend in 1902: 'We have recently done a little experimenting with propellers and are trying to get a closer understanding of how they work. If all goes well the next step will be to apply a motor.'

The story turns to England. The Spencer brothers built an airship. On September 19, 1902 Stanley Spencer made the first flight across London, from the Crystal Palace to Harrow. The *Illustrated London News* said: 'Mr Spencer's absolute confidence in the machine has been amply justified. While in the neighbourhood of Herne Hill he caused the airship to perform numerous evolutions, darting downwards as though falling to earth, suddenly arresting the descent, and again rising.' This airship had a gas-bag 75 feet long, from which hung a bamboo framework carrying a petrol engine of 35 horse-power, a propeller in front, and a basket for the pilot. It flew at about 20 miles per hour.

What it was like to fly in is told by MARIE SPENCER, now Mrs Townsend, of Eastbourne: 'At the Crystal Palace one day in 1902 my Uncle Stanley said "Would you like to come up?" To my great joy, I was quickly lifted into the little basket and we cast off from the ground and rose up into the air. There was no seating, just a little piece of board on which we stood, and as

Illustrated London News

The first attempt to fly the Atlantic, 1910: the airship *America*. The 'petrol-filled equilibrator' trailing in the sea was intended to keep the airship steady and at the same time to store a ton of petrol. Another four tons were carried in a tank aboard ship

the wind got up so did my white silk skirt. As a little girl of nine, there was I standing holding my skirt down, as it wasn't done for little girls to show underclothes. But anyway, I do remember I thoroughly enjoyed the flight; it was lovely – just the feeling of floating over the country and seeing things down below, like looking at a glorified map. Of course, I'd been up in balloons before, in fact the first time was when I was only eleven months old and I went up in my mother's arms, but this was quite a new experience as there was a motor roaring and a propeller whirring round. And, of course, having the motor it was possible to drive the thing and guide it.'

Marie Spencer was thus the first of her sex to fly in an airship. The fact that the ship carried on its side the huge words MELLIN'S FOOD shows that even in those days a commercial could be slotted between the most exciting adventures.

In the next year Orville and Wilbur Wright's experiments in America brought the great breakthrough, in a secluded spot in the sand-dunes at Kitty Hawk, USA, on December 17, 1903.

Britain's first military airship, the *Nulli Secundus*, 1907. From Farnborough she flew with a crew of three to London (top speed 16 m.p.h.) but head-winds prevented her returning to base and her skipper, Colonel Capper, brought his ship 'skilfully to anchor' at the Crystal Palace, said the *Illustrated London News*. She was packed up and went home by road

It was virtually unpublicized because these two were modest fellows who never liked the limelight; years later MR ORVILLE WRIGHT refused to broadcast for *Scrapbook* but sent us this written record: 'I would not think today of making my first flight on a strange machine in a twenty-seven mile wind even if I knew the machine had already been flown and was safe. I now look with amazement upon our audacity in attempting to fly with a new and untried machine under such circumstances. But we had faith in our calculations, and confidence in our system of control. The course of the flight up and down was exceedingly erratic, partly due to the irregularity of the air, and partly to my lack of experience in handling this machine. It would rise suddenly to about 10 feet and then as suddenly dart for the ground. A sudden dart when a little over 120 feet from the point at which I rose into the air ended my first flight. It had lasted only twelve seconds. It was the first in the history of the world in which a machine carrying a man had raised itself by its own power into the air in full flight, and had sailed without reduction of speed and had finally landed at a point as high as that from which it started.'

121

It is amazing to find that a sceptical world simply would not believe what had occurred. The Wright flight was reported very briefly in newspapers but people generally thought it a tall story. As long as three years after the flight a London musical comedy *The Beauty of Bath* was singing of the aeroplane as something of the future:

> *When flying machines BEGIN to fly*
> *We never shall stay at home,*
> *Away we'll skip on a half-day trip*
> *To Paris, perhaps, or Rome . . .*

In 1906 the first flight across the English Channel by a woman was made by MRS BEATRICE GRIFFITH BREWER – but in a balloon. She had Percival Spencer and Frank Butler with her: 'One afternoon when the wind was just right we took off from Wandsworth Gasworks in London, where the balloon had been filled with ordinary coal-gas. From start to finish our trip took about three hours. It was a pleasant day but intensely cold, so cold that the sand-bags froze solid. Sandbags were used as ballast. Normally we tipped some overboard when we wanted the balloon to rise, but this time it was so hard we had to dig bits out and drop them overboard. We left the English coast over Dungeness, and landed about twenty miles from Boulogne. The two men shook me heartily by the hand. I ran up and down the sand-dunes to get warm. A little French padre came up and ran along beside me, firing questions at me, and very excited.'

Crossing the Channel by balloon was a rare occurrence but – a woman! – the exclamation was inevitable. H. G. Wells has his suburban Cockney, Tom Smallways, grousing in *The War in the Air* about balloons dropping ballast all over the place – 'I got three barrer-loads of gravel off my petaters.' The milkman reminds him that '*Ladies*, they say, goes up!'

'I suppose we got to call 'em ladies,' says Mr Smallways. 'Still, it ain't hardly my idea of a lady – flying about in the air, and throwing gravel at people. It ain't what I been accustomed to consider lady-like, whether or no.'

The War in the Air foretold airships – not aeroplanes – flying the Atlantic and bombing New York. In real life Britain's first military airship, the *Nulli Secundus*, bumbled at 16 miles per hour across the Metropolis in 1907 and 'sent London almost wild with delight', said the Press.

Balloons and airships – yes. These were well proved; but aeroplanes! – the Engineering Editor of *The Times* asserted forthrightly that 'all attempts at artificial aviation are not only dangerous to human life but foredoomed to failure from an engineering point of view'. Un-deterred, the Wrights continued to make powered flights in America, while Santos-Dumont, Ferber, and Blériot did so in France.

There was a complete lack of publicity for the *first aeroplane flight in Britain*. This took place in 1907 but was so completely disregarded that it is only lately, in the 1960s, that the research of the aviation historian, CHARLES H. GIBBS-SMITH, has proved that it took place at all. It has hitherto been believed that the first heavier-than-air flight in this country was in 1908 by S. F. Cody. But Mr Gibbs-Smith has evidence that a certain Horatio Phillips constructed and flew his own aeroplane earlier. The machine looked rather like a huge bird-cage, with wings similar to venetian blinds. It had a 7-foot propeller and an engine of 20 horse-power.

'Phillips', says Mr Gibbs-Smith, 'had been demonstrating the high-lifting qualities of narrow cambered wings since 1893. Then in 1904 he made a man-carrier which could not get off the ground. Finally, in 1907, he made his latest design, a multi-wing aeroplane, the wings consisting of a large number of cambered slats. This ingenious contraption took off from a field near Streatham with Phillips on board, and was fully airborne for a few seconds at about 30 miles per hour. There is no doubt that in this event we have the first powered man-carrying take-off, and the first tentative hop-flight in Britain.'[1]

MR GRIFFITH BREWER (husband of the cross-Channel lady) won the International Balloon Race of 1908: 'This was the largest balloon race ever held in England, for the news that aeroplane flying was really within the reach of man was soon to rob ballooning of its interest, until today it is more difficult to arrange a balloon trip than it was in 1908. In that year most people still scoffed at the idea of aeroplane flying. So rooted was our disbelief that, even at the Aero Club in London, when reports came through that Wilbur Wright had gone to France and had flown his machine with a passenger, we couldn't believe them. There must be a catch somewhere. I therefore went over to Le Mans to see with my own eyes the shattering of the impossible.'

He became the first Englishman to fly as a passenger. Wilbur Wright trundled his plane out of a hangar and invited Mr Brewer to sit alongside him: 'The machine was catapulted off the ground. It ran along a rail on a trolley which was left behind when we rose into the air. We climbed up to 20 feet and flew twice round the field at tree-top level at 30 miles per hour. At the turns the lower wing came within 10 feet of the ground. I sat holding on to a strut and could look straight down between my legs at the ground. Two feet above the ground Wilbur Wright cut off the ignition, the propellers stopped immediately, and the plane dropped on the skids, sliding along for 15 yards or so. From being a disbeliever I suddenly became an enthusiast.'

Aeroplane-flying now got off the mark in England. It focused popular attention on such new-style heroes as S. F. Cody, A. V. Roe, and J. T. C. Moore-Brabazon (later Lord Brabazon). Newspaper paragraph, 1909: 'In order to convert the familiar saying "Pigs might fly" from a potentiality into a certainty and thus rid us of a hackneyed phrase, Mr Moore-Brabazon took up in his Short Biplane the other day a healthy young porker. On the hamper in which it travelled was the legend: I AM THE FIRST PIG TO FLY.'

More important in that year was Blériot's first aeroplane flight across the English Channel, a feat of great significance ('We're no longer an island'), not to say daring. Many years later *Scrapbook* invited him to describe the flight (he had never broadcast about it):

'In the early morning of July 25, 1909 I left my hotel at Calais and drove out to the field where my aeroplane was garaged. On the way I noted that the weather was favourable to my endeavour. I therefore ordered the destroyer *Escopette*, placed at my disposal by the French Government, to go to sea. I examined my aeroplane. I started the engine, and found it worked well. Daylight had now come.

'Four-thirty-five. *Tout est prêt!* In an instant I am in the air, my engine making 1,200 revolutions, almost its highest speed, in order that I may get quickly over the telegraph wires along the edge of the cliff. As soon as I am over the cliff I reduce my speed. There is now no need

[1] This new information makes revision of reference books necessary. In newspapers, television, and radio Cody is often mentioned as the first man to fly an aeroplane in Britian; so is J. T. C. Moore-Brabazon. In fact, when Cody flew his plane at Farnborough in 1908 he was an American (he was naturalized British in the next year) so Moore-Brabazon has been credited as the first Briton to fly in Britain, in 1909. Phillips' precedence is now discussed in Mr Gibbs-Smith's book *The Aeroplane* (H.M. Stationery Office) in greater detail than he was able to use when he broadcast in *Scrapbook for 1907*.

to force my engine. I begin my flight, steady and sure, towards the coast of England. I have no apprehensions, no sensations, *pas du tout*. The *Escopette* has seen me. She is driving ahead across the Channel at full speed. She makes perhaps 26 miles per hour. What matters? I am making over 40 miles per hour. Rapidly I overtake her, travelling at a height of 250 feet. The moment is supreme, yet I surprise myself by feeling no exultation. Below me is the sea; the motion of the waves is not pleasant. I drive on. Ten minutes to go. I turn my head to see whether I am proceeding in the right direction. I am amazed. There is nothing to be seen, neither the destroyer, nor France, nor England. I am alone. I am lost.'

Without compass, without radio or visual guidance, he was over the sea with a 25-horse-power engine between him and disaster. He flew blind for ten minutes.

'Then I saw the cliffs of Dover! Away to the west was the spot where I had intended to land. The wind had taken me out of my course. I turned and now I was in difficulties, for the wind here by the cliffs was much stronger, and my speed was reduced as I fought against it. My beautiful aeroplane responded. I attempted a landing, but the wind caught me and whirled me round two or three times. At once I stopped my motor, and instantly my machine fell straight on the ground. I was safe on your shore. Soldiers in khaki ran up, and also a police-man. Two of my compatriots were on the spot. They kissed my cheeks. I was overwhelmed.'

The flight took about forty minutes. The Chief Coastguard of Dover said that 'the speed was almost incredible'. Blériot's monoplane was exhibited at Selfridge's store in London and 120,000 people filed past it in four days.

This was one up to the aeroplane in its rivalry with the airship, and thoughts turned from flying over the narrow seas to the significance of bridging the great oceans when in the following year, 1910, the airship *America* set off from the United States, her captain an-nouncing that she would reach Europe in six days; but she came down in the Atlantic after two. The crew of six escaped in a lifeboat which had been slung beneath the gasbag.[1] The Germans, flying Zeppelins again and again over their country, with forty or fifty passengers a time, seemed to know a great deal about this method of transport (or war?) – from 1910 to 1914 they carried 37,250 passengers without mishap – but to most people in Britain flying in 1910 was a sport, not a method of travel or of warfare, and the aeroplane was definitely more exciting to watch than the airship.

Those daring young men on their flying trapezes took to it like steeplechasers. Aero-sport meetings at Hendon, Blackpool, Doncaster, Bournemouth, and elsewhere attracted crowds to watch the races. An amusing angle on what the public thought of it is taken by a bank-clerk of the time, MR L. R. WILLRIDGE, from gossip he heard across the counter: 'Head-shaking and gloomy looks came from some of the older people. They thought it very disturbing and queer. Not satisfied with experimenting with motor-cars, these young fellers were now experimenting with flying aeroplanes. One lady was heard to say "Mark my words, somebody is going to be killed by these things one of these days." It was going against providence. They said, "Why can't people go by train as God intended us to?"'

Alfred Harmsworth, the *Daily Mail* boss with one eye to the future and another on sales, offered to give £10,000 to the first man to fly from London to Manchester within twenty-four hours. This far-fetched idea was something to chatter about in parlours behind lace-curtains and aspidistras, where Father held forth on the day's news between Daughter's spasms of

[1] An airship was to make the first-ever transatlantic flight, the British *R34* in 1919: see Volume 2 *Scrapbook* for a personal recollection.

Mr Claude Grahame-White, the dashing sportsman of the air, and the first man to fly at night, 1910

1909: 'Bleriot,' said Sir Ernest Shackleton, 'did not go up in any blare of trumpets. In the cold, grey dawn of the morning, before the sun had warmed up things, before it had dissipated the dew-drops, he was in our country. It marks a new era in the world'

Paulhan using the railway tracks to help his aerial navigation between London and Manchester; 1910 drawing by Arthur Burgess

singing at the piano ('When you come to the end of a Perfect Day' – the pop-song of 1910). The family joke was that *Punch* was offering £10,000 for a flight to Mars or a Transatlantic swim. Claude Grahame-White – a cigarette-smoking young devil-may-care, beloved at English aviation meetings – decided to pocket the *Mail*'s money. One morning his Farman biplane (top speed 45 miles per hour) took off from a suburban field and followed the London and North Western Railway, for the plane had no compass or other aids to navigation.

MR GRAHAME-WHITE says: 'In those days there was absolutely no protection for the pilot and it was a very cold frosty morning. I climbed to about 2,000 feet and followed the railway quite easily as it was a fine clear day. I soon passed Harrow, but by the time I got to Bletchley I was so cold that I was afraid I was going to faint. I then remembered that I had taken the precaution to have a flask of brandy in the breast pocket of my fur-lined gabardine jacket and before starting I had removed the screw stopper as I knew I could not take both hands off the controls. I managed to get the flask out of the pocket and took a good swig and before long I felt much better.'

He stopped at Rugby for petrol – 75 miles flown so far, a world record – then flew on, but engine trouble brought a forced landing with only 90 miles to go: 'Within a few minutes hundreds of people came running round the plane and started writing their names on the cotton fabric which covered the wings. Presently some 20,000 people from Birmingham, Coventry, and other towns had joined the already unruly crowd, and I got anxious about the safety of my plane but my mechanics arrived by motor-car and while they attended to the engine I snatched a rest at an hotel in near-by Lichfield. About three o'clock my chief mechanic came rushing into the room where I was asleep and told me that a strong gust of wind had lifted the plane into the air and had crashed it upside down. Very extensive damage had been done.'

They packed up the bits and sent them back to London. Behind the lace-curtains Father said 'I told you so' and remarked that a much more remarkable item of news was that the largest, fastest, most luxurious liner in the world was on the stocks at Belfast and would be launched in due course under the appropriate name *Titanic*. At the Apollo Theatre in London the *Pélissier Follies* had a song for madmen like Grahame-White:

> *Percy had purchased a new aeroplane,*
> *But I doubt if he ever will use it again,*
> *For though sometimes it rose about two feet or higher,*
> *It always developed a sudden desire*
> *To go*
> > *Back, back, back to the land;*
> > *Till one day he found it got quite out of hand,*
> > *The bally thing stopped,*
> > *And poor Percival dropped*
> > *With his back, back, back to the land.*[1]

While Grahame-White and his men were repairing the plane in a hangar near Wormwood Scrubs a rival for the £10,000 arrived, Monsieur Louis Paulhan, whose Farman was prepared for the fray at Hendon. Grahame-White called on him and came away under the impression that they had agreed to notify each other before taking off for Manchester, to make it an even race. Perhaps Paulhan thought otherwise; anyhow, late one blustery April afternoon a

---

[1] 'Back to the Land', words by Arthur Davenport, music by H. G. Pélissier (Joseph Williams).

messenger ran into the Grahame-White hangar crying: 'Paulhan – he's started! Left Hendon nearly an hour ago!'

'The Frenchman's stolen a march on me,' thought Grahame-White. It was an hour before dusk. He decided to start chasing Paulhan at once. His story continues: 'I set course following the railway line north. At the various junctions I had already got the railway people to have the sleepers white-washed for about 100 yards, to show me the route I should take, in case I might otherwise follow the wrong lines. The wind dropped and everything was going perfectly. Below, as I passed over towns I could see everyone in the streets looking up at me. It began to get dark. I wondered: How far has Paulhan got? Where will he stay the night?'

Grahame-White began looking for a landing place. No one had ever flown at night.

'After passing Bletchley I saw a likely field by a signal-box and I landed and asked where I was. The signalman shouted: "Roade, sir, near Northampton, 60 miles from London."

'"Have you seen another aeroplane?" I asked.

'"He passed over here an hour ago."

'I was hungry and half-frozen. I went to a house near by and rested, while my friends who had followed by road gathered round me. We held a conference and while we were doing so news was brought to us from the signal-box that my rival had descended at Trent Valley station, near Lichfield, 67 miles farther on, and was spending the night there. The only chance of catching him was to fly on in the darkness. My friends said it was a foolish risk. Of course, I had no experience of night flying. But I decided to risk it.

'"Now, boys", I said, "get all the lamps off the bicycles and motor-cars and put them along the boundary of the field. There's a hedge yonder I've got to clear. Mark it!"'

At two o'clock in the morning he revved up his engine and a small crowd of rustic bystanders foretold imminent disaster as the machine buzzed like an infuriated May-bug across the strangely illuminated meadow. Then it lifted over the trees and disappeared into the darkness. That night in the Midlands many people awoke as an unprecedented noise was heard throbbing through the darkness. For the pilot it was a desperate bid: 'In the absence of any navigational aids, my only way was to fly at less than 100 feet and try to follow the railway, keeping a sharp watch for signal lights and the glare of trains. The lights of cars following me on the main road to Rugby were a help, too. Suddenly I lost the railway, probably because it had gone into a tunnel. I also lost the motor-cars. Turning, I picked them up again, but I could hardly keep awake now. The drone of my engine seemed to lull me. I was frozen. When in the Trent Valley, as dawn broke, the wind got up badly and the plane began pitching about. There were hills all about, and I felt like a feather in a storm. A gust hit me and turned me right round. I was 50 feet from the ground and had to make a quick decision to land or crash.'

Grahame-White came down, ending the first night-flight in history. He landed near another signal-box. The signalmen along the line must have been exchanging messages that night like a news agency. This one told a frozen and tired aviator that his rival, Paulhan, had just got up from a warm bed and had dashed off from Lichfield. But Lichfield was only 10 miles ahead. Grahame-White had nearly overhauled Paulhan. Only 70 miles to Manchester: could he catch up? Unhappily, his engine needed attention; the mechanics arrived, and while they were working the signalman ran up with another message. Grahame-White climbed on to a motor-car and addressed the crowd that had gathered: 'Ladies and gentlemen, I have just received a message that Paulhan has landed within 5 miles of Manchester and has won the £10,000 prize. The best man wins.' Generous . . . but he must have felt inwardly bitter.

Half a century or so later, it is fascinating to look back on old prophecies. In 1909 the *Illustrated London News* said: 'Our artist, Mr Janos, imagines the cross-channel passage of the future and shows a Royal Mail dirigible.' The steersman wears no overcoat—but perhaps summers of the future were expected to be hot

Paulhan drove from his landing-field on the outskirts of Manchester into the city – by horse-carriage. The *Daily Mail* gave Grahame-White a special silver cup as a consolation prize.

Aircraft were rapidly improved in the next three years; men flew much farther, faster, higher (records in 1913 stood at over 634 miles for distance, 126 miles per hour for speed, and 20,000 feet for height), yet the possibilities of flying for civil communications were largely disregarded and its use in warfare was hotly debated by the experts. In 1910 the British War Secretary argued that 'we do not consider that aeroplanes will be of any possible use for war purposes'. An Air Battalion of the British Army was formed nevertheless in 1911, with sixteen aeroplanes and three balloons, and the Navy flirted with flying that year when Lieutenant C. R. Samson flew a Short biplane off the forecastle of HMS *Africa* – the first British aircraft carrier. The Royal Flying Corps was formed in 1912.

A chance to stop air-bombing in advance of it ever happening, by international agreement, had occurred in 1907. It was thrown away. The second disarmament conference at the Hague was held that year. The French military authorities had already used their airship *La Patrie* for bombing experiments, and the other Great Powers had not overlooked the possibilities of hurling bombs from aloft. At The Hague, Belgium suggested the total prohibition of all explosives dropped from the air. The Great Powers said NO.

Sardonic view of the disarmament conference, 1907. The great Dutch cartoonist, Louis Raemaekers, sees it thus:

Christ: My friend, I represent peace on earth.

The Flunkey: That's possible, but if you don't represent an army, you can't enter the conference

(*b*) THE BREAKTHROUGH OF WIRELESS

Once upon a time people thought that a wireless signal – if they had ever heard of such a thing – must travel in a straight line, and that world-wide communication was therefore impossible. Marconi had his own ideas. Early in the century he took on Professor J. A. Fleming, of University College, London, as his scientific adviser, and had a transmitting station built at Poldhu, in Cornwall, with a power of 12 kilowatts. Marconi then went to Newfoundland with two engineers, Mr Kemp and MR P. W. PAGET:

'We selected as a site for our receiving station Signal Hill, a headland at the entrance to St John's Harbour, Newfoundland. It was a desolate scene – not a shrub or a tree, only a deserted military hospital where Marconi set up his apparatus. We had brought two 15-foot balloons and six kites for the purpose of elevating the aerial. The weather was terrible, but I managed to fly a kite up to 400 feet. The wind howled around the building where, in a small dark room furnished with a table, one chair, and some packing-cases, Kemp sat at the receiving set, while Marconi drank a cup of cocoa before taking his turn at listening.'

Marconi had left instructions for Poldhu to transmit S in morse (*pip-pip-pip*) over and over again between certain hours. Never had men listened for so little to mean so much, for if *pip-pip-pip* was audible in Newfoundland the possibilities for wireless communication were boundless.

MARCONI continues: 'It was shortly after midday on December 12, 1901 that I placed the single earphone to my ear and started listening. The receiver on the table before me was very crude – a few coils and condensers and a coherer – no valves, no amplifiers, not even a crystal. I was at last on the point of putting the correctness of all my beliefs to the test. The experiment had involved risking at least £50,000 to achieve a result which had been declared to be impossible by some of the principal mathematicians of the time. The chief question was whether wireless waves would be stopped by the curvature of the earth. All along I had been convinced that this was not so. The first and final answer to that question came at 12.30, when I heard faintly but distinctly, *pip-pip-pip*.

'I now knew that all my anticipations had been justified. The electric waves sent out into space from Poldhu had traversed the Atlantic – the distance, enormous as it seemed then, of 1,700 miles – unimpeded by the curvature of the earth. The result meant much more to me than the mere successful realization of an experiment. As Sir Oliver Lodge has stated, it was an epoch in history. I now felt for the first time absolutely certain that the day would come when mankind would be able to send messages without wires not only across the Atlantic but between the farthermost ends of the earth.'

Wireless soon became a commercial proposition; in 1907 the first regular telegraph service between Britain and Canada was opened to the public; but something more dramatic than that was needed to awaken *popular* appreciation of what wireless really meant. Could it be the enterprising Captain Bloom? We find him in 1905 touring the music-halls, appearing in naval uniform, placing a receiver on the stage and a transmitter in the stalls, and ringing a bell by remote control, not to mention firing a gun. Press reports about Captain Bloom are undecided whether he was a Dutch, a German, or a Belgian 'wireless wizard'. But he was only a nine minutes wonder. Something more was needed.

It came at sea in 1909. Some 200 British ships had been equipped with wireless sets; one of them, the liner *Republic*, was in collision during an Atlantic fog with an Italian steamer, *Florida*, and the story was soon in every home: how wireless operator Jack Binns of the *Republic* sent out the SOS and stayed at his job all day, transmitting over 200 messages while his ship seemed likely to go down at any moment. When the *Baltic* arrived passengers from both stricken ships were transferred to her in boats. Soon afterwards the *Republic* sank. Wireless had saved about 1,800 people, only six were lost, and Jack Binns had a hero's welcome on his return home to Peterborough.

This was a convincing demonstration, but the next one was positively sensational and guaranteed to get the biggest headlines of all, for it was tied up with that ever-mesmeric subject, murder. In 1910 Dr Crippen, having buried the remains of his wife in a cellar in Camden Town, sailed for Canada in haste and incognito, with his secretary, Ethel le Neve, disguised as a youth. The then master of the Canadian Pacific liner *Montrose*, CAPTAIN H. G. KENDALL, has told us the story:

'My ship was in port at Antwerp when I read in the *Continental Daily Mail* that a warrant had been issued for Crippen and le Neve. Soon after we sailed for Quebec I happened to glance through the porthole of my cabin and behind a lifeboat I saw two men. One was squeezing the other's hand. I walked along the boat deck and got into conversation with the elder man. I noticed that there was a mark on the bridge of his nose through wearing spectacles, that he had recently shaved off a moustache, and that he was growing a beard. The young fellow was very reserved and I remarked about his cough.

' "Yes," said the elder man, "my boy has a weak chest, and I'm taking him to California for his health."

'I returned to my cabin and had another look at the *Daily Mail*, at the description and photographs issued by Scotland Yard. I then examined the passenger list and ascertained that the two passengers were travelling as "Mr Robinson and Son". I arranged for them to take meals at my table. When the bell went for lunch I tarried until the coast was clear, then slipped into the Robinsons' cabin unobserved, where I noticed two things: that the boy's felt hat was packed round the rim to make it fit, and that he had been using a piece of a woman's bodice as a face-flannel. I went down to the dining-saloon and kept my eyes open. The boy's manners at table were ladylike. Later, when they were promenading the saloon deck, I went out and walked behind them, and called out "Mr Robinson!". I had to shout the name several times before the man turned and said to me, "I'm sorry, Captain, I didn't hear you – this cold wind is making me deaf". In the next two days we developed our acquaintance. On the third day out I gave my wireless operator a message for Liverpool:

'*One hundred and thirty miles west of Lizard: have strong suspicions that Crippen London cellar murderer and accomplice are among saloon passengers. Accomplice dressed as boy. Voice, manner, and build undoubtedly a girl.*'

'I remember Mr Robinson sitting in a deck-chair, looking at the wireless aerials and listening to the crackling of our crude spark-transmitter, and remarking to me what a wonderful invention it was. I sent several reports, but our weak transmitting apparatus was soon out of communication with land.'

Captain Kendall knew that the White Star liner *Laurentic* had left England after he had reported his suspicions of 'Mr Robinson', and that *Laurentic*'s superior speed would enable her to overhaul *Montrose* as she reached the Newfoundland coast. 'I hoped that if she had any news for me *Laurentic* would leave it at the Belle Island station to be transmitted to me as soon as I passed that point on my approach to Canada. She had news indeed:

'*Will board you at Father Point. Strictly confidential, from Inspector Dew, Scotland Yard.*

'I replied:

'*Shall arrive Father Point about 6 a.m. tomorrow. Should advise you to come off in small boat with pilot, disguised as pilot.*

'The night was dreary and anxious, the sound of our fog-horn every few minutes adding to the monotony. The hours dragged on as I paced the bridge; now and then I could see Mr Robinson strolling about the deck. I had invited him to get up early to see the "pilots" come aboard at Father Point in the River St Lawrence. When they did so they came straight to my cabin. I sent for Mr Robinson. When he entered I stood with the detectives facing the door, holding my revolver inside my coat pocket. As he came in, I said, "Let me introduce you". Mr Robinson put out his hand, the detective grabbed it, at the same time removing his pilot's cap, and said, "Good morning, Dr Crippen. Do you know me? I'm Inspector Dew, from Scotland Yard."

'Crippen quivered. Surprise struck him dumb. Then he said, "Thank God it's over. The suspense has been too great. I couldn't stand it any longer".'

The detective went to the cabin where the 'youth' was reading. Ethel le Neve could hardly believe her eyes when she recognized Inspector Dew, who had called upon her at the Camden Town house before she fled with Crippen. She, too, was arrested. They were tried in London. Crippen was sentenced to death. Miss le Neve, charged as an accessory, was acquitted.

'The invisible bloodhound', said a newspaper, 'has followed the scent across the high seas.'

The British Government rewarded Captain Kendall with £250.

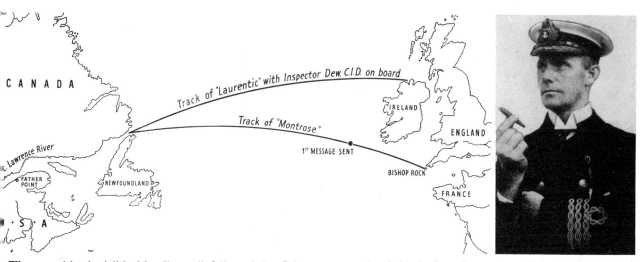

The way 'the invisible bloodhound' followed Dr Crippen across the Atlantic (*map by courtesy Marconi Co*). (*Right*) Captain H. G. Kendall

That maritime Grand Babylon Hotel, the *Titanic*, left Southampton for America one gala day in 1912. The largest ship in the world (46,382 tons), she was very fast, most ornate, gilded and plush-carpeted, and rich socialites of Britain and America were eager to sail on this historic maiden voyage. She carried well over 2,000 passengers and crew. To many in our islands here was the perfect symbol of Rule Britannia and of the stupendous progress of science and engineering and human daring during this accelerating century; man could fly, he could make motor-cars, he could preserve the balance of power with mighty *Dreadnoughts*, and now the engineers said the *Titanic* was 'unsinkable'. Five nights out she hit an iceberg at $22\frac{1}{2}$ knots; 300 feet of her side was ripped open. Shortly before midnight *Carpathia*, 58 miles away, heard *Titanic*'s call for help and changed course. The radio officer of *Carpathia* made these later entries in his log-book:

12.10 a.m. *Titanic* calling CQD.[1] His power appears to be greatly reduced.

12.20 a.m. *Titanic* signals very broken.

12.25 a.m. Calling *Titanic*. No response.

12.28 a.m. *Titanic* calls CQD, his signals blurred and ending abruptly.

At dawn *Carpathia* arrived among the lifeboats and debris floating over *Titanic*'s grave: 711 people were picked up, some 1,500 had been drowned. The liner had foundered in 2 hours 40 minutes; discipline of passengers and crew was good, but boat organisation was poor – some lifeboats got away half-filled, one Pekinese was handed safely into a boat while hundreds of steerage passengers never had a dog's chance. At an inquiry later there were many awkward questions to face (legislation resulted, requiring better provision of boats and boat-drill). *The Times* denounced 'the lavish and unbridled luxury' of an age which demanded such floating palaces racing in a 'mad competition in speed' ($22\frac{1}{2}$ knots through iceberg-frequented seas): 'It is perhaps time that a saner and more ethically sound public opinion were brought to bear upon these questions.'

The official inquiry denounced the spirit of competition and 'the desire of the public for quick passages' which lay behind a long-established practice of liners on the north Atlantic route to maintain speed when in the vicinity of ice at night, trusting to a sharp look-out to avoid danger.

If the *Titanic* disaster was a sudden reminder of the vanity of human calculations, it was also a reminder of the value of applied science; but all Junior Radio Officer Harold Bride of the *Titanic* got for his part in it was a gold watch (his senior, John Phillips, was drowned) and all Radio Officer Cottom of the *Carpathia* took home was a silver medal from the Liverpool Shipwreck and Humane Society and an illuminated address.

But the song-writers cashed in:

> *Be British! was the cry as the ship went down,*
> *Ev'ry man was steady at his post,*
> *Captain, and crew, when they knew the worst:*
> *Saving the women and children first . . .*[2]

– and the Pekinese.

So far we have been examining the birth of wireless telegraphy. Telephony (leading to broadcasting) was a much slower developer. It began in 1902: an American, R. A. Fessenden

---

[1] CQD and SOS were both distress calls then.

[2] 'Be British', written and composed by Paul Pelham and Lawrence Wright (L. Wright Music Co.).

DEDICATED TO THE GALLANT ILL-FATED CREW
OF THE
"TITANIC"

BE BRITISH!

DESCRIPTIVE SONG AND RECITATION

Romanticism: part of
the cover of a song
Lawrence Wright Music Co

Realism: A survivor, Mr
John B. Thayer, made these
sketches while in one of the
ship's boats
Illustrated London News

STRIKES STARBOARD BOW -11.45 P.M.

11.45 P.M.

1.40 A.M.

SETTLES TO FORWARD STACK
BREAKS BETWEEN STACKS

135

of the University of Pittsburgh, managed to make wireless waves carry a human voice over a distance of a mile. By 1907 he could transmit over 100 miles, not only a voice but a violin solo. The quality of his broadcasting was poor owing to the absence of valves, but already (1904) in London the 'oscillation valve' had been patented by Fleming.[1] This was a two-electrode valve, to which in 1905 Lee de Forest in America added a third, thus making the triode, a much more sensitive instrument.

These were laboratory experiments, and the future possibilities were unseen by all but a few like the English scientist Oliver Lodge, the first man who used the word 'broadcast' in this connection. Looking into the future, he said: 'It might be advantageous to "shout" the message, speaking broadcast to receivers in all directions . . . such as for reporting races and other sporting events, and generally for all important events occurring beyond the range of the permanent lines.'[2] But broadcasting was not to make the grade from the laboratory and into the home until after the First World War.

Television was yet farther in the future, but in the Edwardian period we already find an English visionary, A. A. Campbell-Swinton, writing to *Nature* to suggest the use of cathode-ray tubes for both the transmission and reception of images. This was in 1907.

[1] Posterity has done him less than justice. The fame of Marconi is world-wide, but how many people know of this brilliant Englishman? Sir John Fleming, born Lancaster 1849, had superintended introduction of incandescent electric lighting into Britain in the 1890s; became Professor of electrical engineering, University College, London; helped Marconi with first transatlantic wireless experiments; invented the valve.

[2] Report of the Select Committee to Consider the Report of the Radio-Telegraphic Convention signed at Berlin (1907).

1906: *Punch* artist, Lewis Baumer, sees a future for portable wireless telegraph receivers: 'The lady is receiving an amatory message, and the gentleman some racing results'

(c) SOCIAL EXPERIMENTS

Myths grow upon us until they are widely accepted as facts, so much so that it has become traditional in most entertainment and some books to paint the Edwardian era as tranquil, rich, stable, contented. This was one side of the picture but slashing across it came a social break-through as drastic in its effect on our lives today as any of the technological revolutions. Here, at Glasgow in 1906, is one of the resounding voices of change:

'I should like to see the State embark on various novel and adventurous experiments. I am of the opinion that the State should assume the position of the reserve employer of labour. I am very sorry we have not got the railways in our hands. We are all agreed that the State must increasingly and earnestly concern itself with the care of the sick and the aged, and above all, of the children. I look forward to the universal establishment of minimum standards of life and labour.'

This adventurous experimenter is not Keir Hardie or Ramsay MacDonald. It is Winston Churchill, the *enfant terrible* of the Liberal Government in power from 1905 onwards, the most brilliant administration in living memory. After the landslide election of 1906 had given it a truly solid basis for its work (there were 400 Liberal MPs, 157 Conservatives, 83 Irish Nationalists, 30 Labour) the Government began laying the foundation of what is now the Welfare State by enforcing a bold range of social reforms, stiffly resisted by the Tory crust. 'All down history,' Lloyd George cried in their faces, 'nine-tenths of mankind have been grinding corn for the remaining tenth and been paid with the husks and bidden to thank God they had the husks.' He played on the *vox humana* pipes of his wild Welsh organ for all he was worth, which was a great deal. As Chancellor of the Exchequer he even went to His Master's Voice gramophone studio and made a record which was played on machines trundled round the streets during by-elections in 1909. This was the precursor of our present-day political chats and TV blandishments: 'I am one of the children of the people,' preached the voice down the tin trumpet. And verily they called his budget 'The People's Budget'.

He asked for unprecedented millions for social reforms 'to redeem the people from anxieties and suffering which are now so greviously oppressing them', and to pay for all those dread-noughts. Lloyd George's rhetoric got as good as it gave. Lord Lansdowne called him 'a swooping robber gull, particularly voracious and unscrupulous, which steals fish from other gulls.' Our fathers certainly laid it on thick. And over what?

Lloyd George put up income tax from 1s to 1s 2d, he invented a super-tax of 6d on incomes over £3,000, higher duties on tobacco and spirits, new-fangled taxes on motor-cars and petrol, and threatened a taxation of land values.

BARONESS ASQUITH OF YARNBURY (Lady Violet Bonham-Carter), daughter of Mr Asquith, Prime Minister 1908–16, has told *Scrapbook* what venom was thrown upon the Liberal leaders and their families: 'The Lords rejected the so-called People's Budget. This rejection of a money bill was an act without precedent in the last 250 years. My father's government went to the country in 1910, challenging the right of the Lords to veto the decisions of the Commons. It was the last battle for constitutional freedom, and it was fought by the Peers, and indeed by the whole Conservative Party, with a violence and ferocity which overflowed, sometimes absurdly, into the most innocent amenities of social life. Our friends cut us. We were treated by society as pariahs, outcasts, and untouchables. An aunt of mine who apologized to a country neighbour for being unable to bring me over to tea, received the startling reply: "I am indeed thankful that you did not bring Miss Asquith, for had she crossed our threshold we should have been obliged to burn our carpet."

'Untouchable Number One was Mr Winston Churchill. It was felt that as the grandson of a Duke he ought to have known better. Here was a blue-blooded black-leg who had betrayed his class. He was even more bitterly hated than Mr Lloyd George who had poured a devastating fire of invective, wit, and ridicule upon the Peerage. "An aristocracy is like cheese, the older it is the higher it becomes", he said.

'All this turmoil may surprise you if you share the common illusion that the Edwardian era was one of tranquility. The spirit of the age was violent and tempestuous. There were the suffragettes hurling bricks at 10 Downing Street, and attacking ministers with dog-whips, hatchets, and pepper-pots; in industry there was a wave of strikes and lock-outs, and great bitterness between employers and employed. The Edwardian era was, in fact, one of acute contrasts – violence and tranquility, affluence and poverty, and such gaiety as we have never seen since. As a young girl my personal life, steeped in politics and pleasure, was one of enthralling interest and wild enjoyment. I loved every hour I lived. In spite of being laced into a ball dress which I had to hold my breath to get into, with my hair piled into an elaborate pagoda on my head, I danced like a bacchante through the long summer nights, and rumbled home in the small hours (still heavily chaperoned) in a four-wheeler, with my feet in the straw and my head among the stars. But dire, grinding poverty was in the London streets – crossing-sweepers holding out their caps for pennies, children in rags, down-and-outs sleeping on benches in the parks . . . one's conscience was disturbed and haunted.'

These were the years when the Liberals had power to act. Lloyd George's much-wrangled-over People's Budget was swallowed by the Lords, but both the Liberals and Labour were utterly fed up with progressive administration being continually thwarted by an Upper House mainly of high Tories, so the Premier tabled a Parliament Bill for Lords reform, no less. The slogan rang through the land – *The Lords versus the People* – but at the height of this controversy came King Edward's death, and party leaders had a truce. We shall return later to that fantastic *dénouement*, the Affair, as Sherlock Holmes might have said, of the 500 Men Who Didn't Become Peers; meanwhile let us remember that through these years of Liberal crusading, from 1906, they made legislation which has changed the social picture. They set going old-age pensions, town planning, minimum wage-rates for miners. They attacked sweated labour and provided shop assistants with a weekly half-holiday. They brought a new emphasis to child welfare: free meals at elementary schools for children whose education was suffering from lack of food, along with physical training, organized games, compulsory medical inspection. And, most notably, in establishing labour exchanges the Asquith Government brought to the fore William Beveridge as the chief civil servant to organize them.

LORD BEVERIDGE has said: 'It was the root from which all our social security of today has grown. My work on the Insurance Act of 1911 brought me into contact with some of the most constructive minds in Britain, a marvellous chance for a young man to learn how things get done. The first of these creative minds was Winston Churchill. He was determined to do something real about unemployment and he had been told by Sidney and Beatrice Webb that for this he must have "the boy Beveridge" to help him. I'd written a book just before, to show that unemployment was not due to idleness or incapacity of men, but to bad organization of

Drawing by George Soper in *The Wonderful Year* 1909 (Headley)

The birth of the Welfare State: the first old age pensions, January 1st, 1909. Mitigation
of poverty by direct State payment, which has since grown immensely, began in a tiny
way: 5s a week, beginning at 70; or 7s 6d for an old married couple. A weekly income of
10s disqualified anyone from pension

The first leaflet raid on London, by Miss Muriel Matters in 1909

'Women's *only* place in Parliament': the *Illustrated London News*'s caption under a 1906 drawing of the Ladies' Gallery was infuriating to suffragettes. From this fashionable ivory tower they shouted their first protests

industry. So one of Churchill's first acts at the Board of Trade was to get me appointed there for labour exchanges and unemployment insurance. He didn't himself stay very long at the Board, but he had given the definite start to compulsory insurance against unemployment, a brand-new thing in the world at that time.'

The *true* Hope and Glory of those days was, as we ought to see now, in social reform boldly fought for; not in pomp, ceremony, or imperialism.

★   ★   ★

Women were second-class citizens under the law. No vote; no equality; plenty of disabilities (for instance, a man might divorce his wife for adultery but a woman had additionally to furnish evidence of cruelty or desertion). The Lords and Commons were exclusively male clubs with a masculine bias on everything. Valiant Mrs Emmeline Pankhurst said that to get rid of sex disabilities, and to help working women who even more than men suffered from such outrages as wage-slavery, they must first get the vote. This was the social breakthrough at which she aimed. And many Liberals were lamentably lukewarm on this one.

Peaceful pleading for the vote had gone on for half a century; stronger action began in Mrs Pankhurst's Manchester home when a little group founded the Women's Social and Political Union. Their famous slogan was made by accident in 1905 when Mrs Pankhurst's daughter Christabel and a millgirl from Oldham named Annie Kenney were chosen to demonstrate at a Liberal meeting at the Free Trade Hall. First they made a banner – *Will the Liberal Party give Votes for Women?* – intending to drop it from front seats in the gallery, but they failed at the last moment to get those tactical seats so they cut off the first five words from their banner to make it easy to hold up anywhere in the hall.

MRS FLORA DRUMMOND (later known as General Drummond when she became Mrs Pankhurst's *aide-de-camp*, with a habit of wearing a peaked cap and horse-riding at the head of processions) was in the gallery: 'I was not yet a suffragette. Not many women went to political meetings in those days, but I sat in the gallery to hear Sir Edmund Grey outline the policy of the Liberal Government. At question-time I saw two girls, pretty, slender, and well-dressed, rise among the audience. One asked in ringing tones: "Will the Liberal Government give votes for women?" I recognized her as Christabel Pankhurst. The audience were astonished to see Annie Kenney unfurl a banner inscribed *Votes for Women*. Stewards seemed to appear like flies. There was pandemonium, many of the audience shouting, "Answer!" – but the platform remained silent. The girls repeated their question. The stewards tried to pull them down and put their hands over their mouths. They were bundled at last out of the hall. When I saw that the only answer to their question was not a promise of the vote but blows and forcible ejection, I rushed from my seat and joined Miss Pankhurst and Miss Kenney outside, where they started to address the crowd. They were immediately arrested. From that hour I, too, was a suffragette. A week later I met them as they came out of prison. This was the first time women had gone to gaol for the vote.'

Keir Hardie telegraphed to Mrs Pankhurst: 'The thing is a dastardly outrage but do not worry it will do immense good to the cause.'

From then a civil war was on. The suffragettes formed themselves into a large and well-organized army. In 1906 a woman's voice was heard for the first time in history in the House of Commons, during a debate on woman's suffrage instituted by Keir Hardie. The fatuousness of some MPs is well displayed by an honourable gentleman who was speaking as follows while a Pankhurst force seated in the Ladies Gallery was trying to look as un-suffragette as it could:

'Is the House prepared to hand over the government of this country to women, the majority of whom are not breadwinners, who have not to bear the burdens and do not understand the responsibilities of life? (*Voices:* No, No!) Mr Speaker, sir, I am sometimes described in regard to this question as a woman-hater. But I have had two wives, and I think that is the best answer I can give to those who call me a woman-hater. I am too fond of them to drag women into the political arena, and to ask them to undertake responsibilities, duties and obligations which they do not understand. What does one find when one goes into the company of women and talks politics? They say "Stop talking silly politics". And yet that is the type of people to whom honourable members are invited to hand over the destinies of this country.'

At this insufferable point came yells of 'Votes for Women' and 'Stop talking drivel' from the Gallery while banners hitherto hidden in muffs were shoved through the grille and waved in a most provocative manner. The suffragettes were thrown out.

The police became more watchful after that incident, but the suffragettes became more daring. One afternoon in 1908 two furniture vans drove into the Parliamentary precincts. The first was an empty decoy – while the constables were examining it, twenty-one women from the other van 'tripped out and tried to effect an entrance', as *The Times* put it; seventeen were arrested. H. G. Wells used this modern Trojan Horse in his novel *Ann Veronica*. In fiction Ann was the characteristic New Woman, 'nagging the whole Western world into the discussion of women's position', said Wells. Her attitude to politics, policemen, and sex got the novel banned at many libraries. At the same time, best-selling novelist Elinor Glyn's tale of passion-on-a-tiger-skin, *Three Weeks* (not banned), declared that 'women by their greatness, tact, and goodness influence affairs and governments and countries, through men, a thousand-fold more than the cleverest suffragettes could influence these things by securing votes for women.' The New Woman was not universally popular among her own sex, many believing traditionally in 'leaving it to the men'. The Premier's wife, Margot Asquith, expressed herself bitterly about suffragettes; this was hardly surprising when her husband was the target for savage physical blows and when Mrs Pankhurst's storm-troopers raided 10 Downing Street itself, shouting their tiresome slogans.

Chaining themselves to railings is the exploit with which suffragettes are most commonly connected in legend today, but of course they went much further; in fact, when the police were preoccupied with chained ladies for the very first time, in 1908, Mrs Drummond took advantage of their embarrassment and rang the bell of No. 10, the door opened, and the General marched straight in crying 'Votes for Women'. She was, as they say, 'ejected'.

An opinion on these suffragette methods by Sir William Gilbert (of the Sullivan operas) was: 'I think I shall chain myself to the railings of Queen Charlotte's Maternity Hospital and shout "Babes for men".'

King Edward VII's opinion is clear in a note he wrote to the Premier in 1907, when the Channel Tunnel scheme was rejected on grounds of the safety of the country: 'I rejoice to see that you put your foot down regarding the Channel Tunnel. . . . I only wish you could have done the same regarding Female Suffrage. The conduct of the so-called "Suffragettes" has really been so outrageous and does their cause (for which I have no sympathy) much harm.'

Parliament made a concession by passing the Qualification of Women Act (1907) which enabled them to sit on county or borough councils. The next year the first woman mayor was elected, at Aldeburgh, Dr Elizabeth Garrett Anderson. But this was a mere sop to suffragettes. Demonstrations became bigger and more violent, prison sentences heavier. One day Mrs Pankhurst made crystal clear what they were after, in a speech from the dock at Bow Street. When in due course all these battles were over and a new generation had grown up to hear that speech repeated in *Scrapbook for 1908* the BBC received a flood of letters asking for copies of it. So here it is, this heroic thread in the tapestry of our English heritage:

'We shall submit to the treatment – the degrading treatment – that we have submitted to before. Although the Government has admitted that we are political offenders we shall be treated as pickpockets and drunkards. I want you, sir, if you can, as a man, to realize what it means to women like us. We are driven to this. We are determined to go on with this agitation, because we feel it is our duty to make this world a better place for women than it is today. I have been in prison. I was in the hospital at Holloway, and when I was there I heard from one of the beds near me the moans of a woman who was in the pangs of childbirth. I should like you to realize how women feel at helpless infants breathing their first breath in the atmosphere of a prison. That woman was not guilty – she was finally acquitted. We believe that if we get the vote it will mean better conditions for our unfortunate sisters. Many women pass through this court who would not come before you if they were able to live morally and honestly. The average earnings of the women who earn their living in this country are only seven and six-pence a week. Some of us have worked for many years to help our own sex, and we have been driven to the conclusion that only through legislation can any improvement be effected, and that the legislation can never be effected until we have the same power as men to bring pressure to bear upon governments to give us the necessary legislation.

'We have tried every way. We have presented larger petitions than were ever presented before for any other reform, we have succeeded in holding greater public meetings than men have ever had for any reform. We have faced hostile mobs at street corners, because we were told that we could not have that representation for our taxes which men have won unless we converted the whole country to our side. Because we have done this we have been mis-represented, we have been ridiculed, we have had contempt poured upon us.

'No, sir, I do say deliberately to you that I come here not as an ordinary law-breaker. I should never be here if I had the same kind of laws that the very meanest and commonest of men have – the same power that the wife-beater has, the same power that the drunkard has. This is the only way we have to get that power which every citizen should have of deciding how the taxes she contributes to should be made, and until we get that power we shall be here. We are here today, and we shall come here over and over again. If you had the power to send us to prison, not for six months but for six years, or for the whole of our lives, the Government must not think that they can stop this agitation. It will go on. We are going to win.

'Well, sir, that is all I have to say to you. We are not here because we are law-breakers, we are here in our efforts to become law-*makers*!'

Derision, even hatred, was a common reaction to 'Votes for Women': crude mockery in the music-halls, bitter scorn in newspapers, the flippancy of *The Follies*:

> *Our women want the suffrage, so they go and break the peace*
> *With the foolish propaganda of the most im-proper geese.*[1]

[1] 'What a Happy Land is England', words by Arthur Wimperis, music by H. G. Pélissier (Joseph Williams), 1913.

Yet the army of suffragettes grew, their exploits became more intrepid. The first leaflet raid on London was carried out in 1909 by MISS MURIEL MATTERS: 'I was entrusted with the aerial demonstration on the day of the opening of Parliament. That morning I went to Hendon and met Mr Henry Spencer, who had his airship all ready near the Welsh Harp. Written in large letters on the gas-bag were the words *Votes for Women*. We loaded up about a hundredweight of leaflets, then I climbed into the basket, Mr Spencer joined me, and we rose into the air, travelling towards Cricklewood. We ascended to over 3,000 feet. It was very cold, but I got some exercise throwing the leaflets overboard. Mr Spencer occasionally clambered out along the framework to make some adjustment. He was rather like a spider walking across its web, for the rigging was quite open, with nothing between him and the earth, and suddenly I realized that if he fell off I hadn't the first idea how to manœuvre the airship. Not that I bothered much about that, I was far too busy making a trail of leaflets across London. Sad to say, we were blown off our course, we missed the Houses of Parliament, and landed at Coulsdon in Surrey, in the top branches of a tree. But the flight got our movement a great deal of publicity.'

The famous actress, MISS LILLAH MCCARTHY (Lady Keeble) performed one day a Scarlet Pimpernel exploit in her private role as a suffragette: 'I was invited to the Prime Minister's house in Downing Street to play in a charity matinee before the King and Queen. Somehow I got lost in the passages of No. 10. I found myself in the Cabinet Room, alone. All the suffragette in me rose to the opportunity. I opened a box of grease paint I was carrying. I took out the reddest stick I could find, and I wrote across the Prime Minister's immaculate white blotting-pad the words VOTES FOR WOMEN.'

★   ★   ★

The ethics of force being used for political ends presented a hard problem to deeply concerned people. Large numbers of women who refused 'militancy' belonged to the 'constitutionalists', the National Union of Women's Suffrage Societies which had been founded by Mrs (later Dame) Millicent Fawcett long before Mrs Pankhurst started 'militancy'. On many sides of life during the first fourteen years of this century, from suffragettes to industrial strikes and lock-outs, from Boer War to Great War, the morality of force – or the misuse of force, or the non-use of force – was posed, but these issues had nothing like the general discussion they get today.

There was one place, however, which was restored to its ancient function as the public forum for the great moralities and immoralities of life: the stage. The old 'swashbuckling romantic theatre' found itself invaded by writers who 'looked around and saw the terror of modern civilization. The class-war, which had found expression in actual life, was freely dealt with by the newer school'[1] – John Galsworthy, Harley Granville-Barker, Stanley Houghton, St John Ervine, and, towering over all, the astringent Shaw.

'I hate to see dead people walking about: it is unnatural. And our respectable middle-class people are as dead as mutton.' Thus Shaw expressed his theme in the preface to *Fanny's First Play* (1911), and the British public rewarded him by making it a West End winner – 622 performances, comparable with the success of a musical comedy, so the outspoken free-thinker

---

[1] *British Drama*, by Allardyce Nicoll (Harrap).

Bernard Shaw remembered by Lillah McCarthy: he 'doth suffer a sea-change into something rich and strange'

who had found it almost impossible to get a hearing in the Nineties was getting somewhere; and so was the British public. Controversy raged round his plays. It did the social atmosphere of these islands a world of good.

He was naturally on the side of the suffragettes. He denounced 'the horrible artificiality of that impudent sham the Victorian "womanly" woman'. People thought him a terror, but there was another side to Shaw. MISS LILLAH MCCARTHY, the New Woman in several of his plays, says: 'His aim was to make people *think* – I know he made me think – but he never forced conversation when he was alone with his friends, no hectic discussions and no displays of cleverness. He was the best companion in the world. Sunday at his home at Ayot St Lawrence was a day of quiet and rest. In the afternoon he spent a great deal of time in the dark-room developing photographs. In between whiles he would play his pianola. Music seemed to mean more to Shaw than literature. He declared that his master in drama was Mozart. I remember him on holiday in Cornwall, a very strong swimmer; I was not. He used to tell me to put one hand on his shoulder and just swim, on and on. We would find ourselves well out to sea. Then a change would come over Shaw, a sea change. He was vigorous on land, but when swimming he became tranquil. He would say to me as we swam: "We are in another world, Lillah." And if I were afraid: "Have no fear, Lillah, gently and slowly does it." Shaw was always a chivalrous and kind man.'

Winds of change in the drama had their counterparts in music and art. A wonderfully stimulating transformation came over English music – the nation known abroad in Victoria's day as 'the people without music' now had Elgar, Vaughan Williams, Delius, Holst, and a galaxy of smaller but entertaining makers of music arose behind them. This must be reckoned

Walker Gallery, Liverpool

The Old Bedford, a corner of the gallery: to Walter Sickert, who spent many evenings at the London music-halls, this was a favourite, with its yellow and scarlet stucco and its darkly uproarious galleryites. He painted this picture in 1897, and many other versions later.

among the major events of the young twentieth century: the uprising of the musical spirit. Music is the purest and least corrupting of the arts; as life has become faster, noisier and more perilous masses of people have turned to music to balance their existence and save their sanity. Broadcasting, since after the First World War, has taken a key part in this civilizing process; that story lies in *Scrapbook*'s Volume 2, but it is well to bear it in mind as we take stock of the pre-1914 years, and to note the marvellous fact that new springs of creativeness were bursting forth from two totally different directions, the artistic and the technological, so that in due course would come the handshake (to put it figuratively) of Elgar and Marconi, in radio.

Elgar once said to A. C. Benson that he didn't intend his music to be on the musical antiquary's shelves: 'I want the people to enjoy themselves.' He himself did not have to wait for death's hand to crown him with laurels: in 1904 came an Elgar Festival in London and a knighthood; in 1908 his 'First Symphony', launched at Manchester by the Hallé Orchestra, had instantaneous success. It was performed over 100 times in two years. In 1911 he received the Order of Merit.

British pictorial art had a Victorian hangover through King Edward's time. Landseer's stags stood resolutely at bay over many a mantelpiece. There was no great breakthrough in this direction, but there was a foreign invasion. There was also the budding of a genius, which we will take first. The policeman who stood in the Strand one day in 1908 gazing at a piece of sculpture, and who wrote in his Scotland Yard notebook the verdict RUDE, wasn't saying the first word or the last about Jacob Epstein. One of the young sculptor's symbolic figures on the face of the British Medical Association's new headquarters represented, appropriately enough, a pregnant woman: 'A form of statuary which no careful father would care to wish his daughter, and no discriminating young man, his fiancée, to see,' pronounced the *Evening Standard*. Questions were asked in the House. Epstein's chisel was stopped while sermons were preached and leaders were written. The BMA sat in judgment and decided that Epstein could continue. *The Times* agreed: 'The figure is turned towards the wall and is so high up on the building that the particular feature to which exception is taken can scarcely be distinguished except by the aid of an opera glass or telescope, and there is nothing even remotely immodest in the posture or execution of the figure.' Epstein found himself famous, or at least notorious.[1] The *British Medical Journal* said it was ashamed that Epstein owed the foundation of his fame to British hypocrisy.

From its foundations onwards Epstein's career was to be assailed by half-baked moralistic ideas and crude artistic standards; the fact that he lived to be widely accepted as a genius is one token (among many) of how immensely taste has changed and sensibilities have deepened. This applies to the most homely things. The Edwardian home had inherited its décor from her late Majesty's solid reign, when furniture was ornately heavy and on the walls hung pictures of that banal stag alongside such moralizing representations as George Watts' 'Hope', a sad lady squatting on the globe. From around 1900 a new style entered this country: Art Nouveau, as they called it in 'advanced' circles, introduced simpler and more slender furniture and its convolvulus-like sinuous line flowed through wallpapers and ornaments, but Art Nouveau caused no great commotion; the one big blast of controversy came in 1910 concerning some foreign paintings unveiled at the Manet and Post-Impressionist Exhibition at the Grafton

---

[1] He once told me privately how he hated this notoriety all his life; it was the chief reason why he refused to broadcast. - L.B.

Gallery in London. Van Gogh's 'roughly modelled flower pieces', moralized *The Times*, were 'like anarchism in politics, the rejection of all that civilization has done, the good with the bad.' Cézanne 'outraged every canon,' boomed *The Athenaeum*. 'In Gauguin's Tahitian pictures,' said an angry letter in the *Morning Post*, 'I can discover no beauty of form or colour or design.'

'I went to see the exhibition,' says LADY VIOLET BONHAM-CARTER. 'It had caused an outcry almost as though something obscene had been put on view. The pictures which caused all the fuss are nowadays thought quite normal, but in 1910 it was the first time most of these "modernists" had been seen in this country, and I must admit that at first sight it was startling. I was taken round by Roger Fry, the famous critic, and I remember standing in front of a picture by Matisse – three naked women with enormous thighs. I said, "I'm afraid I don't think the lines of their bodies are beautiful". Mr Fry replied: "No, but don't you think the gaps between them are beautiful?". It was the first time I had ever thought of painting as a decorative pattern. I'd only thought that a painting must be representational.'

Picasso's cubism was on the way in, and in the last years before the First World War all sorts of new modes, fauvism, vorticism, surrealism, futurism, wafted across the Channel. It was as though the 'advanced' artists had a premonition as they looked in the mirror and saw the image of life cracked into strange distortions and violent fragments. 'A hurricane has swept through Europe and the tail of it is already wiping our eye,' said Walter Sickert, leader of the Camden Town Group of painters (founded 1911), one of whom, Wyndham Lewis, said: 'It is not enough at the present day to paint a picture in the manner of Tiepolo or of Velasquez or of Manet, but in some new or different manner more appropriate to the beliefs and conditions obtaining in the twentieth century.'

*　　　　*　　　　*

The spirit of Edwardianism is still preserved for everyone to see in a number of large public buildings. Take a look at Selfridge's store (1908) or the Piccadilly Hotel (1905) and you are looking not at a work of art but at the florid face of big business. The Ritz Hotel (1904) has more distinction, as the first steel-framed building in London. The pride and ostentation of a city very conscious that it was the heart of the Greatest Empire is manifest in, for example, London County Hall (1911); looking at it across the Thames, one can almost see the municipal swells in their toppers, riding up in their Silver Ghost Rolls-Royces. Again, the Waldorf Hotel (1908) is a reminder that in King Edward's reign England was embracing France: here is an echo of the elegance of his beloved Paris. All these are whiffs of Edwardianism but there was no really powerful new school of architecture, as there was in music; only a few men were pointing the way to the future, notably C. R. Mackintosh whose Glasgow School of Art, built at the turn of the century, strikes one even now as 'modern'. His ideas had great influence on the Continent, if not in this country.

Even more vital to us today is what happened not about the big buildings but about the smallest. The rich Edwardian era had inherited from the Industrial Revolution thousands of miles of crowded hovels and 'back-to-backs' packed as many as possible to the acre, and no nonsense about health or beauty. In late Victorian times a few enlightened industrialists had reacted against this rottenness by building pleasant 'villages' near their factories, notably the Cadburys at Bournville, and Lever at Port Sunlight, but as a nation Britain had done nothing.

Drawing by Leonora Ison (Daily Telegraph)
Characteristic of Edwardian elegance was the Waldorf Hotel, designed by A. Marshall
Mackenzie and built after some of London's worst slums had been torn down to make
way for the new thoroughfares of Aldwych and Kingsway

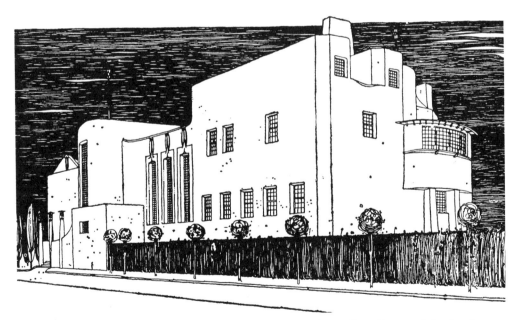

An astonishing leap into the future: this design for a 'House for a Lover of the Arts' was
drawn at the turn of the century by the Scottish architect C. R. Mackintosh. Such art
nouveau in British architecture was extremely rare

149

(*Photo: Cadbury Bros*)
The back-to-back houses in Birmingham that shocked George Cadbury and turned his immense energies towards making decent homes for working people at Bournville

(*Right*) Sir Ebenezer Howard, who inspired the first garden cities, at Letchworth (1903) and Welwyn Garden City (1919)

(*Below*) An avenue at Letchworth, when the idea that factory workers' homes should have gardens and space and beauty was thought Utopian

(Photo: *Letchworth Museum & Art Gallery*)

Social Experiments

George Cadbury was so appalled by the slums in Birmingham that he founded a Trust to develop Bournville into a model suburb (1894). The idea that a town worker's house should have a garden was thought Utopian. Bournville houses were not 'tied' to the Cadbury factory (about 60 per cent of the householders were and are still unconnected with it). At York Joseph Rowntree thought to do likewise, and his son Seebohm, whose revelations about poverty in Britain have been mentioned earlier, wrote to George Cadbury outlining their proposals and received this Quakerly reply: 'Thy letter is most interesting. It is a great pleasure to think of Bournville village as a happy home for many generations of children, where they will be brought up amid surroundings that will benefit them spiritually, mentally, and physically, and I am sure thou wilt find the same in connection with thy suggested Trust.'

The upshot (1904) was New Earswick, just outside York. Its architect, Raymond Unwin, who made tremendous advances in housing, was also responsible for the layout of Hampstead Garden Suburb (1907). Gardens, tree-lined roads, the siting of every house so that it should not spoil the neighbourhood of beauty – these were the standards. The founders of all the above schemes were more than philanthropists: the estates must pay a fair return on capital invested, to be *ploughed back*, so that good housing could be proved a practicable proposition to the rest of the nation (not to mention dividends in health). How strange it seems now that such an obvious proposition had to be proven.

Alongside these suburban developments, but quite distinct, was the garden city idea first put forward by Ebenezer Howard in 1898 – not suburbs fringing the old towns, but new towns. The first was Letchworth (1903, chief architects Barry Parker and Raymond Unwin). Sir Frederic Osborn, the leading authority on this subject, says:[1] 'This was the breakthrough: Howard's idea was to stop the further growth of big cities and to move their excess population and industry to new towns, limited in size by a reserved agricultural belt, where people could live near work and near the country and yet have all facilities for everyday social and cultural life. The town should be built on a site in single public or quasi-public ownership, so that all increases in land value would benefit the community. He proposed that when a single town had reached its limit, further development should be in clusters of towns separated from the first by green belts. Only comparatively recently has Howard's vision become widely understood in this country and abroad.'

Our country would have been a land fitter for heroes to live in after the First World War had there been, before it, something more than a tiny break through the walls of apathy and vested interests surrounding town planning. Asquith's Government made a start with the first Housing and Town Planning Act (1909) but it was a timid start. George Cadbury wrote prophetically to the Minister responsible, John Burns: 'Miserable monotonous suburbs will still be built all round our towns, spoiling the beautiful face of the country. When I think of the millions of little children who will be brought up in these dismal suburbs it is enough to make my heart bleed.'

Today we have many New Towns and other schemes of good housing, yet the sad prophecy of Mr Cadbury is still true in a society which calls itself 'affluent' yet has got its priorities badly wrong.

[1] In a letter to *Scrapbook*.

In Letchworth, alongside its advanced housing ideas, a few old ways lingered on. Some startling experiments with prefabricated houses appeared (*below*), with concrete walls. Liverpool was also leading in housing, and its City Engineer, John A. Brodie, built some prefabricated concrete tenements there in 1904; then in 1905 he designed the house below for erection at Letchworth. Though this was a house of the future, it had no bathroom, as was quite common at that period, and the only lavatory had access from outdoors:

The above house appeared at the Cheap Cottages Exhibition at Letchworth in 1905, and is still standing. It seems to have a claim to have been the first concrete prefab in this country.

CALENDAR OF SIGNIFICANT DATES

1911

Coronation of King George V and Queen Mary (June 22).

King and Queen entertained 100,000 children to a fete at Crystal Palace.

Coronation Durbar in India attended by King and Queen.

Colour film, *The Durbar at Delhi*.

English Women's Golf Championship instituted.

Air battalion of British Army formed.

Investiture of Prince of Wales at Caernarvon Castle (July 13).

Parliament Act accepted by Lords.

Shops Act: compulsory half-day holiday for assistants.

Rutherford postulated the nuclear structure of the atom.

Hopkins proved the existence of vitamins.

Record sunshine summer, 384 hours at Eastbourne and Hastings.

Agadir crisis (July 1–September 22): forces on alert.

Titanic launched.

First escalators in London Underground, at Earl's Court.

Amundsen reached South Pole.

Siege of Sidney Street.

Widespread industrial strikes; also a strike of elementary schoolboys in some towns.

Fol-de-Rols pierrots started at Scarborough.

T. W. Burgess swam English Channel, South Foreland–Cape Gris Nez, in 22 hours 35 minutes: the only previous crossing was in 1875 by Matthew Webb.

Diaghilev Ballet in London, first appearance.

English Folk Dance Society founded.

Sir Edward Elgar received O.M.: his 'Second Symphony' dedicated to memory of Edward VII.

STAGE: *Fanny's First Play* (Bernard Shaw – his longest run, 622 performances); *Bunty Pulls the Strings* (Graham Moffat), 617; *The Count of Luxembourg* (Lehár).

BOOKS: *The Innocence of Father Brown* (G. K. Chesterton); *The White Peacock* (D. H. Lawrence); *Mr Perrin and Mr Traill* (Hugh Walpole); *The Passionate Elopement* (Compton Mackenzie); *Zuleika Dobson* (Max Beerbohm); *The Card* (Arnold Bennett); *Sanders of the River* (Edgar Wallace).

SONGS: 'Alexander's Ragtime Band'; 'Any Old Iron'; 'I'm Henery the Eighth, I am'; 'Joshuah'; 'Just a Wee Deoch and Doris'; 'Little Grey Home in the West'; 'Roamin' in the Gloamin'; 'The Floral Dance'; 'The Gaby Glide'; 'The Spaniard That Blighted My Life'.

1912

Salaries introduced for MPS: £400.

Titanic sank on maiden voyage (April 15).

British telephone system taken over by GPO, except Hull, Portsmouth, Guernsey.

First automatic telephone exchange in Britain, Epsom.

Royal Flying Corps founded.

Captain Scott and party reached South Pole and perished on return journey.

First aeroplane Channel flight by a woman, Miss Harriet Quimby, Deal to Cape Gris Nez.

National Insurance Act came into operation; great protest meetings at Albert Hall.

Doctors pledged not to work Insurance Act.

Daily Herald founded.

Frederick Soddy, at Glasgow University, discovered isotopes.

Review of 80,000 Ulster Volunteers in Belfast.

Great demonstrations for and against Home Rule for Ireland.

Boat race: both boats sank; re-rowed, Oxford won.

First Royal Command Variety performance, Palace Theatre.

Stravinsky's *The Fire Bird*, first ballet to his music to be seen in Britain (Diaghilev).

The Miracle produced by Reinhardt at Olympia.

STAGE: *Hindle Wakes* (Stanley Houghton); *Milestones* (Arnold Bennett and Edward Knoblock); *Everybody's Doing It* (Empire); *Hullo Ragtime!* (Hippodrome).

BOOKS: *The Lost World* (Conan Doyle); *Carnival* (Compton Mackenzie); *Windyridge* (W. Riley).

SONGS: 'Casey Jones'; 'Everybody's Doing It'; 'Ghost of the Violin'; 'Hitchy Koo!'; 'How Do You Do, Miss Ragtime' (*Hullo Ragtime!*); 'I Love the Moon'; 'It's a Long Way to Tipperary'; 'Oh! You Beautiful Doll'; 'Un Peu d'Amour'; 'Waiting for the Robert E. Lee'; 'When Irish Eyes are Smiling'; 'Who Were you with Last Night?'.

The Calendar is continued on page 188

'Mr. R., whose charming residence on the Portsmouth Road was utterly uninhabitable on account of motor dust, has . . .' (*see opposite*)

George Newnes Ltd

The 'simple pleasures' of another age, sketched by Bert Thomas for the *Strand Magazine:* here is a useful key to middle-class vogues—the piano, the mandoline, the moustaches, the boy's Eton collar, the long hair for mother and daughter, the basketwork chair

'. . . rid himself of the nuisance by a simple and inexpensive device.'—*Punch*'s revelation about police traps, which maddened motorists in 1910

The Bystander, 1912

For some readers this must be a nostalgic reminder of the scene on top of a horse-bus—and the smell, at times. Only those old enough to remember it can appreciate the 'effluvia' (as the lady above calls it) of city streets in the horse-traffic age. This cartoon by G. C. Jennis was headed 'The Die Hard Humour of the Surviving Horse-busman' and this dialogue was printed underneath:

Fare: 'Oh! Busman, what a disgustin' effluvia!'
Busman: 'Lor' bless yer, mum, it's quite 'ealthy. They torks about going to Marryanbad and Barritzey to take the cure, but it ain't nothing compared with this 'ere'

Radio Times Hulton Library

The Manx novelist Hall Caine is lampooned, 1910. Enviously, he says 'My time will come too!' as he grinds out his melodramas. The theme of Bernard Shaw's *Arms and the Man* had been profitably (but without Shaw's permission) turned into the musical play *The Chocolate Soldier*, just as *Pygmalion* has more recently had an even more lucrative metamorphosis as *My Fair Lady*. Hall Caine's novels had prodigious sales, and *The Graphic*'s caption under this cartoon asked 'May we not expect to find Hall Caine at Covent Garden?' After all, grand opera was often as melodramatic . . . but all Caine's stories achieved were a few heavy films

The Kaiser, in the uniform of a British field-marshal, rides in London alongside King George V at the funeral of King Edward, 1910

(*Below*) The goliaths of the arms-race: Britain's HMS *Dreadnought* compared with a German Zeppelin. The airship was 445 feet long, the battleship 490 feet

6 GEORGIAN

The Last Years of Peace

One evening in 1910 a star journalist of Fleet Street put on his top-hat and hailed a four-wheeler: 'Buckingham Palace' he shouted, and away they trotted at the speed that chariots had kept up since the Romans (probably a bit faster than the traffic-jammed motor-car can manage today). Years later SIR PHILIP GIBBS sat in retirement over the fire of his country house in Surrey, and the compiler of BBC *Scrapbooks* – who is simply a radio-journalist using electronic methods – held the microphone of a tape-recorder before the most famous reporter of his time.

'I hired the cab with my old friend Percival Eddy, who afterwards became a judge,' said Sir Philip. 'We drove straight into the courtyard at the Palace, where we were known to the police; outside was a vast crowd waiting anxiously to know whether King Edward would die. We parked the cab in the courtyard and prepared to spend the night in it. Eddy took off his boots and put his feet up. I paced up and down outside, smoking a last cigarette. As I was doing this a carriage came through one of the archways and inside I recognized the Prince and Princess of Wales. They were weeping. I ran to the cab and said, "Eddy, put your boots on quickly." We then ran to the Equerry's entrance and there before a fire was a gentleman in a scarlet coat, one of the Gentlemen-in-Waiting. I said, "How is the King?". He said, "The King died a few minutes ago." I made a rush from the Palace to a nearby hotel and 'phoned the news to the *Daily Chronicle*, and we were the first paper to be on the streets that early morning with the Life and Death of King Edward VII.'

The new King wrote in his diary: 'At 11.45 beloved Papa passed peacefully away & I have lost my best friend & the best of fathers . . . I am quite stunned by this awful blow.'

George V was not a flamboyant pageant-lover like his father though he was an absolute stickler over ceremonial, which is a different thing. He wasn't a gay ladies' man either; no more Darling Daisies behind the throne. 'His domesticity and simple life are charming,' declared Lord Esher, visiting Windsor Castle soon after the accession. 'The change that has come over the place! . . . everything so peaceful and domestic.' Alas, public affairs during the new reign were not peaceful, and yet over the perilous stream of life there hung a mist of un-apprehension. The public as a whole had no perception of what they were drifting towards abroad, while inside Britain between 1910 and 1914 a rising turbulence of events was reported in the papers, and there was an occasional glimpse on the silent cinema screen of such a melodrama as the Siege of Sidney Street; but it was a distant tale that was told. If one is to

159

understand one of the greatest differences between life then and life today one must bear in mind that the explosions went off as muffled thuds distant from most people's ears, whereas today every crisis and craze comes crackling white-hot on to everyone's hearth by radio and TV, and every protagonist jostles for our attention. We are a much better informed people, but at the cost of the old peace of mind.

What a field day TV cameras would have had in Sidney Street! Coronation Year, 1911, was only a few days old when The Siege came as a lurid prelude to that year's mixture of pageantry and violence. Not in living memory had Londoners heard soldiers shooting to kill. A group of gunmen whom the Press called 'foreign anarchists' were wanted for robbery and the shooting of three policemen. They had been on the run in the East End for a fortnight. Their leader was known as Peter the Painter. One January night fifty police surrounded No. 100 Sidney Street.

DETECTIVE-SERGEANT LEESON has told *Scrapbook* that the wanted men were believed to be sleeping in a front room on the second floor: 'We cleared the other occupants of the house with difficulty. I well remember the trouble I had with a woman of eighty who objected to being turned out on such a night, for snow was falling. By 7 a.m. every doorway within sight of the house contained an armed policeman. The door of No. 100 was open. I went towards it to put a shilling in the gas-meter in the hall, so that we might see anyone attempting to leave. Suddenly the desperadoes opened fire from the bedroom windows. The first shot hit me in the foot, the second just below the heart.'

MR HUGH MARTIN, reporter of the old *Daily News*, continues the story: 'By the middle of the morning Sidney Street was in a state of siege by 750 police and a detachment of Scots Guards from the Tower, with a machine-gun. The soldiers lay in the street on newspaper billboards, looking very much as though they were trying to score bulls at Bisley. Then I saw a motor-car arrive, with an imposing figure in a silk hat and a fur-lined overcoat with astrakhan collar: the Home Secretary, Mr Winston Churchill. Peeping round corners, he exposed himself with the Scots Guards to the fire, and consulted his staff in tones of the utmost gravity. A couple of field-guns were sent for, and Mr Churchill agreed that a party of Royal Engineers might be useful if mining operations had to be undertaken against the citadel. He even suggested that casualties might be avoided if steel plates were brought from Woolwich to form portable cover for the sharp-shooters – an early version of one of his ideas in the First World War. Soon after one o'clock wisps of smoke began to ooze through the broken windows of No. 100. The firing ceased. The house was alight. A police inspector, with Mr Winston Churchill and a guardsman in close attendance, marched up to the front door and kicked it down. An order to surrender. No reply. The fire engines got to work, and at that moment two field-guns drove up at a gallop, too late.'

SIR PHILIP GIBBS adds: 'I watched these proceedings for several hours from the roof of the Rising Sun, a pub opposite No, 100. In the end I saw an arm come through a burning curtain and fire the last shot, and it appeared that papers were being burnt for they came through the chimneys and floated away. The whole house went up in smoke and flame. Three bodies were found there dead, but there ought to have been four; there is still a rumour – a legend, perhaps – that Peter the Painter escaped and got back to Russia. But there is little evidence about that.'

From Sidney Street onwards, George's Coronation Year was hag-ridden by strife. A bad atmosphere in industry had been left over from the notorious Ton-y-pandy affair in 1910 when mob-violence during a coal-mining stoppage led Churchill to send troops to South

The siege of Sidney Street, the detectives shooting at No. 100: drawing by G. K. Jones in *The Graphic*

Radio Times Hulton Library

(*Below*) The Scots Guards enter the front line

Four cards from a game marketed at a time of radical turmoil. The Premier is labelled with the phrase he used in 1910 when asked his intentions ('Wait and See'). The Chancellor offers the golden eggs of his People's Budget.

Labour leaders are represented as wild men, but even they have coronets—a quip on Asquith's threat to create 500 peers. (The cards, invented by Mr J. Laurence, loaned to *Scrapbook* by Mr F. S. Bass)

Wales to help the police. He was berated as much as he was praised. Now came in 1911 a unprecedented epidemic of strikes, lock-outs, and looting. During a dock strike (the worst since 1889) soldiers in Liverpool fired and two men were killed.

At the height of a bright Coronation summer a storm of anger broke on quite a different level: the old dispute between the Commons and the Lords about the Peers' over-ruling powers. A truce between party leaders after King Edward's death, and their private meetings to try to reach an agreement, had come to grief in 1910; once again the 'people' (no women, of course) had voted at a general election under the blazing slogan *The Lords v. the People*; once again Asquith's Liberals had been returned; now, in 1911, once again – and finally – he put before Lords and Commons his Parliament Bill to establish the supreme powers of the latter for ever.

This is the point of almost unbelievable comedy in Britain's story when the 500 Men Who Didn't Become Peers come marching in like ghosts without coronets. Shortly before King Edward's death Premier Asquith had sounded him out very privately with a proposal that the King should create sufficient new progressive peers to force the Parliament Act through. It was a foxy idea to fox the 'backwoods' peers who always rolled along to Parliament to block progress. It was also an awkward problem for King Edward; he was surrounded by courtiers who gave him conflicting advice; he disliked the idea; wasn't this the monarch entering into politics? He had not made up his mind about it when he died without briefing his heir on the subject, so George V was pitched unprepared into a red-hot constitutional issue. Finally, and reluctantly, he gave the Cabinet a private undertaking to create Peers as necessary.

Asquith wrote out a little list of 500 – they included J. M. Barrie, Thomas Hardy, Bertrand Russell, Gilbert Murray, Joseph Rowntree, and General Sir Ian Hamilton. The names were secret, but the threat of wholesale coronet-distribution was well-known when a packed House of Peers met on a stifling August night (the temperature that day had been 100 degrees) to give their final decision on the Parliament Bill. Many last-ditchers believed Asquith's list to be bluff, until the Leader of the House drew from his pocket a slip of paper: a message from the King's Private Secretary confirming that the King would create peers as necessary. There was a stunned hush. The message was read again. It was sufficient: the Lords, on a division, passed the legislation to clip their own wings. Those who had voted 'for', including thirteen bishops, were thereafter damned by all last-ditchers. 'We have been beaten,' said one, 'by the bishops and the rats.' *The Globe* newspaper consigned them to purgatory: 'We hope no honest man will take any of them by the hand again, that their friends will disown them, their clubs expel them, and that in politics and social life they will be made to feel the bitter shame they have brought upon us all.'

The ghostly 500 faded away. Many were to end their days just plain Mr.

This historic measure, together with the decision that MPs should be paid, lifted Parliament clean away from the ancient status which Mr Arthur Hayday has described earlier in this book as the preserve of 'rich business men, manufacturers, or men of property and leisure'. But the very idea of paying an MP £400 a year depressed *The Times* which predicted a flood of election candidates 'who have no other object in view than to make a living more easily than by honest and useful work'. The same notion was expressed in other words by a character in an Elinor Glyn novel: 'Parliament isn't a place for gentlemen any more.'

The suffragettes held a truce part-way through Coronation Year; then their brand of strife broke out, harsher than ever. They set fire to pillar-boxes. They ripped up census forms (1911 being census year). Mrs Pankhurst returned hers marked NO VOTE, NO CENSUS.

A battle song was written for them, 'The March of the Women', by Britain's foremost woman composer, MISS ETHEL SMYTH,[1] who wasn't the daughter of an artillery general for nothing, as witness her report of action: 'At exactly 5.30 one memorable evening in 1912 relays of women produced hammers from their muffs and handbags and proceeded methodically to smash shop windows in all the big London thoroughfares – Piccadilly, Regent Street, and so on – inspired by the knowledge that exactly at that moment Mrs Pankhurst was opening the ball with a stone aimed at a window of No. 10 Downing Street. As a matter of fact, Mrs Pankhurst was not a cricketer, and in spite of much practice in my garden her stone fell harmlessly in the area of No. 10. But her companion's stone did its duty. Over 200 women were arrested.'

Ethel Smyth did time in Holloway Prison: 'My cell was on the third storey. One day I heard unusual sounds from outside in the prison yard. It was some of the suffragettes exercising and singing as they marched. The windows in prison are about eight feet up. I put my chair under the window, stood an inverted slop-pail on it, clambered on to the top of this erection, and pushed a hand through the bars, in it a toothbrush with which I conducted "The March of the Women". Almost at once the women noticed the waving hand and began cheering, until driven away by a few horrified wardresses.' Ten years later King George was to make Ethel Smyth a Dame of the British Empire. But in 1912 she spent two months in His Majesty's prison. Some of the suffragettes there went on hunger-strike and were forcibly fed, a horrible business.

Premier Asquith had greater trouble on his mind than suffragette violence or industrial strikes, grave as these were. The Kaiser sent a gunboat to Agadir in Morocco and made a landing 'to protect German interests'; the prospect of a German naval base on the Atlantic coast of Africa worried the British Government and snubbed the French who had a foothold in Morocco, and international nerves were so tensed – three years before 1914 – that the British army and navy were put on alert.

'All the alarm bells in Europe began to quiver,' Winston Churchill wrote later.[2] For the first time in a century British ministers 'felt that sense of direct contact with the war peril which was never absent from Continental minds'. Yet the common people enjoying a blazing hot Coronation summer knew little about Agadir and cared less, such was the general unapprehensiveness. At the height of this unrecognized crisis a general railway strike was threatened; Asquith told the unions sternly that the government could not permit a standstill – his stiff line angered the railwaymen, they were not to know that uppermost in his mind was the fear of war any day with Germany. Most of the railwaymen struck. Troops were turned out. During rioting at Llanelly the soldiers fired and killed two men. Swiftly Lloyd George (Chancellor of the Exchequer) negotiated an end to the strike.

The Agadir alert lasted nearly three months, then the armed forces were stood down, including sentries at the ends of tunnels on the South-Eastern and Chatham Railway: their appearance had been a sign of governmental apprehension, for anyone sharp enough to notice them, but most people were too absorbed in holidays supplemented by Coronation celebrations, pageantry in towns, fêtes in villages, decorations everywhere.

---

[1] Ethel Smyth (1858–1944), best known for her operas *The Wreckers* (1906) and *The Boatswain's Mate* (1916); also wrote choral, orchestral, and chamber music rarely heard now.

[2] *The World Crisis*, by Winston S. Churchill (Thornton Butterworth). At the time he was Home Secretary.

Cameras, either movie or still, were once again barred from the Abbey during the 1911 Coronation (the last to be unshared by the public at large; the next, in 1937, was broadcast but not televised), but George's spectacular visit to India later in the year had a considerable photographic coverage and was the subject of one of the first substantial colour films, *The Durbar at Delhi*. It was the King's personal idea to 'crown himself in Delhi' at a great Coronation Durbar, but when the Archbishop of Canterbury pointed out that a Christian service would be essential but would hardly be welcomed by Moslems and Hindus the crowning part of the excursion was dropped. The King had also hoped to pack his crown in his baggage, but an old law was turned up establishing that it is illegal for anyone, even the monarch, to take the crown abroad; so a new Imperial crown of India was made for the occasion. It has not been worn since; today it rests in the Tower of London.

So far as the public imagination could be caught by events-at-a-distance, there was one which did so because it was uniquely fashioned for the year 1911, when the King's eldest son was seventeen, and because that handsome fair-haired Prince assumed henceforth a national and Empire-wide role as Prince Charming: the investiture of the Prince of Wales at Caernarvon Castle.

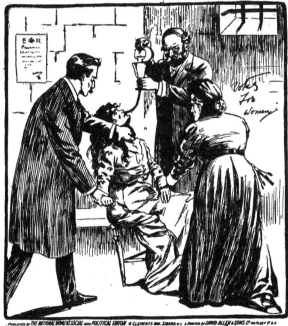

An election poster issued by the militant suffragettes

Illustrated London News
Oxford Street shops assaulted, November 21st, 1911:
223 women arrested

LADY MEGAN LLOYD GEORGE[1] was present: 'I was nine years old at the time, and perched beside my mother I could only see by poking my head in between the feathers and the vast hats, like herbaceous borders in full flower. A tropical sun beat down on the grey walls of the castle, its battlements hung with ancient heraldic devices; it was a blaze of colour, a truly medieval scene. The procession slowly came into sight: prelates in scarlet and purple, Privy Councillors in their encrusted gold coats, the bearers of the regalia and the golden circlet soon to be placed on the Prince's flaxen head. The scene was set – the King, the Queen, and the lone figure, slim, slight, nervous, weighed down with the crimson cloak and the ermine. Behind, I could see my father, Constable of the Castle, chief architect of this pageant.

'The Home Secretary, Mr Churchill, read from a splendid parchment: "Know ye that we have made and created and by these our letters patent do make and create our most dear son, Edward Albert Christian George Andrew Patrick David" – the familiar voice rolled out the titles, and finally – *"Prince of Wales"*! The Prince was then crowned, the ring placed on his finger, the silver rod in his hand. He made a little speech with some sentences in Welsh which my father had patiently taught him. Lastly came a great moment – a fanfare of trumpets, and the King and Queen led the Prince by the hand up the ancient stone causeway to Queen Eleanor's Gateway, where, six centuries before, Edward I showed his baby boy, the first

[1] Daughter of David Lloyd George (Chancellor of Exchequer at that time, Prime Minister 1916–22), formerly Liberal, she later became a Labour MP.

Radio Times Hulton Library

Pageantry in Coronation Year, 1911: the Prince of Wales invested at Caernarvon Castle; 25 years later he became King Edward VIII and abdicated within the year

Prince of Wales, to the chiefs. Now a burst of song rose up and reverberated through the mountains and over the sea: "God Bless the Prince of Wales!" Thousands of Welsh voices chanted the lovely melody, now alas almost forgotten.'

From that throbbing sunny day onwards loyalist Britain took the future King Edward VIII to its sentimental heart. Prince Charming's 1911 investiture now stands in total contrast to the dark night in 1936 when his abdication speech came over the radio and he left the country.

★   ★   ★

The Diaghilev Ballet advanced triumphantly across Europe and reached London in George V's Coronation Year; an artistic revolution had arrived from Russia. Each year thereafter up to the eve of war in 1914 Diaghilev returned. Some of his dancers are now a legend; there is, of course, no completely objective way (in the absence of good films) to compare them with the stars of today; we can only consult people who saw these dancers from the east, and the terms of recollection leave no doubt that this was a profound and unprecedented experience. MISS CATHLEEN NESBITT, the actress, tells of going with the poet Rupert Brooke to see the Diaghilev Ballet:

'I remember one performance of *Le Spectre de la Rose* when Nijinsky's leap across the stage transcended anything he had ever done. He seemed to remain suspended in mid-air for a full minute and then to float down to earth gracefully and delicately like a bird. We were so up-lifted that we couldn't wait to see the rest of the programme. We went out and walked about in the darkness of Covent Garden, and Rupert said, "Now I know how people felt when they saw a miracle. There's something almost terrifying about *seeing* with your eyes what your reason tells you is by natural law impossible. After all, there is a law of gravity."'

The Diaghilev company made their first English appearance in a Coronation Gala at Covent Garden in 1911 when the programme also included a galaxy of opera singers who are likewise fabled in memory: Melba, Tetrazzini, John McCormack, Destinn, Kirkby Lunn. But on this occasion, despite such a king's ransom of talent, it was outshone by the show on the other side of the footlights. The Diaghilev *prima ballerina*, MADAME TAMARA KARSAVINA, remembers that 'The audience that night was really more spectacular than the stage! – the garlands of roses decorating the boxes, the glitter of jewels and evening dresses, the King George and the Queen Mary in the royal box, and the wonderful stateliness in which Queen Mary wore her robes. I remember, too, that my attention was detracted from the interpretation of my part because I couldn't keep my eyes off an Indian rajah who sat there under an elaborate turban, in the most wonderful glittering robes, with pearls and emeralds *woven into his beard*!'

In the Diaghilev company it was not only the dancers who set a new standard. MADAME KARSAVINA says: 'For the first time all the arts which go to form a spectacle collaborated in perfect ensemble.' In colour and artistic design, in music, in balletic conception, the productions were a supreme new experience, and their influence ran far outside the realm of ballet: 'It awakened the love of colour. The art of house decoration, for example, was very much in-fluenced by it. A lot of people painted their walls a vivid blue which, because our designer had introduced it on the stage, was called Bakst blue.'

Today, when we take our own Royal Ballet rather for granted, it needs an effort of the imagination to appreciate the peculiar sub-artistic status of British ballet in those days, sand-wiched between sword-swallowers and the biograph at the music-hall. Ballet companies maintained by two London halls, the Empire and the Alhambra, had a curiously romantic aura (preserved in Compton Mackenzie's novel *Carnival*) due to the associated raffishness of variety, the stage-door johnnies, and the easy-going fact that all that was required was a lollipop that could be enjoyed both by the knuts in the stalls and roistering Cockneys in the gallery. Spectacle, not artistry, was what they paid their sovereigns and sixpences for. Techniques were poor in general, but a few ballerinas danced high above the common level.

ADELINE GENÉE (later Dame Genée-Isitt), prima ballerina at the Empire for many years, tells a story which well illustrates the artistic poverty of British ballet: 'I often wished that *Coppélia* could be seen in this country. One day I was invited to attend a meeting of the directors in the board-room. They offered me a contract to stay another two years at the Empire. I saw my opportunity. Before replying I asked them if they would present *Coppélia*.

'"Who wrote the music?" asked one gentleman.

'"Delibes," I replied. "It was first produced in Paris in 1870."

'"But, mademoiselle! How old-fashioned! Come, come, this ballet is quite unknown in England."

'"Not a very practical proposition," said another director. "The costs would be heavy, the return doubtful. Too risky."

'So then I'm afraid I was guilty of a little bit of, shall I say, feminine diplomacy. I told them if I couldn't have my *Coppélia* they couldn't have me. And with that I walked out of the room.'

She had her way. *Coppélia* was staged at the London Empire in 1906 with Genée as Swanilda. It was a success, though *The Times* reported that the audience found it 'a little difficult to follow'; however, it led the Empire to present a short version of another Delibes ballet, *Sylvia*, in Coronation Year, 1911, starring Lydia Kyasht, brought over from Russia. George Robey, the comedian, was on the same bill. Dancing before a boisterous English music-hall audience was something new for a ballerina accustomed to the aristocratic elegance of the Mariinsky Theatre at St Petersburg (now Leningrad); one evening when Phyllis Bedells danced on with a tribute of fruit which she placed at Kyasht's feet a voice yelled from the audience: '*Have a BANANA!*' – a catchphrase derived from the popular song 'Let's all go down the Strand (and have a banana)'. The English girl burst out laughing, and Kyasht stamped her little foot angrily, crying 'Phyllis, you encourage dem!'[1]

Another incident such as one would hardly expect to see today at the Royal Ballet was when Pavlova was dropped by her partner Mordkin at the Palace Theatre; she jumped up and clouted him smartly across the face, the audience roared (with delight?), the curtain was dropped, the bioscope switched on. Formerly a prima ballerina with Diaghilev, Pavlova had come from Russia in 1910 to freelance in England with a little company of eight dancers and the unhappy Mordkin. She re-joined Diaghilev temporarily during the spectacular Coronation Year season, and was for years thereafter a great favourite here, appearing mostly on the halls. The impression she made is conveyed by MR GEORGE ROBEY: 'One night I stood at the back of the stalls at the Palace Theatre. The whole house was cheering and encoring Anna Pavlova. The only person who was silent was a tall, elderly man standing at my elbow. I turned to him. To my amazement tears were streaming down his face. I said: "Excuse me, sir, but that dance appears to have strangely moved you." He replied: "When I see such perfection of art mated

---

[1] *My Dancing Days*, by Phyllis Bedells (Phoenix House).

with such radiance and beauty, applause is beyond me, I can only shed tears – tears for all the beauty and happiness I have missed in my own long, long, life.'' And he turned and drifted away.'

The tenderness of this Robey memory may surprise people to whom his name is synonymous with music-hall gags and guffaws. The 'Prime Minister of Mirth' was in actual fact a sensitive soul and *Scrapbook*'s microphone caught him in that mood; but in the wink of an eye his sense of the comic returned, especially when we asked him to recall the very first Royal Command Variety Performance, in 1912. 'This miracle,' as he called it, happened at the Palace Theatre, and in a social-history sense it *was* a miracle for royalty to attend a music-hall, not incognito as the late King had done, but with all the strict ceremonial surrounding King George V and Queen Mary. This was terrifying to the buffoons, as Mr Robey recalls:

'Some of my colleagues were overwhelmed by the *solemnity* of the occasion, not to mention having suffered at the hands of the censor who went through our rehearsal with a fine comb. And what, you may ask, did George Robey do? Out of my repertoire I selected one character because I thought the royal family would know him best, for in their travels they had met him

Bertram Park   *Radio Times Hulton Library*

Great stars who have broadcast in the *Scrapbooks*, recalling from their very different angles the entertainment before 1914: Tamara Karsavina, of the Diaghilev Ballet, here seen in *Firebird*, and (*right*) Florrie Forde, of music-hall and pantomime

almost every day – a Mayor – the Mayor of Mudcumdyke. I determined to break the ice and put him over in my usual manner. One joke I was pressed to cut out, but I refused, and lo and behold when the joke in question came the King and Queen laughed as heartily as everybody else. I'll tell you what it is now we're all together. During my talk as the Mayor, I said: "Now they've made me Mayor they've given me a lovely house, not much furniture in it but it's all right – I mean, we hadn't got a bed at first but we soon obviated that . . . took the front door down and put it on a couple of trestles . . . very comfortable . . . true, it was a little bit draughty round the letter box. . . .'

Harry Tate, Vesta Tilley, Harry Lauder, Little Tich, Pavlova, Florrie Forde, Wilkie Bard, and a host of other stars appeared at the Royal Command Performance but NOT the highest paid *comédienne* and darling of the people, the queen of the *risqué*, Marie Lloyd. Too *risqué* perhaps. The joke that went round the town was that Miss Lloyd would retaliate by getting up a Popular Demand Performance.

After the First World War the music-hall was to decline in the face of the rising cinema and radio; the Royal Command Performance of 1911 marked a zenith when its stars were national idols and its songs swept the country – sentimental songs and slapdash songs, Harry Lauder's 'Roamin' in the Gloamin' and Harry Champion's 'Boiled Beef and Carrots' (so popular that working men's cafes advertised 'a Harry Champion, 1s'); and who could beat the lusty ebullience of the busty MISS FLORRIE FORDE's mock-sobstuff in waltz-time? –

> *Oh! Oh! Antonio,*
> *He's gone away!*
> *Left me alone-e-oh,*
> *All on me own-e-oh . . .*[1]

– which years later she belted out in the *Scrapbook* studio at a volume guaranteed to knock microphones for six; then, looking over her shoulder at the years before 1914, she told how every summer she would break away from the music-halls and appear for a spell at Douglas, Isle of Man: 'In the ballroom at the Derby Castle I used to sing to them, between the dances. I've seen 7,000 lads and lassies fra' Lancashire and Yorkshire dancing there in their wakes week – imagine 7,000 doing the old waltzes! It was a grand sight.'

The waltz was in immense vogue. There was one song in marching time which Miss Forde tried out at Douglas, not with any great success; it originated in 1912 when Jack Judge, a music-hall singer appearing at Stalybridge, took a bet that he could write a song and sing it there within twenty-four hours – and won his bet with 'It's a Long Way to Tipperary'.

The end of a lot of things was in sight. Since the Nineties waltz-time had held sway in ballrooms and musical comedies; now came a rude revolution from America, as sensational an onslaught from the west, on its own level, as Diaghilev's from the east: ragtime. MR J. B. PRIESTLEY was in his teens when he first heard it during a visit to the Leeds Empire music-hall: 'Suddenly I discovered it glaring and screaming at me. The syncopated frenzy was something quite new. Shining with sweat, the ragtimers almost hung over the footlights, defying us to resist the rhythm, and drumming us into another kind of life in which anything might happen. I believe that the popular song can be prophetic. It can suddenly reveal great and terrible events to come. Out of this ragtime came fragmentary outlines of a menace to old Europe,

[1] 'Oh, oh, Antonio', by C. W. Murphy and Dan Lipton (Francis, Day and Hunter Ltd.).

170

the domination of America, the emergence of Africa, the end of confidence and any feeling of security, the nervous excitement, the frenzy of modern times.'

> *. . . And if you care to hear the Swanee River*
> *Played in ragtime –*
> *Come on and hear, come on and hear*
> *Alexander's Ragtime Band!*[1]

'It was at a matinee at the London Hippodrome in 1912 that we first sang that song,' says one of the American invaders, MR PETER BERNARD. 'On the same bill was Leoncavallo, conducting his short opera *I Zingari*, and I remember him standing in the wings and listening to the ragtime and he just couldn't believe his ears. In America we'd had it for years; coon-shouting we called it when I was a boy. Then we had a visitor from England, Albert de Courville, the producer. He wanted to take a ragtime troupe to England. So he came to Coney Island, the Blackpool of New York, where there were any number of cabarets. I used to work there. So did Schnozzle Durante and Al Jolson, before ever they became known as film stars, and Irving Berlin. Mr de Courville brought seven of us to England, and with Melville Gideon (later to find great fame as pianist and composer for the *Co-Optimists*) we had our début here as the American Ragtime Octet, singing:

> *OH, ev'ry ev'ning hear him sing –*
> *It's the cutest little thing,*
> *Got the cutest little swing –*
> *Hitchy Koo! H-i-tchy Koo! H-i-i-itchy KOO!*[2]

Such crazy songs played fast and loose, cutting away from old-established moods and rhythms. Ragtime was youth holding its fingers to the nose of tradition. Its vogue is particularly interesting now as one of the first tendencies of young people towards grouping themselves together, devotees of a new idiom which bewildered and appalled their elders. In truth, it wasn't 'new': ragtime had century-old negro roots in the Deep South of America. *Scrapbook* has received letters from listeners who tell of hearing ragtime in Britain much earlier in the century; one remembers a pantomime at Greenwich in 1901 with a song about:

> *Ragtime women with ragtime ways*
> *Wearing ragtime bloomers with ragtime stays . . .*

Debussy's 'Children's Suite', written in 1908, includes the famous 'Gollywog's Cakewalk', a skit on ragging. But all these bits of ragtime had been marginal; the mainstream of life had flowed to smoother rhythms in the first decade of this century, until a few American song-writers, notably Irving Berlin, sensed that the time was ripe for turning the Old World upside down, as well as the New, and they took the early negro idioms of ragtime and cast them into the highly commercial form that captured our music-halls and ballrooms from 1911–12. Among other things, the ragtime invasion was the beginning of the general Americanisation of the British way of life, with American films riding a close second.

Alongside this boisterous new music of youth came new dances – the turkey trot, the bunny

---

[1] 'Alexander's Ragtime Band', words and music by Irving Berlin (Feldman).

[2] 'Hitchy Koo!', words by L. W. Gilbert, music by F. Muir and M. Abrahams (Francis, Day and Hunter Ltd.).

Punch observes a mood of youth in the years before war, 1912–14; (*left*) revue kicks
sentimental musical comedy out of supremacy in the West End theatre; (*right*) the spirit
of ragtime, Miss Ethel Levey. And (*opposite*) . . .

hug, the chicken scramble, and another, denounced in a letter to *The Times* signed 'A Peeress':
'My grandmother has often told me of the shock she experienced on first beholding the polka,
but I wonder what she would have said had she been asked to introduce a well-brought up
girl of eighteen to the scandalous travesties of dancing which are, for the first time in my
recollection, bringing more young men to parties than are needed.' This was the tango.
George Graves called it 'not a dance but an assault'.

'Scandalous travesties' in entertainment were (and still are) reflexes of a people's deeply
changing moods; one of the most dramatic examples of this in all social history is the collapse
of the golden walls of musical comedy before ragtime's syncopated blast. With Lehár's *The
Count of Luxembourg* (340 performances) and Oscar Straus's *The Chocolate Soldier* (500) in
1911–12 there ended a fashion which since the Nineties had reflected the superficial opulence
of its time. We have seen many musical comedies since, but no such unchallenged reign of
waltzing romanticism. Now came a ribald rival: ragtime revue in the West End. The adorably
French Mlle Yvonne Arnaud sang a protest in a musical comedy *The Girl in the Taxi* at the
Lyric Theatre:

> *Horrible dances one gallops or prances*
> *In false time –*
> *Where is the measure of passionate pleasure*
> *Like waltz time?*

172

Punch

The tango craze in the ballroom, as 'letters in the papers from amateur social reformers would have us imagine it' (i.e. shocking)

– but the zippy American Miss Ethel Levey, hobble-skirted, with an osprey in her hair and a bracelet round her black-silken ankle, retorted in *Hullo Ragtime!* at the Hippodrome:

> *Farewell to thee, dreamy waltz,*
> *Go right on your way . . .*

Ragtime revue, a swift-moving miscellany of saucy sketches, spiced with ragtime music and exuberant dances, was the West End rage in the last years of peace. Even at the Empire, sacred old home of variety and ballet, half the bill was now given over to a revue, *Everybody's Doing It* ('Doing what? The Turkey trot!' chortled comedian Robert Hale). The men who wrote these new-style shows were English; one was the novelist Max Pemberton. The ragtime style had come from America but once here it was seized with delight by Young England. They enjoyed the new pep, the break with tradition. Out went the old romanticism; in came topicality. This event-song was banged out in *Hullo Ragtime!* –

> *That Ragtime Suffragette –*
> *Ragging with bombshells and ragging with bricks,*
> *Hagging and nagging in politics –*
> *That Ragtime Suffragette –*
> *She's no household pet.*

173

Oh, mercy, while her husband's waiting home to dine,
She's ragging up and down the line, shouting –
Votes, votes, votes, votes, votes for women!
Oh! That Ragtime Suffragette![1]

*　　　*　　　*

Mrs Pankhurst and her followers stepped up their militancy viciously in 1912–13. Public and private buildings were burned down, the Rokeby Venus in the National Gallery was slashed, bombs exploded, telephone wires were cut, Kew's orchid-houses were destroyed, hundreds of false fire-alarms were given. This anarchy only turned some sympathisers against the militants and strengthened the Government's determination not to be coerced. Under the 'Cat and Mouse' Act the authorities were able to liberate a hunger-striker before she died and re-arrest her as soon as she was fit again, and so *ad infinitum*. The most sombre incident has been described in *Scrapbook for 1913* by MR ST JOHN ERVINE, the playwright:

'At that time I was a young journalist in London. The Editor of the *Daily Chronicle* heard that I had never seen the Derby, and he asked me to go down and give my impressions of this religious ritual. I started off, not very interested because I never have taken the slightest interest in racing, though I'm very fond of animals, especially horses; but I went down to Epsom and I decided that instead of going on the fashionable side of the course, where the grandstand was, I would go on the common part; and I went across to the rails where I found myself standing beside a rather agitated woman. She was very pale and thin, and quite clearly was in a state of mental agitation. I couldn't think why she was there at all. She didn't look the sort of woman you'd see at a race meeting. I paid no particular heed to her; I just stood beside her and looked up the course and saw the horses coming down from Tattenham Corner like express trains. Suddenly this woman went under the rails and as they came up she flung herself in front of the King's horse, Amner, and there was a rather horrid scene. She was knocked on the ground, the horse fell, the jockey went over its head – he might have been killed. The amazing fact about it is that practically nobody on the course saw it, except a few people round where the incident happened. The woman was brought out. She was nearly dead. I don't think anything particular happened to the horse except a few cuts and bruises. The jockey, as far as I could see, was not hurt at all.'

The woman was Emily Davison, M.A., a suffragette. She was fatally injured. Mr St John Ervine rushed back to the *Daily Chronicle* office: 'This was what journalists called a scoop, and a very big scoop. I'd never had one before and I've never had one since, but the whole thing was rather horrible. At that time Mrs Pankhurst and Christabel Pankhurst were having an immense influence on middle-class women, especially young women, and "the Cause" apparently had worked upon Emily Davison's mind to the extent that she was determined to do something that would make the Government enfranchise women. Why she should think that they would do that just because she'd got herself killed on the race-course I don't know, but many of these girls did rather go off their balance.'

Such methods were deprecated by the non-militant suffragettes, the 'constitutionalists'. In 1913 the National Union of Women's Suffrage Societies held a great peaceful pilgrimage

---

[1] 'Hullo Ragtime!', words by Max Pemberton and Albert de Courville, music by Louis A. Hirsch (Feldman).

On the ground at the Derby lies the suffragette Miss Emily Davison, in a white dress; one of the watchers standing at the railing is Mr St John Ervine

(*Below*) They used CND-methods long before the nuclear age: a suffragette 'prison parade'. The demonstrators carry wands tipped with broad arrows

to London, a forerunner of the Aldermaston marches of many years later. DR ELSIE TOMS, of St Albans, writes to *Scrapbook*: 'The pilgrimage came from the farthest corners of the country and finally everyone converged to a demonstration of 80,000 in Hyde Park. One contingent came through St Albans and my mother put up two of the ladies for the night, rather to my father's annoyance for he was against granting women the vote, always excepting his wife and daughter; he felt that *his* females could vote wisely but not other women! The speakers in Hyde Park included Dame Millicent Fawcett, Eleanor Rathbone, Mrs Philip Snowden, Maud Royden, and Susan Lawrence. I still laugh over one incident. My father was worried lest there should be riots in London and when he found that I had gone up to join the march he followed by the next train and looked for me among the thousands of demonstrators forming up behind the British Museum. He failed to find me, but some bold spirit thrust a banner into his hand and for several miles he marched through London carrying a banner advocating a cause in which he did not believe, while he searched for me! When the great crowd in Hyde Park dispersed we met; he was very forgiving and treated me to tea with another girl I had picked up on the march. It was obvious that the demonstration had been an eye-opener to those who thought that the suffragettes were all "wild women".'

Of course they weren't. It is too easy to generalize. Nor were all young people ragtime-mad. New trends were slow to spread. But a fascinating aspect of the years 1910–14 is that the young generation (up to, say twenty-five or thirty years of age) were exposed to powerful rising influences which excited them especially; they were not a self-consciously isolated group as teenagers can be now, but they began to take their own line more than the previous generation which had generally followed where Victorian Papa and Mama led them. This tendency has since gone much further. Its emergence on the eve of the Great War has a terrible poignancy in view of the fate that awaited that generation.

Youth sniffed an exhilarating tang in the air: to be young alongside so many expanding forces, to run excitedly out of the house to watch an aeroplane crawling across the sky 'like clockwork angels of the blue' as G. K. Chesterton put it, to shout 'Votes for Women' or nurse a secret passion for ragtime, to share the fledgling days of the gramophone and the motor – it was all exciting then in a simple way, a naïve way it may seem now compared with our astronaut-and-computer age. Who in the 1960s would think of writing a song to a telephone girl?

> *Kitty, Kitty, isn't it a pity*
> *That you're wasting so much time*
> *With your lips close to the telephone*
> *When they might be close to mine?*[1]

And motoring was now out of its childhood and into its muscling-up adolescence. The affluent young man who could afford £175 for one of Mr W. R. Morris's new bull-nosed Morris Oxfords was no end of a dog. This car, first marketed 1913, had a slogan '50 miles an hour, 50 miles a gallon'.[2] Morris was turning out some 350 a year at Oxford, and Austin was stepping up production of his cars at Birmingham to over £500,000 worth a year. For the less affluent there were now motor-bikes in many varieties. The number in this country rose from about

[1] Song from revue *Hullo Tango!*, 1913–14, written and composed by Harry Gifford, Huntley Trevor, Tom Mellor, and A. J. Lawrence (Francis, Day and Hunter Ltd.).

[2] The first Morris Cowley was not in production until 1915.

The Last Years of Peace

25,000 in 1909 to nearly 124,000 five years later. Some of the young ladies were even taken for rides on the back of motor-bikes by young gentlemen. Some were known as flappers.

Flapper is a pre-war term, not post-1918, as is commonly thought, though it gained greater currency in the Twenties. As early as 1907 the novelist Ian Hay wrote of 'the years of flapperdom', and by 1914 in *The Passing Show* revue Elsie Janis was singing:

> *Florrie was a flapper, she was dainty, she was dapper,*
> *And her dancing was the limit, or the lid.*
> *When her dainty skirt she'd swish up*
> *They say she shocked the Bishop.*
>   *I don't believe she did it,*
>   *I don't believe she did it,*
> *But he told the Missis Bishop that she did.*[1]

[1] 'Florrie was a Flapper', words by Arthur Wimperis, music by Herman Finck (reproduced by permission of Francis, Day and Hunter Ltd.).

Punch, 1912

The cartoon as a record of social change: the girl in the 'daring' one-piece costume is saying 'Excuse me—you probably don't know, as you've only just arrived—but, according to the regulations of this silly place, you mustn't walk across the beach without a garment that covers you from head to foot'

In town there were 'young' fashions. A young man preferred the clean shave to Father's whiskers, the new safety razor to the old 'cut-throat' (Gillette had produced his first safety blade in 1904). Shoes were fancied instead of boots, sock with bright colours, the trilby rather than the topper. And we mustn't forget those curious pieces of white cloth buttoned round the ankles, known as spats (spatterdashes). They may seem ludicrous now but they looked very dashing then. Tight ankle-length skirts were ludicrous, too, for it was practically impossible for a woman, so hobbled, to jump on a bus, but at any rate they were a few inches further from the ground than hemlines had been for centuries, and thus more hygienic than the old pavement-sweepers. The pouter-pigeon figure of generations past was disappearing along with its most brutal corseting. And the shedding of some of the layers of petticoats had now gone so far that it was celebrated in this illuminating event-song which tells social-history in the saucy way of 1910:

Mother told me, so did Aunty,
So did people ev'rywhere,
Proper folk were never scanty
In the way of underwear!
Heathen dress was slight and shady
But they wished to have me note,
Any perfect British lady
ALWAYS wore a petticoat!

Refrain:

Petticoats for women
Once were full of grace;
Some of them had flounces,
Some of them had lace;
Then the fashions altered,
Don't know why or how,
So we don't wear our petticoats now![1]

A marked increase in games for girls was noted in *Tatler* (1909): 'The flapper brigade is a force (at golf) which grows every year.' On many sides there were breaks with restriction and taboo, in more senses than the physical. Bernard Shaw's six-letter word in *Pygmalion* (1914) – 'Walk! Not bloody likely, I'm going in a taxi!' – made a sensation, but it was the rejoinder from another character in the play that drove the point home: 'I really can't get used to the young ways.'

New freedoms were beginning to appear *before* the First World War. What the war did was to accelerate existing emancipations swiftly towards a totally different scale of values in the Twenties. The term 'birth control', for example, was first printed in an American journal *The Woman Rebel* in June 1914. It was coined by Mrs Margaret Sanger, American advocate of contraception. The ignorance which had so lamentably smothered this subject in Victorian times, whatever the Queen may have thought about it (she had nine children), continued to a great extent in Britain, but the enlightenment sown in Victoria's reign by such victimized

---

[1] Sung by Gracie Leigh in *The Quaker Girl*; words by Adrian Ross and Percy Greenbank, music by Lionel Monckton (Chappell).

pioneers as Charles Bradlaugh and Mrs Besant was slowly breaking through. One of the most significant statistics of the period covered in this book is that the birth-rate (England and Wales) tumbled down from 29.6 per 1,000 of population in 1896 to 23.8 in 1914, despite fromidable opposition to birth control; in 1905 the Bishop of London denounced it as a 'gigantic evil', and in 1908 the Lambeth Conference of Anglican Bishops called on all Christians to stop 'the use of all artificial means of restriction, as demoralising to character and hostile to national welfare.' By 1914 a government enquiry found that contraception was common in the upper classes. Information on methods was passed by word of mouth and from class to class; there were a few books and pamphlets under the counter. The whole subject was odiously hush-hush. This was the situation when war came – and wars always put special stresses on social conventions towards sex, free love, etc. Sensational newspapers predicted a crop of 'war babies' (illegitimate children). Dr Marie Stopes resolved to write a book because 'I felt that psychologically the time was ripe to give the public what appeared to me a sounder, more wholesome, and more complete knowledge of the intimate sex requirements of *normal* and healthy people than anywhere available.' Her famous *Married Love* came out in 1918.[1]

*   *   *

The first great Picture Palace boom came just before the Great War. *Scrapbook* research has given us a rather startling index to the rise and fall of this form of entertainment: we have noted earlier that in 1906 London had one cinema (Colonel Bromhead's), by 1914 the number had soared in the LCC area to 308, but by 1965 in the same area it had sunk to just under half as many: no doubt the consequence of television. Even in the 1930s, usually regarded as the golden age of the cinema, there were fewer cinemas in London than the 308 in 1914, but many of these early picture palaces were 'flea-pits' improvised in old buildings.

£13 millions of capital was invested in British cinemas and studios by 1914, but our reference to this subject must be in unabashed sentiment rather than in cold statistics, for to take a girl to the pictures was yet another of those experiences that gave life a new tang, especially for the young – a spice of daring in the unaccustomed and exotic semi-darkness, while everything that appeared on the screen was deliciously fresh to the unjaded eye, in its excitement and above all its *fun*. Oh, to be with Mabel now that Keystone Cops are there, the cowboys on the trail, and all's well in a flickering world!

The new mythology was creating its gods and goddesses; in place of the anonymity of the brief films of a few years back there now appeared the star system, with longer and sometimes better films . . . Bronco Bill the cowboy, John Bunny the fatty comic, and the girl soon to be 'The World's Sweetheart' – of whom MR ADOLPH ZUKOR, the famous American producer, has told *Scrapbook*: 'I was convinced that the cinema had got to employ and exploit stars, that this was the one sure way to lift it from a peepshow level. Mary Pickford, twenty years old, had been known in her earlier films as "The Bioscope Girl". I said to her "Miss Pickford, I will put your name on the films and advertise you, and pay you 20,000 dollars a year."'

In 1913 not more than 15 per cent of all films shown here were British. The Americanization of the British way of life was opposed by a trickle of home-grown films, usually with a

---

[1] *The Birth Controllers*, by Peter Fryer (Secker and Warburg) gives a full account of one of the most capricious sides of human behaviour.

Punch

The effects-man behind the cinema screen, 1913. The showman is saying: 'Ere, I say, it be 'orses 'ooves, not 'orns or 'ail-storms'

distinctive English flavour: they favoured treatments of popular novels by Hall Caine, Marie Corelli, Rider Haggard, and, of course, Dickens. It was a pity that no British producer spotted the cinematic potentialities of that little Cockney named Charlie Chaplin who had been appearing on the halls; during his tour of America in a show called *A Night at an English Music-hall* the Keystone Company snapped him up for Hollywood at 150 dollars a week, and his first comedy picture to reach England, *Making a Living*, was shown here in June 1914.

Cecil Hepworth, the foremost British producer, was featuring stage top-liners (for example, Forbes Robertson in *Hamlet*) but like the Americans he also made his own film stars; one of them, MISS IVY CLOSE, ex-*Daily Mirror* beauty queen (and mother of present-day producer, Ronald Neame), says: 'Alma Taylor and Chrissie White were already with the Hepworth Company when I joined in 1912. My first picture was *The Lady Shalott* with a cast of two and forty extras. As the Lady I floated down the Thames in a sort of gondola while the cameraman stood on the bank turning the handle. When the director wanted extras he rang up the Gaiety Theatre and asked if the girls and boys of the chorus would like to be on the pictures; they jumped at it for six shillings a day.'

A deep impression was made on the public by 'actuality' (as with TV today): films made on the Shackleton and Scott expeditions to the Antarctic did something that had never been possible before, they showed just what life and non-life looks like at the other end of the world, and, above all, they told the real stories of two national idols, bringing them close to Everyman for the price of a seat at the Picture Palace or a lecture at the Town Hall. To look at Antarctica, so terrible, so beautiful, was a revelation, for this had been the 'Unknown Continent' at the beginning of the century, since when had come a dozen years of spectacular adventures – the Heroic Age of polar exploration it has been called – and heroic it was in terms of hand-to-hand fighting against implacable Nature by men stretching endurance to the limit in their quest for the coveted Poles. Peary had first taken the North Pole for the USA, fairly easily, but the South Pole was a far tougher proposition, hidden behind mountains and protected by the worst weather in the world. Amundsen won it for Norway, closely followed by Scott. Shackleton never reached the Pole, but the public hero-worshipped him for the boldness of his explorations and for his own appealing nature, combining adventurer with mystic: a superb leader who could bring his men back from terrible sufferings and say 'We had pierced the veneer of outside things. . . . We had seen God in his splendour, heard the text that Nature renders. We had reached the naked soul of man.'

Such saga-figures of the Heroic Age excited the public, and especially the young generation, rather as do the American and Russian astronauts nowadays (perhaps more). They too were probing the unknown, at high risk, and they were surrounded by strong nationalistic sentiments – but, unlike the explorers of space whose personal endeavour is closely dependent on their use of complex technologies, the first men to penetrate the ends of the world were on their own: it was indeed hand-to-hand fighting. Apart from cinematography, the technological developments which had begun a revolution in the civilized world – wireless, motorcar, aeroplane – played such small parts in the conquest of the polar regions that it is worth summarizing them as a measure of the first baby steps of science in that direction:[1]

First, *flying*: In 1897 a Swedish balloonist, Andrée, tried to fly from Spitzbergen to the North Pole. He disappeared. A third of a century later, in 1930, skeletons were found 480 miles from

[1] I am indebted for help in research here to the Marconi Company, the Austin Motor Company, and the Scott Polar Research Institute at Cambridge. L.B.

the Pole, together with Andrée's equipment, including negatives from which good aerial pictures were obtained. In 1902 Scott, on his first expedition, used a captive balloon for reconnaissance; when his ship *Discovery* reached the barrier of ice skirting the Antarctic continent he went up to 1,800 feet and surveyed the ice rising towards the south. Shackleton (a young member of that expedition) ascended to take aerial photographs. Scott wrote: 'As I swayed about in what appeared a very inadequate basket and gazed down on the diminishing figures below I felt some doubt as to whether I had been wise in my choice.' After this, no expedition made use of flying; the Australian, Douglas Mawson, intended to take an aeroplane on his Antarctic exploration of 1911–14 but it crashed on a trial before his ship *Aurora* sailed.

Second, *the motor-car*: Shackleton was the first to try it, using an Arrol-Johnstone car with a 12 horse-power engine, on his 1907–9 expedition. After brief, hectic trips at 15 miles an hour over the ice, the car proved inadequate. The wheels, though shod with wood and steel projections, lacked the necessary traction. The machine was abandoned. It had proved that a petrol engine could be used in Antarctic temperatures – but not car wheels. So the next step was the caterpillar tractor: in 1910 Scott, en route to his tragic venture south, took in the *Terra Nova* three Wolseley motor-sledges so equipped. They ran near base only, then broke down. Scott wrote: 'The dream of great help from the machines is dead.' Next, Shackleton took a 'motor-crawler' on his 1914 *Endurance* expedition but it was abandoned after the ship foundered, crushed by the Antarctic floes, leaving the men on the ice to get back to civilisation as best they could.

Third, *wireless*: the first explorers to reach the Poles, Peary and Amundsen, had no wireless on their expeditions. Nor did Scott: the news that his party had perished on their return from the Pole took over a year to reach the inhabited world. Later, in 1914, Shackleton's attitude to wireless was characteristic of the man and his times: he took no transmitter in *Endurance*, only a receiver, partly because he doubted a transmitter's utility in the far south and partly because he was a rugged individualist who dreaded that wireless inter-communication would put him at the beck and call of interfering authorities in London. His wife once said he was 'an eagle who couldn't be confined to a barnyard', and an eagle is a lone bird. When the *Endurance* was caught fatally in the ice, Shackleton, isolated with his men far from land, may well have wished for a transmitter to summon help; it could have cut short nearly a year of awful, if heroic, struggles. Admittedly, the type of transmitter then used in such small ships was unlikely to be heard from a point so far south, but radio experts now believe, in the light of modern knowledge, that there was an outside chance of a signal getting through.

The only effective use of wireless telegraphy in polar exploration before the First World War was by Mawson, in 1911–14, when he linked his base on the Antarctic continent with a station he had set up on Macquarie Island 1,000 miles away, which in turn relayed messages on to Tasmania. For the first time a polar explorer was not isolated. Receiving time signals, Mawson was able to calculate with precision his exact longitude. He also investigated the effect of aurora on wireless communication.

The marginal use of various new scientific aids by the great men of the Heroic Age compares dramatically with the 1958 expedition led by Vivian Fuchs whose caterpillar-tracked Snocats drove right across the Antarctic continent, in touch by radio all the way, aided by aircraft, and hailed by a Press reception when they paused at the South Pole! – a far cry from the experiences of Amundsen and Scott. Yet perhaps it was the very fact that the pioneer explorers relied so much on themselves alone, rather than on machines, that made them outsize humans in popular

'By motor-car to the South Pole – how Lieutenant Shackleton will invade the Antarctic'
– so runs the *Sphere*'s heading to their artist's drawing, 1907. 'The expedition', it says,
'will be aided by the use of a motor-car specially built for the task at the Arrol-Johnstone
works, Paisley. Great hopes are being entertained, but it is recognized that its employment
is an experiment and the chance of success is far from being centred in any such novel
means of locomotion.' In fact, Shackleton reached in 1909 the then 'furthest south' (97
miles from the Pole), on foot.

> we shall stick it out
> to the end but we
> are getting weaker of
> course and the end
> cannot be far.
> It seems a pity but
> I do not think I can
> write more —
>   R. Scott
> Last Entry —
> For God's sake look
> after our people

The last entry in Captain Scott's diary, written in his tent in the Antarctic

An experiment in mechanization and a caterpillar-tracked forerunner of tanks in the First World War: a motorized sledge made by Wolseley for Captain Scott's Antarctic expedition of 1910–12

esteem. The *New Statesman* made this comment (January, 1914), eloquent of moral attitudes just before the First World War:

'If it be true that "we live by admiration, hope and love", it is also true that everyday modern life, with its substitution of machinery for effort, its worship of comfort, and its highly artificial conditions, does not effectively display some of the virtues which we do best to admire. The modern world has a real need for heroisms from outside itself; a need often catered for in crude ways, from the football arena to the cinematograph hall, but genuine none the less. The polar explorers have supplied this need on its highest plane. Nothing in human nobility can outdo some features of the Scott epic; and despite all the rabid and nauseous sentimentalizing over it, it must have left a deep, abiding, and ennobling impression on every thoughtful mind in the nation. Nor does Scott's case stand alone. Can anyone doubt the value of Sir Ernest Shackleton's lectures to the thousands of British schoolboys who heard him so gladly? The very bareness of the polar stage, the failure of machinery, the stark pitting of humanity against the elemental forces of Nature, lend a unique eloquence to these examples of courage, self-devotion, endurance, loyalty, discipline and mutual help.'

On the mind of youth, especially, such qualities had a powerful influence, qualities very soon to be found on a large scale in the mood with which that generation went to war, a mixture of loyalty and lightheartedness. It must be almost inexplicable to youth today that the British marched cheerfully into a war now seen as a horrible disaster. Some of the reasons behind the mood have been indicated earlier: the mist of unconcern over international affairs bred an over-sanguine spirit ('It'll all be over by Christmas'); the excitements of the motor-bike and ragtime era, and the adolescent aeroplane time, all gave the peacetime air a flavour of excitement for the young, and it was contagious, and God knows how many lads were to mistake war for yet another excitement until illusions were blown up for ever in France. Most of all, patriotism and service to others were powerfully impressed on boys before the war; you could see it in the new Boy Scouts, or by turning the pages of the *Boy's Own Paper*, or in the enormous success of Arthur Mee's *Children's Encyclopaedia* with its glowing stress on good deeds and national heroes from Drake to Scott.

Scott's story was absolute tragedy and complete failure, in one sense, yet when at last in 1913 came news that he had reached the Pole in 1912 only to find the Norwegian flag planted there shortly before by Amundsen, and on the trek back the polar party of five had perished, the influence of this story on youth was anything but tragic. They read of Dr Wilson tending his frost-bitten and starvation-sick companions and writing in his diary: 'This is the most fascinating ideal I think I have ever imagined, to become entirely careless of your own soul or body in looking after the welfare of others.' Oates had walked out into the blizzard to become a nation's hero, and Scott's last letters to his wife, found in the tent beside his body, provided a text for a generation itself destined for hard self-sacrifice: 'What lots and lots I could tell you of this journey! How much better it has been than lounging in too great comfort at home.'

This was the note which came to some of the ragtiming youth of Britain as an inspiration – and there's nothing incongruous in putting their fun and their idealism side by side, for this is the essence of youth, or should be.

Turn next to Hendon aerodrome on a summer evening not long before the war and you will find a scene filled with the 'modern' details which appealed strongly to that generation. It is described by the enterprising CLAUDE GRAHAME-WHITE: 'Twenty or thirty thousand people used to flock out to Hendon to see the Grahame-White Circus, as some people called it. When I first bought the field at Hendon it was nothing but farm-land. I laid out an aerodrome with grandstands, car-park, and restaurants, and our flying meetings and demonstrations there became great social functions. One of the planes I built was the Grahame-White Flying Charabanc, with which I announced that I would take up seven passengers. Such a load was unheard of, and many "experts" predicted that I would never get off the ground, for the engine was only 100 horse-power. The flight was successfully made not with seven, but with nine passengers. It's true that some of the passengers were simply perched on the wings, there wasn't room for them all in the cockpit, but they went up and came down safely. We also did the first parachute demonstrations from any aeroplane in flight.[1] Mr Newell, the chap who dropped, didn't have his parachute strapped on his back as they do nowadays, he simply folded it up on his knee haphazard. He sat on the undercarriage and at 3,000 feet he was shoved off with a hefty kick from behind.'

Mr Grahame-White adds (and, remember, this was only weeks before the war came): 'At night the planes went up stunting, their wings festooned with flashing electric lights. We even had demonstrations of bomb-dropping at a dummy battleship on the aerodrome, using bags of flour as bombs. But most people of my acquaintance regarded a flying machine as unlikely to be of any use in war, or indeed to influence in any way the future of transport.'[2]

Wilbur Wright said later: 'We thought we were introducing into the world an invention which would make further wars practically impossible.' If there was one thing the pre-war world believed in it was *Progress*. Engineering, science and medicine were striding forward. Poverty was retreating. The Liberal Government had begun to lift the undernourished classes out of the ditch. The widespread malnutrition revealed when so many Boer War volunteers were found to be medically unfit was responding to social reform and better knowledge: a milestone here was when the Cambridge biochemist Sir Frederick Gowland Hopkins showed that the food factors he called 'vitamins' are essential to health. (Incidentally, if Captain Scott had known about vitamin C the endurance of his Polar party would have been greater and they might have come back.) One way and another, the nation's health was progressing: the United Kingdom death-rate which had been 20.7 per 1,000 of population at the beginning of the Nineties had declined to 14.9 by 1910–12. It is now (1965) 11.5.

'Progress' took its most significant step, so far as its ultimate effects are concerned, when Rutherford, researching at Manchester University in 1911, discovered the nuclear structure of the atom.[3] Earlier, he had written: 'If it were ever possible to control at will the rate of disintegration of radioactive elements an enormous amount of energy could be obtained from a small quantity of matter.'[4]

These highly technical observations were not 'popular news'; few people heard of them. But H. G. Wells did. He wrote a novel of the future called *The World Set Free*, an ironical title for us living now in that future; by 1954, said Wells, men would have built an atomic engine,

[1] In Britain; the first drop in the world was made by Capt. Albert Berry at St Louis, USA, 1912, from an aeroplane; drops from balloons dated from 1797 when Garnerin parachuted over Paris.

[2] The Government had started building a few planes at Farnborough, for the new Royal Flying Corps, notably the B.E.2, soon to become famous in the war. A. V. Roe was making his Avro 504, similarly to have extensive use soon.

[3] Lord Rutherford (1871–1937), New Zealander; while professor of physics at McGill University, Canada, from 1898, did research into radioactivity; in 1907 went to Manchester, in 1919 to Cambridge where he led a team on nuclear physics in the 1930s.

[4] In his book *Radioactivity*, 1904.

replacing all old sources of power. The atom would be used to drive aeroplanes. There would be invented what Wells called 'the atomic bomb'. He described an aviator dropping the first one – 'He hoisted the bomb over the side', so small was it. But when it exploded: 'It was like looking down upon the crater of a small volcano.' Thereafter Wells saw the whole world flaring into a monstrous phase of destruction: 'Power after power about the armed globe sought to anticipate attack by aggression. . . By the spring of 1959 from nearly two hundred centres roared the unquenchable crimson conflagrations of the atomic bombs, the flimsy fabric of the world's credit had vanished, industry was completely disorganized and every city, every thickly populated area was starving or trembled on the verge of starvation.' This was the extraordinary prophecy Wells published early in 1914. He went on to argue that only when men recoiled from world-disaster would they meet to create a republican World State, realizing that 'The old tendencies of human nature, suspicion, jealousy, particularism and belligerency, were incompatible with the monstrous destructive power of the new appliances the inhuman logic of science had produced.'[1]

The lines with which Rupert Brooke greeted the 1914 war faced the facts of life in a very different way:

> *Now, God be thanked Who has matched us with His hour,*
> *And caught our youth, and wakened us from sleeping . . .*

. . . which is often assumed today to have been merely a romantic attitude, but it was actually based on a young man's leftish dislike for the rich materialism which 'progress' had bestowed on some sections of society ('I'm always on the side of the strikers!' he once said); Brooke longed for a crusade which would be better than 'lounging in too great comfort at home' – Captain Scott's last words had greatly stirred many young men. And behind the romantic poet that posterity sees across the years there also stands the man of gaiety that his close friends knew. As a last memory of the last days of peace *Scrapbook* turns to this other profile, for here is a great deal of the spirit of his generation, its exuberance and love of homeland. One of those friends, the actress MISS CATHLEEN NESBITT, tells us that 'Rupert had what he called "a tearing hunger to do and do and *do* things."' Early in 1914 he went on a world tour. In Mataiea, a Pacific island, he was overtaken by homesickness and wrote a poem about 'the things I have loved' far away at home, then came back via America, preceded by a letter to Miss Nesbitt, telling how he longed to sight Plymouth from his ship: 'Plymouth – was there ever so sweet and droll a sound? – Drake's Plymouth, English Western Plymouth, city where men speak softly and things are sold for shillings and not for dollars, and there is love and beauty and old houses, beyond which are little fields, very green, bounded by small piled walls of stone, and behind them the brown and black-splintered haunted moor.'

Miss Nesbitt continues: 'He came home to that wonderful cloudless June of 1914, quite dizzy, he said, with the thoughts of all he wanted to do. "I want to see 1,000 plays and walk 1,000 miles and kiss 1,000 girls and write 1,000 poems." We went to everything from Chekhov to the newest revue – he had a passion for ragtime. He declared that "Hitchy Koo!" was the silliest and most delicious tune he'd ever heard. But he never could stay for long in a city. He would suddenly disappear with a rucksack and a book of poems in his pocket for a week's tramping. He was always eager to communicate his enjoyment of things. He once went to a village post-office in the middle of a walking tour and sent me a telegram: *Cathleen Nesbitt,*

[1] *The World Set Free* by H. G. Wells (Macmillan).

Apollo Theatre, London. I say, have you realized how good John Milton is? He brought to soldiering the same zest that he brought to everything. He was enchanted to find himself in the Royal Naval Division. "We are Winston's pets", he wrote, "and will be in the thick of everything."'

Like many thousands, he had to leave those things he had loved:

> *. . . voices that do sing;*
> *Voices in laughter, too; and body's pain,*
> *Soon turned to peace; and the deep-panting train;*
> *Firm sands; the little dulling edge of foam*
> *That browns and dwindles as the wave goes home;*
> *And washen stones, gay for an hour; the cold*
> *Graveness of iron; moist black earthen mould;*
> *Sleep; and high places; footprints in the dew;*
> *And oaks; and brown horse-chestnuts, glossy-new;*
> *And new-peeled sticks; and shining pools on grass; –*
> *All these have been my loves. And these shall pass,*
> *Whatever passes not, in the great hour,*
> *Nor all my passion, all my prayers, have power*
> *To hold them with me through the gate of Death.*[1]

CALENDAR OF SIGNIFICANT DATES

1913

News reached England of Scott expedition tragedy in 1912.

'Cat and Mouse' Act, enabled Government to release hunger-striking suffragette prisoners and re-arrest them.

Great march of non-militant suffragettes.

Miss Emily Davison, suffragette, died after throwing herself under King's horse at the Derby.

Miss Emily Duncan, first woman magistrate, West Ham.

Strike of taxi-drivers over cost of petrol (8d a gallon).

First Morris Oxford cars produced.

Doctors reverse decision not to work Insurance Act.

Commons voted for, but Lords rejected, Home Rule for Ireland.

International Aero Exhibition, Olympia.

Aerial Navigation Act prohibited flying over certain areas, mostly of naval and military importance.

Stainless steel developed by Brearley at Sheffield.

---

[1] From *The Great Lover*, by Rupert Brooke (Sidgwick and Jackson). He died in 1915 on Greek island of Scyros, *en route* to the Dardanelles.

First fishing trawlers equipped with wireless, *Caesar* and *Othello* of Hull.
Birmingham Repertory Theatre founded by Sir Barry Jackson.
Departmental Committee on Tuberculosis recommended drastic steps to counter disease.
Unprecedented season of Russian ballet and opera, Drury Lane, with Chaliapin's English début in *Boris Godounov*; also first *Sacre du Printemps* (Stravinsky).

STAGE: *Androcles and the Lion* (Bernard Shaw); *Hullo Tango!* revue at Hippodrome.

BOOKS: *Trent's Last Case* (E. C. Bentley); *Sons and Lovers* (D. H. Lawrence); *General John Regan* (George A. Birmingham); *The Amateur Gentleman* (Jeffrey Farnol); *Sinister Street* (Compton Mackenzie); first English translation of Freud's *Interpretation of Dreams*.

SONGS: 'Friend o' Mine'; 'Kitty the Telephone Girl' and 'Get Out And Get Under' (*Hullo Tango!*); 'Hello, Hello, Who's Your Lady Friend?'; 'Hold Your Hand Out, Naughty Boy'; 'Peg o' My Heart'; 'The Sunshine Of Your Smile'; 'You Made Me Love You'; 'Up From Somerset'.

1914

Imperial wireless telegraph chain started with stations in England (Leafield and Devizes) and in Egypt and India.
George V first monarch to attend FA Cup Final.
Ulster crisis and Curragh 'mutiny'.
Gun-running at Larne for Ulster Volunteers (April 24).
Gun-running at Howth for National Volunteers (July 26).
Sir Ernest Shackleton's Antarctic expedition sailed in *Endurance*.
Britain declared war on Germany (August 4).
Despatch of British Expeditionary Force to France.
Retreat from Mons (end of August).
Battle of the Marne (September 6–12).
Battle of the Aisne (September 13–28).
Battle of Ypres (October-November).
King George V visited the Western Front.
German bombardment of English east coast towns (December 16).
First bomb dropped on Britain, at Dover (December 24).
Vaughan Williams's 'London Symphony'; Gustav Holst wrote 'The Planets'; Rutland Boughton's opera *The Immortal Hour* produced at Glastonbury.
Russian ballet and opera at Drury Lane, new productions *Prince Igor*, *Le Coq d'Or*.

STAGE: *Pygmalion* (Bernard Shaw); *The Land of Promise* (Somerset Maugham); *The Passing Show* revue at Palace.

BOOKS: *Sinister Street* cont. (Compton Mackenzie); *Quinneys'* (H. A. Vachell); *The Wisdom of Father Brown* (G. K. Chesterton); *Dubliners* (James Joyce); *The World Set Free* (H. G. Wells).

SONGS: 'Florrie Was a Flapper', 'I'll Make A Man Of You' and 'Gilbert The Filbert' (*The Passing Show*); 'Keep The Home Fires Burning'; 'Sister Susie's Sewing Shirts For Soldiers'; 'The Army Of Today's All Right'; 'They Didn't Believe Me'; 'When We've Wound Up The Watch on The Rhine' (*Business as Usual*); 'Your King and Country Want You'.

Illustrated London News

Preparing for the civil war that everyone expected: in the early summer of 1914 Ulster Volunteers are drilling in the grounds of the Duke of Abercorn's residence at Newtown Stewart

7 THE UNEXPECTED WAR

The Bells of Hell go Ting-a-Ling-a-Ling
(For You But Not For Me)[1]

'Never was a fairer prospect of peace and friendship between two sets of men bred to a profession of arms than was presented when two squadrons of the British Navy lay at their moorings surrounded by the German Fleet.'

This placid scene in 1914 was at Kiel Yachting Week, only six weeks before war came. ADMIRAL SIR WILLIAM GOODENOUGH, at that time captain of HMS *Southampton*, continues his description of the fraternization of the two mightiest navies in the world: 'The Kaiser, when visiting the British flag-ship, wore the uniform of a British Admiral of the Fleet, and said with that somewhat exaggerated phrase of speech to which he was addicted that he was proud to wear the uniform worn by Lord Nelson. His brother, Prince Henry, an honorary Admiral in our own Fleet, said: "This is what I have long hoped for, to see a portion of the British and German Fleets lying side by side in friendship in Kiel Harbour."'

[1] Soldiers' Song, First World War.

Officers and men were being freely entertained both aboard and ashore when the unexpected happened: 'The Kaiser was out in his racing yacht and was hastily recalled to be told that his great personal friend, the Archduke Ferdinand of Austria, lay murdered at Sarajevo. The Kaiser sat alone in the boat sent for him, a dramatic figure plunged in gloomy thoughts. He left Kiel for Berlin the next morning, having said little except to express his personal horror at the loss of his friend, and the necessity of affording protection to crowned heads by condign punishment.'

A Serbian youth had shot the heir to the throne of Austria–Hungary. A pebble had started an avalanche, but it was to be a month before the big rumble began to reach the ears of the common man in Britain where such people as were sensitive to political stresses were turning their eyes across the Irish Sea: private armies were openly but illegally drilling – the Ulster Volunteers (the 'Carson Army') in the north, the National Volunteers in the south – and civil war seemed likely over the Asquith government's proposal to grant home rule to all Ireland. It was not until the end of July that the big headlines began to switch attention to the continent of Europe. Austria: war on Serbia. Russia mobilizing. German ultimatum to Russia. France mobilizing. The 'balance of power', vaunted for years, was collapsing. Yet to anyone who has known the brinkmanship atmosphere of Munich in 1938, and war 1939, and Cuba 1962, to look back on 1914 is to see an unexpected war. No one, from Dad and Mum paddling at Blackpool to the Prime Minister reading telegrams at Downing Street, had any experience of what world war could mean; the Government's anxiety was deepening – yet it was by no means certain that Britain's *entente cordiale* with France would bring her in to war. It carried no promise to do so. The influential editor of the *Manchester Guardian*, C. P. Scott, was counselling neutrality; so were such men as Keir Hardie, George Lansbury, Ramsay MacDonald, and Gilbert Murray.

On the last day of July the Commons met to discuss the Irish situation, only to hear Premier Asquith push that subject aside: 'We meet,' he said, 'under conditions of gravity which are almost unparalleled in the experience of every one of us. The issues of peace and war are hanging in the balance.'

LADY OXFORD AND ASQUITH, his widow, has said: 'There was gravity and bewilderment on every face. I got up to leave the Speaker's Gallery, but the earnest Ulster ladies crowded round me.

'"Good heavens, Margot!", they cried, "what can all this mean? How fearfully dangerous! Don't you realize that the Irish will be fighting each other this very night?" Answering, as if in a dream, I said: "We are on the verge of a European war".

'That was on the Friday before the August Bank Holiday. The weather was beautiful. On Sunday I called at the house of Prince Lichnowsky, the German ambassador. I found Princess Lichnowsky lying on a green sofa with a dachshund by her side; her eyes were red and swollen from crying, and her husband was walking up and down the room, wringing his hands. He caught me by the arm. "Oh, say it is not true, there's not going to be a war! Dear, dear Mrs Asquith, can nothing be done to prevent it?" The Princess got up and looked out of the window. "Look at this beautiful, wonderful England," she said, "and to think that we are going to fight against her!" She pressed her forehead against the window-pane. I kissed her and left the room. All that day my husband and Sir Edward Grey, the Foreign Secretary, were sending cables to Germany in the hope of finding a way out.'

At dusk Grey, standing at the window of his office overlooking St James's Park, spoke his solemn epitaph: 'The lamps are going out all over Europe; we shall not see them lit again in our time.' When Germany declared war on France the British Government sent to Berlin an ultimatum demanding an assurance of respect for Belgium's neutrality, which they had both guaranteed in a treaty of 1839; but the German generals were bound to the wheel of the long-prepared Schlieffen plan which their paper-wars had already proved in theory to be the quick way to victory, i.e. through Belgium into France.

A wireless signal from London informed His Majesty's ships that the British ultimatum to Germany would expire at 11 p.m. (midnight in Berlin) on August 4. LADY OXFORD has given *Scrapbook* an intimate picture of what happened at 10 Downing Street while Germany's reply was awaited that evening: 'I went down to the Prime Minister's room. Henry was sitting at the writing-table. He looked grave. I went and stood behind his chair. "So it's all up?" I said. "Yes", he answered, "it's all up." I sat down beside him with a feeling of numbness in every limb. A messenger from the Foreign Office came in with despatch boxes. He put them down and went out. Henry remained at his writing-table. He was leaning back with a pen in his hand. What was he thinking of? . . . his sons? . . . I got up and leant my head against his; we could not speak. After dinner I joined my husband, Lord Crewe, and Sir Edward Grey, in the Cabinet Room. The night was hot; the windows were all open. We sat without speaking and listened to the distant sound of thousands and thousands of people singing and cheering outside the railings of Buckingham Palace. Other members of the Cabinet came into the room. We sat in silence while the clock on the mantelpiece ticked out the hours. Then Big Ben struck. The crowd outside seemed to be singing and cheering everywhere. But inside the Cabinet Room it was silent as dawn. I left to go to bed. No reply from Germany. We were at war.'

'Land of Hope and Glory' roared through the London streets that night, and echoed long thereafter through concerts, music-halls, and homes. It was the perfect song for the mood of jubilation in which masses of people greeted the war, as Germany's invasion of 'little Belgium' caused a swift rise in emotional temperature. But now comes a curious epilogue to our story, told earlier, of how that song was written in 1902 by Benson and Elgar.

MRS CARICE ELGAR-BLAKE says: 'When the war broke out we were living at Hampstead, and my father joined the Special Constabulary and became Inspector Elgar. It was a time of patriotic songs, and "Land of Hope and Glory" was heard everywhere, but my father felt somewhat concerned about its suitability in the new circumstances. On August 22 he wrote a letter to Mr Benson: "Could you write another stanza befitting the times we are in? The people have adopted our effort as the second National Anthem, and it does good, but the words are not quite apropos at the moment." He added in another letter: "Of course, *wider still and wider* should come out – it is liable to be misunderstood now."'

Sir Edward Elgar sent to Benson, as an indication of the spirit of words he would prefer, a poem by an American, Colonel John Hay, called 'The Vengeance is God's'. This produced the following revealing reaction from the Fellow of Magdalene, Cambridge:

'My dear Elgar, I'll turn to again and see if I can do anything but I'm not strong in the vengeance line, and indeed I don't see what there is to avenge as yet – we have hemmed in Germany tight all round for years in the good-natured unsympathetic way in which we Anglo-Saxons treat the world, and the cork has blown out! What I do feel with all my heart is that *bullying* must be stopped – but bullying mustn't be met by bullying and if we only end in being more militaristic than Germany, *je m'y perds!* Anyhow, thanks to you, and I'll try again. Ever yours, A. C. Benson.'

Elgar's rejoinder was: 'There's no vengeance for us – the idea, tersely put, is "If it is God's work (Heaven knows there's enough *preaching* being done) it is our place to do it." '

Benson wrote new words, Elgar received them with 'A million thanks – excellent!' and prepared them for the publisher. Then came this letter: 'My dear Benson, one hurried line to say that the new version of "Land of Hope and Glory" must be held back for a little time. Clara Butt is singing the original version at the patriotic concerts and on all circulars has printed the old stanzas. So we must wait. Forgive this bad writing, I have left my pen at the Police Court! Yours affectionately, Edward Elgar. (I may add – Inspector, "S" Division, Metropolitan Police.)'

The new words were put away in a drawer to await Clara Butt, and there they have remained ever since, unsung except once when we told this story on the radio. The lines replacing 'wider still and wider', and intended more to meet the mood of 1914, are below:

> *Land of Hope and Glory, Mother of the free,*
> *How shall we uphold thee, who are born of thee?*
> *Gird thee well for battle, bid thy hosts increase;*
> *Stand for faith and honour, smite for truth and peace!*

Not very inspired. The ordinary soldier of the British Expeditionary Force, moving to the ports for embarkation, seems to have echoed the buoyant spirit of the day more aptly, if unmartially, by preferring to sing as he marched such cocky music-hall songs as 'Hullo, hullo, who's your lady friend?'. It was a triumphal departure as the crowds cheered the troopships and the men shouted their cheery catch-phrase:

'Are we downhearted?'

'No!'

'Shall we beat 'em?'

'YE-E-E-S!'

GENERAL SIR BRIAN HORROCKS, then an eighteen-year-old lieutenant with the BEF, says: 'This was, I should think, the last time there was any romance and glory attached to war. As I marched through those cheering crowds I felt like a king among men. It was all going to be over by Christmas, and our one anxiety was to be on the spot in time. When I left Chatham I had ninety-five men under command, but on arrival at Southampton there were ninety-eight – three men had hidden under the seats so as not to miss the battle. It seems extraordinary now but that was the spirit.'

Lloyd George said: 'Never was there a war so universally acclaimed.' In Germany the Kaiser commanded a national day of prayer: 'I commend you to God. Go to church and kneel before God and pray for His help for our gallant army.' In Britain the Archbishop of Canterbury announced a service of intercession with God. J. C. Squire wrote later:

> *God heard the embattled nations sing and shout:*
> *'Gott strafe England' – and 'God Save the King'.*
> *'God this' – 'God that' – and 'God the other thing'.*
> *'My God,' said God, 'I've got my work cut out'.*

Queues stood at the recruiting offices under the poster of Kitchener's moustached face and summoning finger, *Your Country Needs You*. The spirit of voluntary service was so lively that Kitchener's Army, as it was called, quickly attained the figure which became its second nickname, the First Hundred Thousand. A headline in *The Times* strikes the chord of the day – 'Boom in Recruiting'. One of Kitchener's recruits analyses their motives – MR J. B. PRIESTLEY: 'To most of us the call was really little to do with "King and Country" and flag-wagging and hip-hip-hurrah. It was a challenge to what we felt was our untested manhood. In centuries gone by other men who had not lived as easily as we had, had drilled and marched and borne arms – couldn't we? Yes, we too could leave home and soft beds and the girls to soldier for a spell, if there was some excuse for it, something at least to be defended. And here it was. In those first months we believed that war still held movement, colour, adventure, drama.'

Among other things it was a horses' war. Each infantry division had 5,600 horses to draw the supplies and guns for its 18,000 men, then there were the cavalry, and the remounts necessary

The *Sphere*'s war artist sketched a cavalry charge that occurred in a French village street, before the war got bogged down in the trenches. One of the hussars said afterwards, 'It was just like you see on the pictures' which must have been putting it mildly

Cartoon by the Dutch artist, Louis Raemaekers
'Death demanded the best, and got it'

to replace casualties: 53,000 horses went out with the BEF in 1914 (with six horse hospitals) and this figure rose later to 450,000. Even more astonishing and saddening, it is computed that the Allied and German armies eventually dragged over 2,000,000 of these creatures into the morass with them. From the outbreak of war a thorough requisitioning of animals went on in Britain; within twelve days some 120,000 were earmarked for war service. *The Times* carried an advertisement: 'If your horses are commandeered by the Government why not use instead the Standard 9.5 horse-power light car? – price £185.'

The BEF was splendidly trained and equipped, though it had only eighty motor vehicles and no equipment for trench warfare. But no one expected trench warfare. 'All my thoughts,' said the British Commander-in-Chief later, 'were concentrated upon a war of movement and manoeuvre.'[1] He got it, at first – with 2,000,000 Germans swiftly invading Belgium and France, and with mix-ups so incoherent that it was difficult to know just where the front line was. There were cavalry clashes in the old classic trumpet-blowing style, as former PRIVATE A. E. WEBB, of the Lancers, remembers:

'We were advancing up a ridge, and suddenly we got the order to gallop. We saw the Germans in front of us, firing at us from behind the stooks in the corn-field. We heard the order on the bugle to charge, and we put our lances under our arms and went mad for them. We rode straight through them. We were shouting, screaming, and bawling our heads off, not taking any notice of anything except for going for the first German we could see. We were charging with our lances down and I saw one particular German which I went for. I put my lance through him and unfortunately I left it there. I couldn't pull it out. I nearly came off my horse. I immediately drew my sword. We turned about, but the few Germans that were left were taken prisoners. I didn't have any occasion to use it.'

The autumn months of 1914 are sign-posted with those names which 'are for ever England' – Mons, the Marne, the Aisne, Ypres – terrible Ypres, the most sickening, bloodiest battle-field the world had ever known. Thousands of British families bought maps of Europe and packets of flags to mark the front line. As it bulged into France and towards Paris they had to swallow the conclusion that the Union Jack would not be flying in Berlin by Christmas after all. The BEF was half-destroyed, but the line held and the Channel ports were saved. The German juggernaut was brought to a standstill by the hard resistance of men and through something overlooked by all the makers of the Schlieffen Plan for quick victory: winter was coming, and with it the rain, and *mud*. The war became bogged down. British, French, Germans, Belgians dug themselves in.

'There was something sublime in the endurance of all these soldiers of all these nationalities,' says SIR BRIAN HORROCKS. 'Movement had disappeared from this terrible war. From the Alps to the North Sea millions of men dug like beavers and disappeared underground to lead an almost troglodyte existence for years on end.'

MR J. B. PRIESTLEY adds: 'Now came disillusionment for us who had joined up in a fine spirit of adventure. The frenzied butchery of this war, indefensible even on a military basis, was eventually to kill at least 10,000,000 Europeans. After being dressed in uniform, fed, and drilled, cheered and cried over, these 10,000,000 were then filled with hot lead, ripped apart with shell splinters, blown to bits, suffocated in mud, or allowed to die of diseases, after rotting too long in trenches that they shared with syphilitic rats and typhus-infected lice. Death, having come into his empire, demanded the best, and got it.'

---

[1] *1914*, by Lord French (Constable), 1919.

This war was so utterly different from any previous war, and life in the trenches was so remote from civil life, that the front-line soldiers became psychologically divided from the folks who were keeping the home fires burning, as Ivor Novello's popular song put it. This division is shown particularly by an absolute difference in quality between the songs of Civvy Street and those of Flanders. Unknown warriors developed a knack of improvising songs; the lyrics of over sixty of them have been published[1] and these ditties, many of then ribald parodies, some sentimental ballads, are a commentary on the soldier's life all the more valuable because it is artless and devoid of the 'commercial angle' of the pop-song-world. It came from the heart. It continued the centuries-old British habit of folk-song-making by peasants living hard lives near the earth and the sea; now Tommy found himself up against hardships as close to pitiless earth as men could get. Hard times make humble men improvise song to fit the day; in easier times they are quite happy to leave it to the merchants of Tin Pan Alley. John Brophy, himself a 1914 soldier, writes: 'These songs satirised more than war: they poked fun at the soldier's own desire for peace and rest, and so prevented it from overwhelming his will to go on doing his duty. They were not symptoms of defeatism, but strong bulwarks against it.'

> *Far from Ypres I want to be,*
> *Where German snipers can't get at me,*
> *Damp is my dug-out,*
> *Cold are my feet,*
> *Waiting for whizz-bangs*
> *To send me to sleep.*

Compare the heroics of the following commercial song sung by starry-eyed ladies back home in 1914. The stress on games betrays, surely, an assumption that war was still a sport:

> *We've watched you playing cricket*
> *And every kind of game,*
> *At football, golf and polo,*
> *You men have made your name;*
> *But now your country calls you*
> *To play your part in war,*
> *And no matter what befalls you,*
> *We shall love you all the more;*
> *So come and join the forces*
> *As your fathers did before.*

Refrain:

> *Oh! We don't want to lose you,*
> *But we think you ought to go;*
> *For your King and your country*
> *Both need you so,*
> *We shall want you and miss you,*
> *But with all our might and main,*
> *We shall cheer you, thank you, kiss you,*
> *When you come back again.*[2]

[1] *The Long Trail*, by John Brophy and Eric Partridge (André Deutsch), is the best collection.
[2] 'Your King and Country Want You', words and music by Paul Rubens (Chappell).

Bruce Bairnsfather, himself in the trenches in 1914, reflected the British soldier's humour by inventing Old Bill, here remarking 'Poor old Maggie, she seems to be 'avin' it dreadful wet at 'ome.' (*The Bystander*)

How remote was London from Ypres . . . and where was that war in the air so often predicted by H. G. Wells? On September 22, 1914 the Royal Flying Corps set things going by dropping three missiles on Zeppelin sheds at Düsseldorf but the Zeppelins seemed in no hurry to retaliate. As a precaution London street lighting was reduced and suburban trains ran at night with blinds drawn. This apart, there was virtually no war discomfort on the Home Front in 1914; no air-raids yet, no conscription, no rationing, no shortages. The title of a new London revue summed it up: *Business as Usual* . . . and better business for those industrialists connected with war supplies.

Britain entered hostilities with sixty-three aircraft in the Royal Flying Corps and ended it in 1918 with about 3,300 in the Royal Air Force. War was a forcing ground for technology – radio, for example – but housewives did not know that they were deprived temporarily of a splendid invention to reduce their hard domestic chores. The name of their eventual benefactor was obscured by the war and full credit has never been done him. Back in 1913 Mr Harry Brearley, a metallurgist in the Sheffield laboratory run jointly by Brown and Firth, the steel firms, was testing metals for rifle barrels and he forgetfully mislaid an experimental piece of steel containing a higher proportion of chromium than had ever been used before; it lay about the place for some time and when he found it he was surprised that it had not rusted. He told cutlery manufacturers about it, for he knew that the most tiresome of household chores was cleaning knives with bath brick, or manually turning the handle of a cleaning machine, but the war broke out before stainless steel knives could be marketed. The entire output of this new steel went to the war effort, principally for aero-engine valves. After the war the cutlery-makers got busy.[1]

[1] Information from Firth-Vickers Stainless Steels Ltd.

Though business was as usual on the Home Front in 1914 the atmosphere of life was far from normal. Patriotic fervour of the 'We don't want to lose you but we think you ought to go' kind swept the country alongside a hate-the-Hun gospel whipped up on recruiting platforms and in cartoons, and brought to the boil by stories of German atrocities. Any shop with a Teutonic-looking name over the window was liable to be stoned. An over-zealous censorship did not help the public towards a sober understanding of what the new warfare meant. The tallest of stories circulated – a Russian army landed at Aberdeen with snow on their boots and travelled through Britain to the Western front – and spies were round every corner. An antidote to such spasms of hysteria was laughter, and when that unique music-hall comedian MR HARRY TATE appeared in *Business as Usual* at the Hippodrome Theatre with his sketch 'Fortifying the Home' he did the same job of mocking wartime absurdities as Tommy Handley's *ITMA* did in the next Great War with Handley's mad telephone calls to the Ministry of Aggravation; in fact, Tate, his moustache semaphoring and his indignation bellowing at the enormities of life, was the surrealist Englishman, the direct ancestor of *ITMA* and the *Goons*. Fortifying his 1914 villa by improvising machine-guns from mangles ('The place is surrounded by SPIES – one never knows what's going to happen'), he phones the War Office:

'Hello, is that you, Kitchy? How's your *father*? All well at home? They're HERE! I want reinforcements! No, not three-and-*fourpence*! Reinforcements! I want every man – every man, woman, and dog. If the men can't shoot them, the dogs can bite them, and if the dogs can't bite them the women can TALK them to death!'

★   ★   ★

More than two centuries had passed since the fire of an enemy had scorched any part of our land, so it was a nasty shock when on the misty morning of December 16, 1914 the German battle-cruisers *Derfflinger* and *Von der Tann* bombarded Scarborough with 12-inch and smaller shells. More than a shock, this was the beginning of the end (carried through by Hitler) of the old tradition that our wars were fought far away.

MRS FOSTER, formerly Dorothy Cass-Smith, daughter of the then Harbour Master at Scarborough, gives us a schoolgirl's-eye view: 'We lived inside the lighthouse and at break-fast time we heard a noise very like loud thunder. Father thought that it would be safer if we left the lighthouse, so he told mother to take me down the pier. Mother and I looked over the parapet and saw two big ships in the distance and guns flashing, a bright orange, like a furnace door being opened. As we were going down the pier we saw the men coming off the trawlers like a lot of scared rabbits, and we all went down together and sheltered under this parapet. The shells were flying over us and we could see the houses tumbling down like sandcastles. The Grand Hotel was hit two or three times. The noise was so tremendous because it rever-berated against the castle hill. All of a sudden there was a lull and Mother said "We haven't any money and we've left the deed box behind, so shall I go back?" She returned to the light-house but within five minutes she was back; she said "I didn't go in because just before I got there a shell went right through the lighthouse tower."'

MR G. F. HYDE, at that time a reporter on the *Scarborough Evening News*, says that some people jumped to the conclusion that a German invasion was imminent: 'The newspapers had been full of pictures of refugees on the Belgian roads, and I saw pretty much the same thing that day. Motor-cars and all sorts of horse-drawn vehicles and handcarts were going along the roads carrying loads of bedding, and conveying bedridden invalids. The damage was widespread. It was afterwards computed that between five and seven hundred shells had fallen on the town and the immediate district.'

The assaulting battleships eluded the British Navy, slipped northwards to shell Whitby and the Hartlepools, and then got away. They had killed 149 people and injured about 600. The Germans' chief purpose was propagandist. The *Kolnische Zeitung* said: 'The attack will bring home to the English the fact that their great fleet is unable to protect them.' The *Berlin Lokalanzeiger* reported 'terrible panic' at Scarborough, 'the most important harbour on the east coast of England between the Humber and the Thames, protected by a mole and batteries.' In fact it hadn't a single gun. Perhaps the best reply to the attack on civilian morale lies in a story told by the present Lord Rea, whose father was then MP for Scarborough:[1] 'When a shell whistled through the drawing-room of our house our elderly housemaid struggled up through the debris to my mother's bedroom and said: "Have no fear, madam; we are in God's hands and Cook's in the cellar".'

Shortly after this naval raid came the first-ever air-raid on Britain. Just when Britons were buying their turkeys at 10d a pound, singing the latest comic ditty of 'Sister Susie's Sewing Shirts

[1] In a letter to *Scrapbook*.

The German navy's raid was turned to use in a recruiting poster; (*right*) the direct hit on Scarborough lighthouse

for Soldiers', and festooning the home with greenery and bunting, on the morning of December 24, 1914 a certain Lieutenant von Prondzynski looked down from a German Taube aeroplane and saw Dover Castle 5,000 feet below him: he lifted a bomb over the side and let go. It missed the castle by 400 yards and landed in a garden adjoining St James's Rectory, excavating a hole four or five feet deep, smashing some rectory windows, and making a near-miss of a gardener named James Banks who thus became the first civilian ever to have a personal story of '*my* bomb'. He told the *Dover Express and East Kent News*: 'I was up a tree in the rectory garden, cutting branches for Christmas decorations when I heard the whirr of an aeroplane. Then I saw a blinding light and heard a very loud explosion. I was thrown to the ground.' He was not hurt.

Von Prondzynski turned seawards, chased by two British aeroplanes, said to be armed only with pistols. He made his escape to a hero-worshipping reception in Germany. In England fragments of Mr Banks' bomb were mounted on a shield and presented to King George V, to mark, rather curiously, this historic occasion.

'Dover remained cool under the attack,' the local paper assures us.

So, at the end of 1914, people on the Home Front in general had hardly an idea of real war. The Zeppelins were not to come until 1915, and through all that war the havoc unleashed on Britain was a fleabite compared with that of the Second World War; yet economically, politically, and morally the consequences of four long years' embroilment in international anarchy were so convulsive that after sacrificing the cream of its youth Europe was faced with a shambles to clean up after 1918 – and how badly the nations did it we saw in the Twenties and Thirties.

★   ★   ★

'Business as usual' in the first years of the war is well illustrated by the frontispiece to the present book: Sickert's 'The Brighton Pierrots' was painted in his studio but a preliminary ink-sketch was made on the spot on a summer's evening in 1915. This fact has led us to check the blackout situation.[1] We find that towards the end of 1914 reduced lights were ordered in Greater London, Birmingham, Grimsby, Lowestoft, Southend, Clacton, and the Kent and Sussex coastline. Then came airship raids (the first, January 19, 1915, killed three people at King's Lynn, one at Yarmouth); thereafter the partial blackout was extended to coastal areas from Scotland to Dorset but it was not until mid-June 1915 that the Chief Constable of Brighton issued a specific local order prohibiting lights on the Brighton Marine frontage from one hour after sunset to an hour before sunrise. The outdoor entertainers could thus perform until about 9 p.m. in summer. The party painted by Sickert were Ellison's Entertainers, run by Joe Ellison, father of John Ellison, a well-known broadcaster today. Mr Bill Tupper, of the Theatre Royal, Brighton, remembers them, and says: 'It was certainly "business as usual", in fact more so, as Brighton was inundated with evacuees (rich ones) from London and it was very difficult to find any accommodation in the town.'

---

[1] Research with the help of Town Clerk of Brighton, Miss Lillian Browse, Mr John Ellison, *Brighton & Hove Gazette*, and the Home Office.

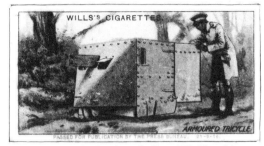

Collection, Saffron Walden Museum

Collecting cigarette-cards was for years every schoolboy's hobby. These two in a war-time series show London motor-buses in France transporting troops towards the firing line and (*right*) an armoured motor-tricycle, a card passed by the censor in 1916 with a legend on the back that 'these baby fortresses have proved of great service'

How bombs were dropped overboard in 1914, and (*inset*) the first Englishman who ever had a 'bomb story' to tell: Mr J. A. Banks of Dover

The artist of a German magazine had a grandiose conception of the first air-raid on Britain, Christmas Eve, 1914. Actually it was by a single plane

At the end of 1914 the cartoonist of the German *Kladderadatsch* promised the shape of things to come. In fact, the havoc wrought by Zeppelin and aeroplane raids on Britain in the whole of the war was small (1,413 people killed) compared with Second World War standards

THE HISTORY OF A PAIR OF MITTENS.

The feminine craze for knitting 'comforts' for soldiers received this comment from *Punch* in November 1914

The war that had become bogged down in trenches from the Alps to the North Sea by Christmas 1914

As it is now: Charles Brewer revisits the spot where he took part in the Christmas truce. The farmer says he still ploughs up cartridge cases here

(*Below*) As it was: photograph of corpse-strewn no-man's-land taken in 1914 by Josef Sewald from the German side. The willow trees were approximately where the British line was.

8 PARABLE

The Christmas Truce of 1914

Author's note: Of all events chronicled in the *Scrapbook* programmes none has appealed to my own temperament as intensely as this. I believe it belongs to the mysteries and miracles of the human spirit. I believe it is a parable for posterity. I feel gratitude for having had the opportunity to tell this story in deeper detail and to more people than ever before. For these reasons I write this chapter from a more personal angle than the rest of the book. Facts are sacred: these I strive to find and give objectively, but in this case what happened was outside 'normal' expectations so I intend to allow myself some conjecture on the significance of the events in no-man's-land.

L. B.

In the beautiful German town of Augsburg one evening some years ago an old soldier of the First World War tuned his radio to the BBC. He listened to *Scrapbook for 1914*. When it came to an eye-witness description of an unofficial truce in the trenches the years fell away from him and he was back in no-man's-land himself that Christmas, fraternizing. He wrote to a German newspaper about the programme, saying that the radio did a service to peace on earth when it brought to its wide audience the facts about such an event, in which he had himself taken part. I shall return to him later, for he is one link in an extraordinary chain of events.

Several different editions of *Scrapbook for 1914* have been broadcast, the latest in 1964.[1] When preparing the first in 1934 I found that surprisingly little information had been published about the truce. Here was an event so entirely out of key with the frozen hatred of December 1914 that I felt I must tell what happened, and why. I had a chat with my BBC producer about it.

'I'm wondering where on earth I can find someone who can tell me what happened, from personal experience,' I said, 'and how the men felt about it. Any ideas?'

Sometimes, but seldom, the story is right under the programme-maker's nose. Charles Brewer replied: 'As a matter of fact, I took part in it myself.'

So I persuaded Brewer to tell in *Scrapbook* his story of that dark day when all the movement and the early romantic excitement had gone out of the war, and great armies had gone to earth,

[1] This programme has also been put on the market as a long-playing record, Fontana 493 015 FDL.

and the long bestial attrition of trench war had begun, when by some instinctive impulse the firing ended along the Anglo-German front and men climbed from the muck and celebrated Christmas together in no-man's-land. The response of listeners, in the Press, and in our post-bag, showed that this story had struck a chord deep in the human heart. Many wrote in terms similar to those used by a listener at Geneva: 'When the broadcast closed I said to myself that the radio could be the most powerful peace-maker in our times. Nowhere in all Europe have I heard anything to compare with this . . .' – an over-optimistic judgment, perhaps, since the world has scarcely become increasingly pacific since broadcasting began. Yet it was abundantly clear from letters, foreign and British, from old listeners and young, that the account of the Christmas truce had made many people feel that the BBC's motto, 'Nation shall speak peace unto nation', is more than pious jargon.

Reaction from Germany at that time (1934) was nil, for Hitler had recently taken over radio and Press, and such a story of fraternization between 'enemies' was not in accord with Nazi ideology; but years later, after another war, the BBC again broadcast our story of the Christmas truce and this time the mail brought me a cutting from a German newspaper, a review of the *Scrapbook* written by that ex-enemy ex-soldier at Augsburg. I wrote to him. He replied, and it transpired that at Christmas 1914 he was in a stretch of the front line near Fleurbaix in the Pas de Calais exactly opposite where Brewer was entrenched! – so when a revised edition of this *Scrapbook* was planned in 1964 we decided this time to bring together the memories of Charles Brewer, in 1914 a nineteen-years-old lieutenant in the Bedfordshire Regiment, and Dr Josef Sewald, in 1914 a twenty-four-years-old non-commissioned officer in the 17th Bavarian Reserve Regiment.

I also decided to do further research, extending my review from what occurred among humble soldiers in the mud to what happened that Christmas in the seats of the mighty. It seems not to be generally known that there was a top-level proposal for a truce *before* the Sewalds and Brewers of the front line took the initiative in 1914. At a time when the world was (as *The Times* said) 'fuller of wounded and broken men than ever in its history,' the Holy See put the idea to the warring powers. On December 12, 1914 the British Roman Catholic paper *The Tablet* said: 'As far as our government is concerned it may be taken as a foregone conclusion that the merciful suggestion of the Holy Father will meet with the most sympathetic consideration. In fact, as far as the western front of the war is concerned there should be little difficulty. The position is not so simple on the eastern front for this reason, that for the Russians Christmas Day is not celebrated on December 25. It must also be remembered that Germany's latest ally, Turkey, does not recognize Christmas Day at all.'

Was it beyond the wit of man to get round these objections which, in comparison with the magnitude of the proposal, were quibbles? The Pope used every diplomatic persuasion, but a few days later the *Osservatore Romano* reported that while the majority of the governments 'sympathetically adhered' to the suggestion the necessary unanimity was lacking. It has since been disclosed[1] that the project met with sympathy 'in principle' from Britain, Germany, and Belgium, but with refusal from France (for military reasons) and from Russia (owing to the difference of date).

What governments would not do, ordinary men did.

---

[1] *Benedict XV: The Pope of Peace*, by Fr. H. E. G. Rope (1941).

Brewer of the Bedfordshires   Sewald of the Bavarians

A photograph taken in the German lines by Sewald

A soddened and ravaged country looms through the mist—'the Flanders fog', Sewald calls it. He took this picture. A few men on both sides smuggled 'forbidden' cameras up to the front, and thanks to them we have these views; there were as yet no official photographers on the spot

Imperial War Museum

A group of British and German soldiers fraternizing between the trenches, Christmas 1914

The Christmas Truce of 1914

MR CHARLES BREWER says: 'Christmas Eve was a still, frosty night with a clear half-moon. For once it wasn't raining. As we looked over the top row of soddened sandbags we could easily see the German trench and barbed wire not 100 yards away, across the slimy churned-up morass of no-man's-land. A body or two lay out there. Everything was still, except the occasional tok-a-tok-a-tok of a machine-gun. In my own strip of water-logged trench a chilled sentry stamped and beat his mittened hands. Suddenly he saw a group of glistening lights appear on the German parapet.

'"Look out!" he called to his mates. "Keep yer perishin' 'eads down. I bet it's a sniper's trap."

'They fetched me up from my dug-out and I had a good look. I saw that the lights were on a Christmas tree. Farther along the line I could see more Christmas trees sparkling. Then came a sound new to the western front – "Silent Night", splendidly sung across there:

> *Stille Nacht, Heilige Nacht!*
> *Alles schläft, einsam wacht*
> *Nur das traute, hochheilige Paar . . .*

'We gave the Jerries a cheer, then one of our chaps said: "Ere, let's sing 'em something back! Come on! –

> *We are Fred Karno's army,*[1]
> *The ragtime infantry,*
> *We cannot fight, we cannot shoot,*
> *What blinkin' use are we?*
> *And when we get to Berlin*
> *The Kaiser he will say*
> *'Hock! Hock! Mein Gott!*
> *What a bloody rotten lot*
> *Are the ragtime infantry!'*

Any German who understood English must have been astonished by a Tommy's choice of song for Christmas Eve, unless he understood the English sense of humour. (Incidentally, one German ex-officer tells me that he can recall no such ironical and self-mocking ditties ever being sung by their soldiers: 'Our songs were very sentimental or very patriotic.' One wonders whether any other nationality had the sardonic type of soldiers' song – the French? – the Americans? – the Russians?).

DR JOSEF SEWALD takes up the story of the 1914 truce: 'I shouted to our enemies that we didn't wish to shoot and that we make a Christmas truce. I said I would come from my side and we could speak together. First there was silence then I shouted once more, invited them, and the British shouted "No shooting". Then a man came out of the trenches and I on my side did the same and so we came together and we shook hands – a bit cautiously!'

MR BREWER continues: 'When dawn broke, we saw several Germans standing on top of their parapet, and waving to us. We also clambered out, picked our way through the wire, and there in no-man's-land, disregarding the dictates of Imperial systems and the propaganda of a screaming Press, we solemnly shook hands, and wished each other the compliments of the season. We gazed at each other almost shyly. So here were the fellows we had been sitting

---

[1] Fred Karno was a popular comedian in whose party Charlie Chaplin appeared before going into films. The above words were sung to a hymn tune!

opposite for two months – the fellows whose slightest visible movement had meant the pressure of a trigger behind one of our own loopholes, the recoil of an explosion, and 100 yards away perhaps the spurt of blood and brains.'

Football was played in no-man's-land. Photographs were swopped. The truce spread for miles along the front. At one point bagpipes provided Scottish music for this Christmas, despite English objections that bagpiping was tantamount to reopening hostilities on Fritz. At another point a hare appeared between the lines and was wildly chased by British and Germans. The opportunity was taken by both sides to pump out waterlogged trenches and repair parapets. Not a shot was fired. And there was the most moving incident of all, thus remembered by Dr Sewald:

'An English lieutenant said there was a comrade who had been killed the previous afternoon, and they wished to bury this man. I said "Why not? – of course you can do it", and so they brought the dead man, laid him on the ground, and we all laid a handful of earth upon him and together prayed the Lord's Prayer: "Vater unser, der du bist im Himmel, Geheiligt werde dein Name".'

Mingled voices, in German and English, spoke the ancient words about Thy Kingdom coming.

The truce lasted all Christmas Day in some parts of the line, in others it continued the best part of a week. 'We swopped coat buttons and exchanged bully beef for cigars,' says Brewer. 'That was responsible for the biggest laugh, when amid the amazement of our men at finding every German with a well-filled cigar case, our Sergeant, "Rags" Nicholls, said "Blimey, it's a millionaire's battalion".'

Sewald fills in the picture from the German side: 'The soldiers would kneel down and hold up their heads to be shaved by the English, and on the other side the German soldiers shaved the English soldiers; it was laughter and joy, and it was as if there never had been any disturbance between the feeling of these thousands of young men. The Generals did of course know nothing, and we were very careful to make it impossible that any news got back to the staff officers.'

When carols broke out both German and British joined in. Says Brewer: 'It was something we all knew; we all joined in . . .'

> *Oh, come all ye faithful*
> *Joyful and triumphant . . .*

And Sewald adds: 'We sang louder and louder, and all at once it was like a hymn that arose out of the trenches to the sky. Christmas united the enemies. It is wonderful that the thought of Bethlehem united the men. The men heard the voice of 2,000 years back, but the rulers did not. And so war went on for four years. And millions of young men had to die . . . had to die.'

★   ★   ★

To record this story in 1964 I travelled to Augsburg and met Dr Sewald in his study, a white-haired old man with a fair grasp of English. He spoke the above passage slowly, simply, with the emotion of a full heart, and at the end he repeated three words on the spur of the moment – 'had to die' – and the sadness and compassion in his voice I shall never forget.

The truce—drawn by an artist for the *Times History of the War*, and (*right*) by Captain Bruce Bairnsfather of the 1st Royal Warwickshires, who was there: he called this drawing 'Swopping buttons'

During that journey of mine across Europe Charles Brewer took me to a field near Fleurbaix: here, he said, was our trench and over there 100 yards away was the German line. In the side of a sodden ditch he found the exact spot where the entrance to his dug-out was on that Christmas Eve when he was called up to look at the strange lights on the Jerry parapet. It is a flat, wet, chilly land. A couple of miles across the fields, I caught sight of a village church tower and I remembered something else Dr Sewald had told me. He said that his regiment, the 17th Bavarian, had alternated with the 16th in and out of the trenches, and the German troops who happened to be 'resting' in that village behind the line at Christmas 1914 included a *meldegänger* (runner of messages) in the 16th Bavarian Regiment whose name was Hitler. Had the turns of duty been the opposite way, Hitler would most probably have been in the front line at Christmas when his mates were fraternizing with the enemy.

With this rather startling thought in my mind, as I stood on that earth where men 'had to die' in two great wars my thoughts turned to what might have happened if the Pope's 1914 proposal had been accepted and an *official* truce on all fronts had brought a breathing space in which sanity might have turned our destinies away from the decimation of human values, lives, and riches: no Somme, no Passchendaele, no Verdun, no four years of increasing hatred in the 'fight to a finish', no harsh Peace of Versailles to sow the seeds of Hitlerite vengeance, no Second World War. A dream? – yes, but I wonder whether history might have been different had kings and governments been activated by the spirit of the humble men in no-man's-land and had shared the dreams of ordinary soldiers. Siegfried Sassoon, the soldier-poet who scribbled his verses in the trenches with a disenchantment so contrasted to the earlier eager romanticism of Rupert Brooke, wrote:

> . . . *Soldiers are dreamers; when the guns begin*
> *They think of firelit homes, clean beds, and wives.*
> *I see them in foul dug-outs, gnawed by rats,*
> *And in the ruined trenches, lashed with rain,*
> *Dreaming of things they did with balls and bats,*
> *And mocked by hopeless longing to regain*
> *Bank-holidays, and picture-shows, and spats,*
> *And going to the office in the train.*[1]

My dream is that if the Kaisers, Tzars, Lloyd Georges, and Clemenceaux of that power-drunken and politics-befouled Europe had been required to spend December 1914 freezing – and dreaming – in the trenches they would have paid more serious attention to Pope Benedict XV. It is worth noting that the British commander-in-chief of that time, Sir John French, wrote of the Pope's proposal: 'I have since often thought deeply over the principle involved in the manifestation of such sentiments between hostile armies in the field. I am not sure that, had the question of the agreement of an armistice for the day been submitted to me, I should have dissented from it. I have always attached the utmost importance to the maintenance of that chivalry in war which has almost invariably characterized every campaign of modern times in which this country has been engaged.'[2]

As it was, when news of the unofficial truce reached the High Command on both sides reprimands were issued, but it is significant that no great wrath seems to have blown up.

---

[1] From *Dreamers*, by Siegfried Sassoon, 1917 (Faber and Faber).

[2] *1914*, by Lord French (Constable), 1919.

Pope Benedict XV who wanted an official truce

Field-marshal Sir John French who might have agreed to one

Sewald says that the ticking-off he received from the adjutant of his regiment was mild. Brewer was scolded by no one. Others who took part agree that such a truce could not have happened later in the war when positions had hardened. A 1914 captain, now a retired general, says that when he first saw the men go into no-man's-land he thought the truce was to bury the dead: 'And I didn't think that was wrong, I thought that from the days of the Peninsular War it had always been understood as a recognized part of war. Then, when it turned into fraternization it was just a common feeling of Christmas.'

Why did the men return to fighting within a few days? To have defied reprimands would have been mutiny and these men had no intention of facing the consequences, for they believed doggedly that their cause was right and were prepared to carry on (on both sides, for while the Britisher knew he was fighting aggression, the German was persuaded by his country's propaganda that Germany had to invade France to prevent a choking Franco–Russian encirclement of the Fatherland). The fact remains that when they sang carols and swopped fags in no-man's-land they divested themselves for a time of the mantle of power and patriotism that is a soldier's uniform, and were just men. Only a strong impulse could do that. It is, of course, impossible to assess with certainty the motives of these thousands of soldiers, but some are surely evident: the disgust with trench warfare, the tradition of holding truces to bury the dead, the ancient pagan habit of festivity at the year's end, combined with what Dr Sewald calls 'the thoughts of Bethlehem'. Whether they counted themselves Christians or not these men were acting in the Christ-born spirit of that day, spontaneously, instinctively, in many cases probably with no solemn thoughts at all. They were Common Man, not saints or even padres, but the most impressive thing about their climbing over their parapets and meeting one another was that they showed *trust*. They stood at a point in history where, as the Pope hoped, all Europe might pause 'to bring a healing balm to the wounds inflicted'; in the quietening of the guns humanity might have thought twice before resuming the plunge towards what H. G. Wells was to call two years later 'a war that has lost its soul – it has become a mere incoherent fighting and destruction'.

In their no-man's-land of 1914 they stood, as we stand half-a-century later, at a point where neither patriotism nor power nor politics is enough – nor megatons.

Peace on earth will only be reached when men and women of all nations can get together, in mind even more than in body, from the highest to the lowliest, and can meet as did the fraternizers of Flanders in *trust*, discovering in their common humanity something to conquer their differences; then they can take the one further crucial step which was not taken either in 1914 or in the partial truce of the Vietnamese 'holy year' of 1966: to refuse to pick up those guns again, but rather (as *Punch*'s artist puts it in his drawing of the modern no-man's-land) to make every day a holy day.

THE END

The Bystander

Christmas morning, 1914: 'How it dawned for many', by Bruce Bairnsfather

"*Mother, why can't they make <u>every</u> day a holy day?*"

Punch, January 1966

Cartoon by Illingworth

INDEX

PLAYS, MUSICALS, BALLET, CONCERT PARTIES

The Admirable Crichton, 69; Androcles and the Lion, 188; The Arcadians, 101, 116; Arms and the Man, 38, 157

The Beauty of Bath, 112 n, 122; The Belle of Mayfair, 86, 99; The Belle of New York, 36, 45; The Blue Bird, 116; Bunty Pulls the Strings, 153; Business as Usual, 199, 200

Candida, 46; The Catch of the Season, 70, 98 n; Caesar and Cleopatra, 87; A Chinese Honeymoon, 68, 101; The Chocolate Soldier, 117, *157*, 172; Coppélia, 86, 168; The Count of Luxemburg, 153, 172; The Country Girl, 69

The Devil's Disciple, 45; Diaghilev Ballet, 153, 154, 167; The Doctor's Dilemma, 86; The Dollar Princess, 116

An Englishman's Home, 112, 116; Everybody's Doing It, 10, 154, 173

Fanny's First Play, 144, 153; Firebird, 154; The Flag Lieutenant, 88; Florodora, 36, 41, 45, 46; Fol-de-Rols, 94, 153

The Gay Lord Quex, 46, 49; The Geisha, 36, 44; Getting Married, 88; The Girl in the Taxi, 172; The Girls of Gottenberg, 87, 96; The Grand Duke, 44

Hindle Wakes, 154; His House in Order, 86; Hullo Ragtime!, 154, 173; Hullo Tango!, 188

John Gabriel Borkman, 45; Justice, 117

The Land of Promise, 189; The Liars, 45

Man and Superman, 71; The Madras House, 117; Major Barbara, 71; Merry England, 69; The Merry Widow, 87, 96; Milestones, 154; The Mollusc, 87; Mrs Dane's Defence, 46; Mrs Warren's Profession, 69

The Orchid, 70; Our Miss Gibbs, 96, 116

The Passing of the Third Floor Back, 88; The Passing Show, 177, 189; Pélissier's Follies, 46, 87, 94, 127, 143; Peter Pan, 70, 102; The Playboy of the Western World, 87; A Princess of Kensington, 70; Pygmalion, 178, 189

The Quaker Girl, 96, 117, 178 n; Quality Street, 69

Riders to the Sea, 70

San Toy, 45; The Silver Box, 86; The Speckled Band, 117; Strife, 116

Tom Jones, 87; The Toreador, 68; Trelawny of the Wells, 45

Véronique, 70; The Voysey Inheritance, 71

The Walls of Jericho, 70; Waste, 87; What Every Woman Knows, 88; When Knights Were Bold, 87; The White Coons, 94; Widower's Houses, 38

You Never Can Tell, 38, 45

SONGS

Absent, 68; The Absent Minded Beggar, 61, 68; After the Ball, 68; Alexander's Ragtime Band, 153, 171; Algy, or the Piccadilly Johnny, 44; All Through the Motor-car, 16, 17, 44; Always, 46; The Amorous Goldfish, 44; Any Old Iron, 153; Arcady Is Ever Young, 116; Archibald, Certainly Not!, 116; The Army of Today's All Right, 189; Asleep in the Deep, 45

Back to the Land, 127; Be British, 134, *135*; Because, 69; Bedelia, 70; Beer, Beer, Glorious Beer, 46; Bill Bailey, Won't You Please Come Home, 69; A Bird in a Gilded Cage, 46; Bobbing Up and Down Like This, 46; Boiled Beef and Carrots, 116, 170; By the Light of the Silvery Moon, 116; By the Side of the Zuyder Zee, 86

Casey Jones, 154; Chinee Soger Man, 46; The Church Parade, 70, 98; Come to the Ball, 117; Coronation Day, 43, 68

Don't Go Down the Mine, Daddy, 117; Down at the Old Bull and Bush, 70; Drake Goes West, 117

Everybody's Doing It, 154

Flanagan, 117; The Floral Dance, 153; Florrie Was a Flapper, 177, 189; Friend o' Mine, 188

The Gaby Glide, 153; The Galloping Major, 86; Get Out and Get Under, 188; The Ghost of the Violin, 154; Gilbert the Filbert, 189; Ginger, You're Balmy, 117; Good-bye, Dolly Gray, 46

Has Anybody Here Seen Kelly?, 116; Hello, Hello, Who's Your Lady Friend?, 188, 194; Hitchy Koo!, 154, 171, 187; Hold Your Hand Out, Naughty Boy, 188; The Honeysuckle and the Bee, 69; A Hot Time in the Old Town, 44; How Do You Do, Miss Ragtime?, 154

I Do Like to Be Beside the Seaside, 91, 116; If I Should Plant a Tiny Seed of Love, 88; If Those Lips Could Only Speak, 86; I Hear You Calling Me, 88; I'll Make a Man of You, 189; I'll Sing Thee Songs of Araby, 46; I Love a Lassie, 71; I Love the Moon, 154; I Love You So, 87; I'm Afraid To Go Home in the Dark, 88; I'm Henery the Eighth, I am, 153; I May Be Crazy, 69; In a Persian Garden, 44; In the Shade of the Old Apple Tree, 71; In the Twi-twi-twilight, 87; It's a Long Way to Tipperary, 154, 170; I Want to Sing in Opera, 117; I Wouldn't Leave My Little Wooden Hut for You, 71

Jolly Good Luck to the Girl Who Loves a Soldier, 87; Joshua, 153; Just a Wee Deoch and Doris, 153; Just Like the Ivy, 69

Keep the Home Fires Burning, 189; Kitty, the Telephone Girl, 176, 188

Land of Hope and Glory, 69, 75 et seqq., 193; Let's All Go Down the Strand, 116; Lily of Laguna, 45; Little Grey Home in the West, 153; Louisiana Lou, 68

Mighty Lak' a Rose, 68; Mother o' Mine, 70; Mr Chamberlain, 86, 112; My Ain Folk, 70; My Girl's a Yorkshire Girl, 88; My Hero, 117; Moonstruck, 116; My Mother, 116; My Old Dutch, 34